The School of Compassion

The School of Compassion

A Roman Catholic theology of animals

Deborah M. Jones

GRACEWING

First published in 2009 by

Gracewing
2 Southern Avenue, Leominster
Herefordshire HR6 0QF

UK ISBN 978 0 85244 731 4

Cover picture: *St Anthony Blessing the Animals, the Poor, and the Sick* (83.MS.49), leaf 2 by the Master of St Veronica. The Paul J. Getty Musuem, Los Angeles, California

Typeset by
Action Publishing Technology Ltd, Gloucester, GL1 5SR

Contents

Notes: The Jerusalem Bible is referred to throughout, unless otherwise mentioned.

Foreword

Roman Catholicism: A Compassionate Voice for Animals?

by Andrew Linzey

There is a caricature of Roman Catholic attitudes to animals that goes something like this: animals are just animals – here for our use. They don't have value in themselves like human beings – they are not persons with moral rights, they don't have immortal souls, and what we do to them isn't really a moral issue. Perhaps we shouldn't inflict grotesque cruelty, but to go further than that is really sentimentality and emotional over-indulgence. Only humans really matter – fretting about animals in a world in which children are starving is just irresponsible.

Like most caricatures, this one has some justification. The dominant voices within the Catholic tradition, like Christianity as a whole, have not been favourable to animals. The Aristotelian notion that animals exist for us has been taken over and developed, implicitly or explicitly, by most of the major thinkers, from St Thomas Aquinas to Luther. Historical Christian thinking has reinforced instrumentalist attitudes to animals by interpreting 'dominion' as meaning a God-given licence to do with animals as we please. Unsurprisingly systematic theology has relegated animals to the margins of theological enquiry. And moral theology has followed suit by virtually ignoring the non-human as a legitimate field of ethical exploration. At its worst, then, Catholic tradition has defined animals as outside its circle of theological and moral concern.

But that is only part of the story: the same tradition which has formally excluded animals has also given birth to a range of sub-traditions which draw on the more animal-friendly motifs within the biblical narratives. When viewed less partially, we can see that these narratives acknowledge animals as fellow-creatures; created indeed on the same day of creation, like us they are included within the divine covenant, and have significance in themselves as God's creatures independently of human interests. These and other insights are developed inter alia in the remarkable early Christian writings about animals (sometimes disparagingly known as the 'apocryphal writings'), and have been lived out in the thought and practice of many saints of East and West.

Here we face a paradox which should engage thoughtful Catholics everywhere: while the Church in its systematic and moral theology has largely ignored animals, the same Church has continued to canonize saints whose behaviour has extolled the virtues of kindness, conviviality, and moral generosity towards others creatures. The depictions of generous and friendly relationships with animals, for example in the lives of St Francis of Assisi and St Philip Neri, should not be regarded as hagiographical gloss. Rather they are enduring testaments to a long tradition of including animals within the sphere of Christian spirituality, and are practical demonstrations of how union with the Creator should, if authentic, lead to an intensified communion with God's other creatures.

During the last forty years, we have witnessed an increasing ethical sensitivity to animals that has largely taken the Western world by surprise. Some Catholics have responded defensively to this developing sensitivity by emphasizing human prerogatives, fearful lest concern for animals will dethrone human interests. But what is desperately needed is a reflective theological response that relates the insights and resources within the Christian tradition to an issue of contemporary concern.

The joy of this book is that it helps Catholic Christians to re-engage with the issue of animals by utilizing the riches from within their own tradition. Its author does not minimize the dominant negative voices, nor pretend that all is well in the way Catholic authorities have sometimes formulated official positions, but it is the work of a faithful Catholic theologian opening up the tradition to an issue of increasing moral sensitivity. Tradition has been defined as the 'seedbed of creativity'. For Catholics this should always mean searching and developing the tradition so that the fullness of truth can be apprehended. And what Dr Deborah Jones has discovered is a remarkably more complex, infinitely richer, and considerably more animal-friendly Catholic tradition than might be supposed by the usual caricatures.

This book is the fullest systematic treatment of the moral status of animals within the Roman Catholic tradition. It is the result of thoughtful scholarship, wide reading, and, most of all, insightful theological exploration. It builds on the work of others, like myself, and provides a stream of fresh perspectives on our lives with God's other creatures. It is a deeply Catholic work, and I pray that it strikes a deep chord within the worldwide Catholic community.

The Revd Professor Andrew Linzey, Ph.D., DD, is a member of the Faculty of Theology in the University of Oxford, Director of the Oxford Centre for Animal Ethics (www.oxfordanimalethics.com) and Honorary Research Fellow of St Stephen's House, Oxford. He is also Honorary Professor at the University of Winchester, Special Professor at Saint Xavier University, Chicago, and the first Professor of Animal Ethics at the Graduate Theological Foundation, Indiana.

Part One

Animals in the Roman Catholic Tradition

Chapter One

Introducing the challenge

There are well over one billion baptized Roman Catholics worldwide. Think of the impact that such a number of people would make on the way that animals are treated if the Roman Catholic Church were officially to adopt a 'pro-animal' theology of animals.

Once such a 'pro-animal' theology were accepted, to convey the new teaching effectively, the hierarchical magisterium would need to promulgate it in papal encyclicals and bishops' pastoral letters, put it on the curriculum of schools and seminaries, and publish it in future editions of the *Catechism of the Catholic Church*. For the sake of untold billions of suffering, sentient animals, it is surely pressing that such a theology should be formulated. Because it concerns the food we eat, the clothes we wear, and the livelihood of untold numbers of people, pro-animal teaching may require *metanoia* on a grand scale, perhaps more than the Church dares to risk. But that does not mean that it should not try. The challenge of this book is to see if such a theology is possible, given the historic and present state of thinking within the Church. To avoid getting lost in the rarified reaches of abstract theologizing, it will concentrate largely on those aspects that can most usefully develop the appropriate ethic, a way in which humans can relate to, and treat, animals.

We begin with a brief review of the roots of the current range of views within the Church on the created world, and, specifically, on animals. Old and New Testament references are noted, but only those which were to effect the development of religious thought on the subject to a significant degree. The same is then briefly applied to those figures in the pre-Christian Greek philosophical tradition who were to contribute to Christian thought on the purpose and nature of the non-human animal creation. Appropriate Christian theologians in the early Christian era are also given 'thumb-nail' sketches of their views on the animal creation, culminating in the greatest and most influential of them all, St Thomas Aquinas, whose writings permeate much of this book.

Theologians, however, are not alone in influencing thought and belief. Another source, or stream flowing into the river of mainstream Catholic Tradition, is that of movements and traditions which originate in charismatic, or spirit-filled, individuals, many of whom founded monastic Orders. From the sands of Egypt to the West coast of Ireland, some of these visionary figures related to animals in a personal and highly positive way, recalling and exemplyifying the 'peaceable kingdom' of Eden before the Fall. That pre-lapsarian mythic world was altogether other and different from ours today – ours with its instrumentalist use of created beings. While the restoration, or renewal, of Eden is a biblical vision for the whole of creation, including therefore, all animals, in a future-realized eschaton, these saints lived it in an already-realized manner.

The first part then turns to a third stream, that represented by the magisterium. The sayings and teachings about animals by popes and cardinals are explored in the search for a defined doctrine. Apart from articulating and defining official teaching, one way in which the magisterium leads the Church is through legal processes. Those which relate to animals are looked at, including some of the strange medieval proceedings in which animals are credited with responsibility for their actions.

Finally, this first part finishes by examining the unique contribution to a theological consideration of animals provided by the tradition of the Catholic Church within the

British Isles. The British culture, influenced as it is by Anglicanism and its heritage of literary romanticism, produces the first society in the world for the prevention of cruelty to animals, and the first Catholic society for animal welfare in the world. Maybe through this tradition a universal Catholic theology can be discerned and/or developed.

The Catholic Church (that is, the hierarchical magisterium of popes, bishops and their approved theologians) does not take on board 'new' theologies – although insights from them can be gradually absorbed – so that pursuing novel and original ideas would not be fruitful. What the Church might be open to, however, are elements from the tradition, biblically based, and consistent with precedence, but seen in a new light and with a new emphasis. It may be that there is a satisfactorily coherent pro-animal theology already present and being taught; in which case the task of this book is to identify it.

To that purpose Part Two examines as closely as possible the relevant teachings as laid out in the most recent official compendium of Roman Catholic doctrine, the *Catechism of the Catholic Church*. Finally, by exploring major themes and ideas from the past, and analysing current relevant teaching, the goal of the book, expressed mainly in Part Three, is to present elements that could help to ground a pro-animal theology for the Roman Catholic Church.

The first challenge

The first challenge is one that requires a major shift in perception – from seeing animals and the natural world in general as a mere backdrop for human salvation, to seeing them as the focus of attention and as deserving consideration in themselves. With the ecological crisis, and with pressure from the secular world, this shift in perception is already beginning – slowly and falteringly, with human-centredness – anthropocentrism – still clinging to its claim for supremacy. Until very recently, little intellectual energy in any of the Churches has been expended on theological consideration of the natural world, or, specifically, of the world of animals. The Dominican scholar Fergus Kerr points out that between Peake's biblical commentary of 1962, where there was no entry for Animals in the index, to the 2001 *Oxford Biblical Commentary*, where there is an entry and nine topics listed, scholars have begun to recognize the theological importance of animal creation. What the new attention to animals is showing is that the Christian Churches' attitude to animals is all complexity and contradiction. As the foremost pioneer and exponent of contemporary Christian animal theology, Andrew Linzey, points out, the tradition that has 'both justified animal abuse' has also 'provided a moral critique of that abuse at the same time'.[1]

While so little has been written in the Church's tradition specifically about animals, it is necessary, at least at the beginning, to broaden the subject out to the whole physical world of nature. Certain early philosophers and theologians set up the natural, physical world, matter itself, in dualistic opposition to what they believed to be the only really important world, the spiritual. Doctrines which privilege the spiritual and rational,[2] over nature and matter, often owe more to the pervading influence of heresies such as Gnosticism and Manichaeism than to the religion founded by Christ.[3]

The responsibility of the Christian Church

The natural world, the world that includes species of animals of every sort, is not, in this post-lapsarian world, in a happy state. For the rapid extinction of species, the industrialization of animal abuse, and environmental despoliation, human exploitation is much to blame. The Christian Church, as the dominant influence in the history of the West, for many centuries known as Christendom, is reputedly responsible for much of this state of affairs. Christopher Bartlett, one critic, alleges that 'For most of its past, up to the present, institutionalized Christianity has condoned – even sanctified – the human reign of terror on earth through scriptural reference and expedient doctrine.'[4] For a Church that is founded to seek, love, and worship God, it is perhaps surprising that anthropocentrism, rather than God-centredness – theocentrism – should play such a leading role in Catholic teaching and theology.

There is, conversely, the important fact that Christianity's waning influence in the developed world – with the corresponding rise of secularism – has coincided with the steepest rate of increase in the degradation of nature and in the largest-ever number of animals subjected to exploitative treatment. But that does not exculpate the Church from having imbued society over centuries with values and concepts which have led to the present condition.

What led Christianity to develop those values and concepts? The roots go back to the earliest influences, the Hebrew and Greek pre-Christian traditions. Both, in themselves, and in relation to this subject, are problematic. The Hebrew tradition presents a God who both tenderly cares for his creation, and yet is so transcendent, so removed from creation, that space is created for the development of a scientific, objective approach to nature. The Greek tradition presents a pantheistic system sympathetic to the natural world, while at the same time introduces rational and analytic philosophy which distances human beings from non-rational nature. These contradictions need to be explained to see if anything of value can be salvaged from them.

Despite some glorious nature passages in the Psalms, in Job, in the Song of Songs, and elsewhere, particularly in the Wisdom literature, the Hebrew Scripture tradition that comes to dominate, the priestly tradition, largely focuses on the events of human history, especially that of the chosen people of God. There are very few passages that speak of the right of animals to protection from human cruelty, only 'a single, wretched passage that the righteous person has pity on his animals, and the command not to muzzle the ox while threshing'.[5] For this Hebrew tradition, nature plays a secondary role, in reaction to the influence of the pagan apotheosis of nature held by the peoples among whom the Israelites lived.[6] The very identity of the Israelite people is forged upon their separatedness from these other peoples. So the Hebrew tradition stoutly rejects the cosmological myths of pantheism. Their creation myths instead are based on belief in a Creator-God who is totally distinct from the creation, a distinction that can lead to the objectification of that creation.

This separation between the supernatural – the uncreated realm of grace and spirit – and the material world of creatures, is a significant part of Christianity's Hebrew heritage.[7] It means that nature becomes, literally, 'disenchanted', allowing 'man to perceive nature itself in a matter-of-fact way'. This in turn enables the development of natural science and 'makes nature itself available for man's use'.[8] Cardinal Schönborn, the Editor-in-chief of the 1994 *Catechism of the Catholic Church*, agrees, suggesting that 'The Bible is the first messenger of enlightenment. In its own way, it disenchants the world, strips it of its magical, mythical power, "de-mythologizing" and "dis-deifying" it. Are we aware' he asks ingenuously, 'that without this dis-deification, modern science would be impossible?"[9]

His then colleague (now Pope Benedict XVI), Joseph Cardinal Ratzinger, sees the danger of this approach, and notes that Christianity has been charged with having 'transformed all the powers of the universe, which were once our brothers and sisters, into utilitarian objects for human beings'.[10] He accepts that while this may be good for the rise of modern science, the consequence of it may have led people 'to misuse plants and animals and, in fact, all the world's powers for the sake of an ideology of progress that thinks only of itself and cares only for itself'.[11]

For Johan Metz, the rise of modern science begins in the late medieval period with the waning of the Greek influence on Christianity and its 'divinized world-understanding' and 'cosmocentric' cultural orientation. In early Greek cosmogony, the sky-god Uranus mates with the earth-god Gaia to form the world *and* the gods – linking the two inseparably. This evokes a need in people for ritual worship of natural phenomena – until a more rational culture considers that such phenomena occur independent of divine activity. An 'anthropocentric' cultural orientation develops which leads to our present age, when the world, now fully 'hominized', appears, ironically, to be 'dehumanized'.[12]

It is ironic that Christianity possesses the supreme counter-weight to this objectification of nature. The doctrine of the Incarnation reveals God as not only the transcendent Other, but also as the intimately Immanent. It is doubly ironic that this doctrine of the Incarnate God has seemingly replaced that of the wholly Transcendent God in modern Catholic culture, at the same time as animal cruelty is being practised on a more widespread and intense scale. But perhaps it has yet to work itself through to the stage when animals can be considered. The work of the Holy Spirit has also received less attention historically, than has the authoritarian nature of the Divine Judge – perhaps because of the potentially anarchic effects on individuals.

The Hebrew Scriptures are not responsible in themselves for this interpretation of revelation, but rather what 'exegesis, theology and preaching have often made of them'.[13]

What really matters is whether either Greek pantheism or Hebrew transcendence theology affected the decent treatment of animals within their social cultures. While the ancient Greeks may have held nature in greater spiritual reverence, that does not seem to have caused them to question their harsh treatment of animals. While Odysseus may have bonded with his faithful dog Argos, Homer's gods require the sacrifice of vast numbers of animals. Pantheism also provides no sense of the giftedness of creation, nor that of responsibility for it on behalf of a Creator who provided it with a beginning and therefore can summon it to an end.[14] This sense of responsibility, kindled on appropriate occasions by prophetic voices, provides a check on the exploitation of creation and the hubris of humans.

Let us look now at specific texts in the Scriptures, both Old and New, but only at those which were most salient in shaping the Christian views of animals, for better or worse, throughout the Church's history. But first, they need to be put in context.

Notes

1 Andrew Linzey, 'Animal Rights', in *A Dictionary of Ethics, Theology and Society*, edited by Paul B. Clarke and A. Linzey (London and New York: Routledge, 1960), p. 32.

2 Called by Santmire, the 'metaphor of ascent', see H. Paul Santmire, *The Travail of Nature: the ambiguous ecological promise of Christian theology* (Philadelphia: Fortress Press, 1985) and by Fox, the 'fall/redemption paradigm', see Matthew Fox, *Original Blessing: a primer in creation spirituality* (New York: Jeremy P. Tarcher/Putman, 2000 [2nd edition]).

3 See Christopher Derrick, *The Delicate Creation: towards a theology of the environment* (London: Tom Stacey, 1972), esp. chapter three.

4 Christopher Bartlett, 'A Conversation with Andrew Linzey: on Christianity and animals', in *The Animals' Agenda*, 9.4 (April, 1989), p. 7.

5 Drewermann, *Der Todliche Fortschritt* (Regensburg, 1981); cited in Frank Crüsemann, *The Torah: theology and social history of Old Testament Law* (Edinburgh: T&T Clark, 1996), p. 261n.

6 John Zizioulas, 'Priest of Creation', *Environmental Stewardship*, edited by R.J. Berry (London: T&T Clark International, 2006), p. 275.

7 Denial of it 'would be to deny the Christian faith itself', Henri De Lubac, *A Brief Catechism on Nature and Grace* (San Francisco: Ignatius Press, 1984), pp. 20–2; cited in Paul McPartlan, *The Eucharist Makes the Church: Henri de Lubac and John Zizioulas in dialogue* (Edinburgh: T&T Clark, 1993), p. 28.

8 Harvey Cox, *The Secular City* (New York: Macmillan, 1965), pp. 22–3.

9 Cardinal Christoph Schönborn, St Stephen's Cathedral, Vienna, lecture given on Sunday, 2 October 2005, 'Creation and evolution, to the debate as it stands'; translated and reported on Zenit news agency daily emailing service, 12 December 2005. For more information about Zenit, see <www.zenit.org/>.

10 Joseph Ratzinger, *'In the beginning'* ... *a Catholic understanding of the story of creation and the fall* (Edinburgh: T&T Clark, 1990), p. 34.

11 Ratzinger, *'In the beginning'* ... *a Catholic understanding of the story of creation and the fall*, p. 34.

12 Johan Metz, *Theology of the World* (1969), p. 74.

13 Robert Murray, *The Cosmic Covenant* (London: Sheed & Ward, 1992), p. 162.

14 John Zizioulas, 'Priest of Creation', *Environmental Stewardship*, edited by R.J. Berry (London: T&T Clark International, 2006), pp. 273–90.

Chapter Two

The Hebrews and the Greeks

The Old Testament

The fifth century BC is an amazing time. It is then that the first serious philosophical reflections on the subject of the relationship between human beings and animals begins anywhere. In Greece, the schools of the philosophers Empedocles and Pythagoras, with their vegetarian theories,[1] are flourishing and, further East, Hinduism is abandoning animal sacrifice, and Buddhism is preaching against violence to animals.[2] The priestly writers and redactors of the Hebrew Scriptures are compiling the law codes and texts which form the core of the Torah, the first five books of the Old Testament.[3] The creation account in Genesis 1:1–2:3 belongs to this priestly tradition. This single passage is accorded a highly privileged position in the Christian tradition, providing a basis for the development of a doctrine of creation, especially one *ex nihilo*.[4] The Genesis cosmogony of 1:1–2:3 sits as the priestly editors' preface to the story of Israel for a people in exile.[5] Genesis 1:26–8 opens the key themes of progeny and land for Genesis chapters 1–11, whereas the following chapters, 12–50, describe the Patriarchs' *lack* of land and *problems* with their progeny.[6] It also introduces the concept of humankind's creation in royal terms, using words found in Mesopotamian royal inscriptions – 'image' and 'likeness' and the verbs 'rule' and 'subdue' (which will be examined in detail in Part Two. Also explored further will be the order of creation in Genesis 1 – the structure of the six days of God's work –

which is traditionally seen as a series of steps leading to the most perfect and important of all the creatures, the human being).

What is regrettable is that the older, Yahwist, account of creation in Genesis, found in chapter two, is less emphasized in the Christian tradition. For here, the human being is less separated and distinct from other creatures, but arises out of the very substance of arable soil (*adamah*) in order to serve it (*abad*) and protect it (*samar*). *Abad* has the same Hebrew root as the word used in Isaiah to refer to the 'servant of the Lord', and *samar* with the word 'keep' used in the Aaronic blessing 'May the Lord bless you and keep you'.[7] Both terms are complementary, referring to the dignity of the vocational activity of human beings as 'maintaining, working and keeping', as distinct from the drudgery imposed – for the good of the gods – on the human race, according to Israel's Sumerian neighbours.[8] There is also a religious connotation associated with *abad*, in terms of 'serving God' in, for example, Deuteronomy 4:19, and in the priestly texts, especially of the tabernacle duties of the Levites (Numbers 3:7–8; 4:23–4, 26, etc). Also '*samar*' is used of guarding, in the ordinary sense, but also in the legal texts in connection with observing religious commandments and duties, as in Leviticus 18:5, especially of protecting the tabernacle from intruders in Numbers 1:53. These point 'to the interplay of tabernacle and Eden symbolism'.[9]

Both animals and humans are fashioned from the earth in the same way, and both made 'living souls' (*nephesh hayya*) – but with no 'image of God' metaphor separating human from animal. The Hebrew usage of 'souls', as the breath infused into both humans and non-human animals, carries no necessary implication of a continued personal existence beyond death, other than, as in Ecclesiastes 12:7, the return of the breath to God and, as in Ecclesiastes 3:19–21, the return of the body to dust.[10] The subject of 'eternal soul' in relation to animals has become problematic with the later Aristotelian linkage between rationality and soul. Before modern ethological studies proved the reasoning ability of several species of non-human animals, rationality – and thus eternal life – was believed, as we shall see in later sections of this book, to refer exclusively to the human being. Walter (now Cardinal) Kasper argues that modern anthropology shows that 'Body and soul are not simply two factors existing alongside or in each other, but form an indivisible whole. Man [and animal] is wholly body and he is wholly soul and both are at all times the whole man [and animal] ...' It is not 'having' a body or a soul but 'being' simultaneously body *and* soul.[11] Does that mean that animals, 'being' soul in the same way that humans are, can look forward to a life after bodily death? While the eschatological redemption of creation as a whole is implied in Romans chapter 8 (as will be shortly examined), the personal fate of individual animals after death has not been authoritatively defined. However, it is certainly possible to argue that,

> If it is necessary that each sentient being must have the possibility of achieving an overwhelming good, then it is clear that there must be some form of life after earthly death ... Immortality, for animals as well as humans, is a necessary condition of any acceptable theodicy; that necessity, together with all the other arguments for God, is one of the main reasons for believing in immortality.[12]

Andrew Linzey concurs, and is dismissive of any theology which hubristically decides who or what is qualified for eternal life. 'The divine prerogative is total and absolute' in the matter of the gift of eternal life. Linzey draws a case for animal redemption 'from the nature of God revealed in Christ', one that takes sides 'with the weak, the vulnerable and the innocent' – all of which describe animals, who 'whatever other things [they] may have to fear, divine justice is not among them'.[13] Numerous practical questions arise, such as to what degree of sentience in the chain of being counts as 'animal' for the purpose of according eternal life; how exactly is eternal bliss to be experienced by them; and where is this to take place? None of these can be answered with any assurance, and it would be foolish and arrogant to try. Perhaps the neatest summary would be simply to allow that 'God cannot be outdone in love', and to leave it at that.

Adam's naming of the animals is not an act of power, as was thought in the nineteenth century, but an act of affection, a bonding, enabling a relationship between man and fellow creature, in the same way that God names Israel and Adam names Eve.[14] There may be an element of conscious differentiation in the action, as in Bechtel's psychologizing theory of the Genesis myth representing the maturing of the child to the adult, where this naming of the animals by Adam is the child's 'first experience of differentiation of self from others', also 'an experience that stimulates [Adam's] intellectual capacity to use language for communication'.[15] But that does not diminish the element of relationship between the self and the other.

It is only through the Fall that hostile alienation occurs between people, people and animals, and between animals. *That* that happens is often asserted in Catholic theology, but for an account of *how* it happens it is helpful to turn to St Simeon, the New Theologian of the Eastern Church, as he describes, in terms of unrestrained pathetic fallacy, the revolt of nature, at the moment of the Fall, against the fallen Adam:

> The heaven prepared to fall on him and the earth did not wish to bear him. But God ... did not allow the elements to unleash themselves immediately against man. He ordained that creation should remain subject to man and that, having become perishable, it should serve perishable man for whom it had been created. However, when man is regenerated then creation also will be regenerated and become likewise incorruptible and, in some sense, spiritual.[16]

The Jesuit scholar Robert Murray, also, regrets the concentration that has been paid to the priestly Genesis creation account to the exclusion of all others.[17] This account, when allied with Stoic ideas, 'was to encourage a view of other creatures as if they were all essentially ordered to the good of

humankind and had no intrinsic finality of their own'.[18] Unlike
Psalm 104, where 'nature exhibits a providential harmony of
which man is an integral part',[19] in Genesis 1, 'Teleology
pervades a process of creation whose goal and crown is man.
All is directed to his benefit; the earth and its creatures are his
to rule.'[20] In another creation account, in the Book of Job,
however, human beings are incidental. 'The God of Job celebrates each act and product of his creation for itself, an
independent value attesting his power and grace. Job, representing mankind, stands outside the picture, displaced from
its centre to a remote periphery.'[21] Job is driven into the
wilderness where 'undomesticated and unbounded, [the]
denizens of the margins revel in their heedless vitality and
wanton freedom, which rests on a providence of grace'.[22] Job
is not over and above these creatures, controlling or hunting
them – but one with them, part of the same creation under
God.

However, as will be seen, it is the priestly Genesis text
which predominates in Christian theology. Barr suggests that
the insistence in the Genesis creation story that all that was
originally created was *good* 'would be a powerful motive for
all sorts of action to control and limit the exploitation and
pollution of it'.[23] However, he does acknowledge that the
priestly account of creation is 'a story built upon a process of
separation and ordering' which suggests that there is something 'in common' between this and the scientific principle of
order. It is indisputable that 'separation' was a key motif in
post-exilic Hebrew religion, not only between animals and
human beings, but between Jew and Gentile, male and female,
and clean and unclean species of animals. Such separation is
taken up in Christian theology with the theory of the 'essential difference' between the clerical and lay states, and
materially, in an architectural detail, with the separation of the
chancel from the nave by a screen (to prevent access by the
laity), and then of the altar itself by railings (to prevent access
to the altar by dogs which roamed churches at will).

Noah's story is also significant in the Tradition, if to a lesser

degree. The theme of creation being renewed is seen as a type
of the eschatological Messianic renewal of creation. As a
consequence of the Fall, the original creation, at first seen as
'good' (1:10, 18, 21, 25, 31) is now known to be corrupt
(6:12). Other texts link it with the original creation.[24] For
example, the vegetarian diet envisaged for both people and
animals (1:29–30) in the peaceable kingdom of Eden, gives
way in a fallen world to the reality of predation and carnivor-
ousness (9:2–6). The 'fear' and 'dread' of Genesis 9 are words
often used in military contexts, or when rulers behave other
than the 'good shepherds' that they are appointed to be. In
Jeremiah 23:4, these 'good shepherds' will tend sheep which
will 'no longer be afraid or terrified'.[25]

But there is another chain of significance, as noted by
Anderson, where the link-word 'remember' in 7:24–8:1 is
evocative of the priestly emphatic use of the word in Exodus
2:23–5, where God *remembers* the oppressed Hebrews in
Egypt.[26] In fact Anderson discerns a chiastic pattern between
Genesis 6:9–9:19 in which 7:24–8:1 is the key, or pivotal
passage: 'But God remembered Noah and all the beasts and all
the cattle that were with him in the ark' (RSV). This linking of
animals with Noah in the mind of God has been little
remarked upon in the Christian tradition which prefers to
separate the human from the animal creation wherever possible. This is even noticeable in the chapter headings in editions
of some Bibles, which give 'God's covenant with Noah', and
omit all else![27]

The 'remembering' passages are one way in which creation
is integrated into the historical narratives of the Hebrew Scriptures. In fact it is so embedded that the land is a central – if
not *the* central – theme of biblical faith.[28] The land, in the
Deuteronomic tradition, does not belong to the Israelites:
'The land belongs to [God], and to [God] you are only
strangers and guests' (Leviticus 25:23) – which is a long way
from saying that the land and all its resources belong to the
human race, which is the Church's traditional (and current)
view. This will be returned to later in this book.

Another way of linking creation with the historic narratives is by the repeated motif of covenants. Indeed, for Robert Murray, the idea of there having been an original pre-biblical binding of the cosmic elements by a covenantal oath – breached by rebellious divine beings and re-established by God in the biblical and christological 'eternal covenant' – is central to the thesis of his 1992 work *The Cosmic Covenant*. The Messianic restoration of the 'cosmic covenant' – bringing eternal universal shalom (peace, order and harmony) – is for Murray a much broader enterprise than simply the saving of individual human souls. However, historically, the various covenants have been taken up separately and with a disparity in the weight accorded to them.

The Adamic covenant (Genesis 1:28, repeated in 9:6b) in which human beings are given dominion over animals, has been greatly privileged in the sense of being frequently used as a 'proof text' for the human treatment of animals.

The Mosaic covenant is another privileged one, which, while making provision for animals to rest on the Sabbath (Exodus 20:10), also mandates holocausts and communion sacrifices of animals (Exodus 20:24) as well as the punishment (by stoning to death) of bulls found guilty of goring humans (Exodus 21:28–36).

The consequences of the Noachic covenant (Genesis 9:9, recapitulated both in Hosea 2:18 and Isaiah 54:9–10), however, in which God makes a covenant with 'every living creature ... everything that lives on the earth', have rarely been drawn. However, it is apparent that the Noachic covenant of Genesis 9 is ambivalent. While all creatures (and *kol*, 'all', is used no fewer than nine times) are included within the covenant, there is at the same time the mandate to sacrifice animals, a fact implied by God savouring the smoke and then appearing to be appeased. With that and the embargos on the consumption of animal blood and on the shedding of human blood, it could be that the priestly writers were tracing their religious taboos and practices back into the earliest times, a plausible suggestion made by Wenham.[29] Certainly, the ban on consuming blood is out of respect for life, and the Creator of the life, of the animal.

In the legal codes, the separation of food and sacrificial animals into 'clean' and 'unclean' has been interpreted in the Christian allegorical tradition as symbolizing virtues and vices (the 'clean' animals being virtuous, the 'unclean' symbolizing vices). However, virtue is not the point. The anthropologist Mary Douglas describes how those animals which predate on others, thereby ingesting blood, are 'unclean', as a priestly proscription against eating flesh with blood in it is given out of honour for the life that is in the blood, the God-given life. This is linked with ethical behaviour, with behaving justly for, as Douglas puts it, 'holiness is incompatible with predatory behaviour'.[30] She also argues that both the animals sacrificed and the people permitted to make the sacrifices, the priests, have to be without blemish, 'clean' – that is, conforming to a certain 'perfect' standard, with neither too much nor too little of something. That corresponds with the ethical requirements of justice: too much of something, such as laws, could be burdensome; too little of something, such as power or provisions, could cause suffering too.[31] One other key passage in the Hebrew Scriptures which has been given heightened significance in Christian Tradition is that of the vision of Isaiah 11:6–9, a description of the Messianic renewal of creation. This will be dealt with more fully later in this book.

The New Testament

While there is little in the Gospels to suggest an explicit or specific policy towards animals, there is much that can be generally inferred about the compassion of Jesus which could, considering his integrity and consistency of character, be reasonably applied to animals. It is true that two of the better-known sayings about birds are followed by mention of God according greater value to people 'Are you not worth much more than they are?'(Matthew 6:26), and, 'You are worth more than hundreds of sparrows' (Luke 12:6). But what is of note, however, is that both bird and human are valued by God and differentiated only by degree. The wish of contemporary Christian vegetarians[32] to include Jesus in their number is problematic, as it is not supported in the Gospels, where he is recorded as encouraging fishing and the eating of fish. Jesus, so far as we know, shares the paschal lamb and eats meat at the many dinners to which he is invited. Maybe he did not – we cannot know. Similarly, attempts to devalidate the story of Jesus sending two thousand pigs[33] to their deaths are only of recent origin. Phelps[34] argues that the destruction of such a large number of pigs, which must have belonged to a wealthy Gentile, would have been politically explosive and so could not have happened literally. The interpretation he favours is that the pigs, symbolizing Gentiles being driven into the sea, or vanquished, is a legend that originates in anti-Roman nationalism and attaches itself to Jesus. However, such an interpretation is not traditional.

The animal-related texts of greatest significance in Christian tradition have been the following two: the wilderness reference in Mark's Gospel (1:12–13), and, to a lesser extent, the passage about cosmic salvation in Romans 8:19–25.

The wilderness (Mark 1:12–13) A brief account in Mark's Gospel refers to Jesus being 'with the wild animals' (Mark 1:13). This has led to interpretations ranging from the solitary Jesus being simply in proximity to dangerous animals but safe from them, to some of the patristic commentators actually linking the animals with Satan.[35] Some early commentators suggest that the Devil actually appears in the shape of wild animals, 'as if animals were somehow an appropriate vehicle for displays of devilish activity'.[36]

The reference in the same verse (Mark 1:13) to Jesus being ministered to by angels could recall, for Mark's original readers, a passage from Psalm 91:11–13, 'For he will give his angels charge of you to guard you in all your ways', followed by, 'You will tread on the lion and the adder, the young lion and the serpent you will trample under foot.'[37] The dating of the Gospel can also affect the reading. If it originates in the AD 60s, when Christians are being torn to pieces under Nero's persecution,

> It is not difficult to imagine Mark including the unusual phrase 'with the wild beasts' in order to remind his Roman readers that Christ, too, was [figuratively] thrown to wild beasts, and as the angels ministered to him, so, too, will they minister to Roman readers facing martyrdom.[38]

There is another interpretation in the tradition, however, which gives the word 'with' (μετα) more of the meaning of 'being at peace with' or even 'in companionship with' as when it is used in reference to Jesus being 'with' the disciples in Mark 3:14, and elsewhere.[39] The oldest patristic passage showing Jesus in the wilderness at peace with the animals is a Syriac homily under the name of St Ephrem c.306–373 – but which could date from two centuries later: 'He went about with the animals which knelt and worshipped him: and the angels praised him on earth as in heaven.'[40]

Kerr suggests that the four words in Mark are meant to evoke various texts, such as Hosea 2:18: 'In that day I will make a covenant for them with the beasts of the field and with the fowls of the air and with the creeping things of the ground.' The picture would be that

> having his first great struggle with all that is temptingly demonic, Jesus is being supported not just by angels *but also* by wild animals – at this new start, this re-creation of human-ity, which is what Mark's story is going to be all about, here we have Jesus being sketched as Adam, the original human being, back in harmony with the creatures of the animal kingdom.[41]

Job too is told that, as a truly righteous person, '[you] shall not fear the wild animals of the earth ... [They] shall be at peace with you' (Job 5:22–3). Eschatologically, the messianic age would herald peace between animals and humans, as described in Isaiah 11:6–9. In other words, the peaceable kingdom, or Eden restored,[42] is heralded in Mark's Gospel by this encounter between the new Adam and the wild animals. That is indeed the reading given in many of the apocryphal writings from the second to the ninth centuries. Some of these anticipate the wilderness scene by having the child Jesus perform miracles on behalf of animals. We shall return to this interpretation later in the book.

Romans 8:19–25 'The whole creation is eagerly waiting for God to reveal his sons ... creation still retains the hope of being freed ... from its slavery to decadence ... From the beginning till now the entire creation has been groaning in one great act of giving birth ...'

With the phrase '*pasa ktisis*', the *whole* creation, this text could have been seminal for a thorough soteriology (salvation theology) of animals and the rest of creation. However, since Origen interprets *ktisis,* creation, solely as *human* creation[43] the Church has largely followed this anthropocentric path. So what does the term *ktisis* really mean? It could be used to refer to creation as a whole,[44] to the corporeal Christian alone,[45] to human beings in general,[46] to Gentiles, or the heathen world,[47] or to human history.[48] G. W. F. Lampe is speaking for the traditional, post-Origen view that, in Scripture, nature is merely a setting for human history, providing the human being with the mortal body, but as 'he [the human being] alone of all creatures is made in the divine image', uniquely capable of responding to the Creator and 'capable of fellowship with him', he alone experiences redemption.[49] For Lampe, the redeemed living Christian is to tend the creation in a better way, as God's agent or steward, than in his or her unredeemed or fallen state, and it is for that better treatment for which the rest of creation waits. Then, with a want of logic, he claims that, as only human beings are capable of falling into disobedience, the new creation is reserved only for human beings. The new life described by Paul (Romans 8:18–25) is 'life in the Spirit ... the transference of believers from the sphere of the flesh to that of God's Spirit'.[50] This traditional dismissal of nature and, with it, of the animal creation, from the activity of Christ has led to the belief in an unbridgeable gulf between human beings and animals, and to the consideration of animals as of no more consequence than the rest of inanimate nature.

There is a view, more recent than Lampe's, that considers the 'groaning of creation' to refer not only to the pain of childbirth, or the process of transition from one state to another, but also to a sense of lamentation, of nature mourning and bewailing the loss of innocence. Braaten argues that human sin and divine judgement (the curses of Genesis 3:14–19 whereby the snake, man, and woman are cursed, but the ground is only indirectly so, 'on account of Adam') are the cause for creation's lament. As in Joel chapters 1 and 2, where God summons Israel to repent and lament and then offers salvation, so here creation groans until, 'finally joined by God's people', ... 'God will save both creation and people alike'.[51]

Paul's interpretation, in 1 Corinthians 9:9, of Deuteronomy 25:4, as allegory,[52] could be regarded as expressing his low consideration of animals. Paul denies that God really cares for oxen and claims that 'oxen' really means Christian evangelists like himself. As Gaffney explains: 'It was for many centuries a common practice among Christians, confronted with biblical passages whose prior import conflicted with their own notions of what a divine revelation might decently contain, to resort to allegorism.'[53] Allegory itself does not necessarily imply that the spiritual interpretation alone matters, only that it is higher or deeper,[54] but here Paul actually denies the literal meaning any validity. This interpretation is at variance with that of the sages of the Talmud, who defend the literal meaning of the Deuteronomic text with references to Psalm 32:7, where 'the salvation of the Lord extends equally to "man and beast"' and to Job 38:41 which describes God providing for the raven and its young.[55] While many of the rabbinic sages support the opinion that animals are specially created in order to serve the material, and even moral, needs of human beings,[56] there is nevertheless an ethical precept in Jewish texts and tradition of *tsa'ar be'alei chayim*, the mandate 'not to cause pain to any living creature'.[57] The adoption of this into Christian ethical practice would make a useful contribution to a consistent ethic of life.

Greek philosophers before Christ

As mentioned, the fifth century in Greece saw the flourishing of the great philosophical schools, including those of the vegetarian philosophers Empedocles and Pythagoras. Foremost is the Academy of the influential philosophical giant, Socrates (469–399 BC). It is to Socrates that the first expression of the concept of nature being created solely for the benefit of human beings has been traced.[58] Xenophon's *Memorabilia* has Socrates, in conversation with Euthydemus, explaining how everything, for example, light and darkness, food and drink, 'are all divinely ordered for the safety and convenience of man'. Euthydemus questions whether animals are also involved in this, to which Socrates replies 'Yes, and is it not evident that they too receive life and food *for the sake of man?*'[59] Socrates does ban meat-eating from the three highest of his ideal cities – allowing it only in the 'city of luxury' – not from motives of kindness to animals, but only because meat-eating inevitably involves ritual sacrifice which he argues is a form of 'bartering' with the gods.

However, it is Plato (428–348 BC) who dominates the philosophical scene for centuries to come, including long into the Christian era. Christian theologians were attracted to the quasi-monotheism of Plato's concept of the Good, and take his rationalism as their guide, assuming that knowledge of the natural world can be gained by reason alone. This elevation of the faculty of reasoning to the highest possible level is a major cause of Christianity's dualistic approach to nature. Plato himself inherits the dualistic thinking which supposes that animals lack reasoning and humans uniquely possess it.[60] The mid sixth-century philosopher Alcmaeon states that 'Man

differs from the other animals because he alone has understanding whereas animals perceive, but do not understand.'[61]
Anaxagoras (500–428 BC), too, holds that humans are the
masters of animals because of humans' unique experience,
memory, expertise and technical knowledge, but he does not
deny that animals possess intellect (*nous*).[62] For Plato all
animals, human and otherwise, have souls – meaning an
animating, incorporeal self capable of surviving after death –
and animals' souls contain a reasoning part and even one
capable of a primitive form of belief (*doxa*).[63] This attribute is
shared with human slaves: 'A precarious form of true belief
can be found in the nature of a beast and of a slave.'[64] Moreover, in an inverted form of evolution (Darwin-meets-
Pythagoras), Plato gives to the central speaker in his *Timaeus*
dialogue the belief that humans preceded animals, resulting,
through reincarnation, in animals manifesting human characteristics gained in a former existence.[65] As the ideal function of
a Form is to fulfil its *telos* (purpose), and as the function of the
'Form of Man' is to accommodate a rational soul, intellectual
and moral degeneration (from that of the rational male
human being) is reflected in progressively 'lower' forms of life
– with first the female human body (!), then that of birds, then
'footed beasts', snakes and finally fish and shellfish.[66] All the
creatures, human and animal, have the same kind of soul as
that of the world itself, that which is demonstrably alive by the
motions of the planets. All were created by a Demiurge who
made a world that was, while containing elements that seem
to be imperfect, nevertheless the best of all possible worlds.
For Timaeus, as for the other believers in transmigration,
Pythag-oras and Empedocles, a vegetarian diet is necessary to
avoid harming 'members of our own family'.[67] Whether Plato
himself believes in this myth, with its comic and far-fetched
elements, is debatable, but Sedley concludes that it does
provide a guide to Plato's views, and is scientific in the sense
that it 'locates afterlife punishment in the natural kingdom,
not in a mythic other world'. [68] Anthony Kenny notes that the
Timaeus was the most influential of Plato's dialogues for

centuries in the medieval period, and that it was even a set text in the early days of the University of Paris.[69]

Another of Plato's Socratic dialogues, the *Protagoras*, provides an alternative creation myth, this time describing the emergence of the non-human animals from the archaic slime all naked and defenceless. Epimetheus, one of the two demigods who had been given the task of equipping them for survival, used up the whole supply, so that when human beings emerged, there was nothing left for them. The more practical demigod, Prometheus, then stole fire and the use of the arts from the gods, and provided humans with both technology and an affinity with the gods. Thus morality is explained as a 'survival tactic for a threatened species' and 'our war on the rest of nature comes to seem like a justifiable struggle', one that the gods seem to have really intended us to win.[70]

However, it is Plato's disciple Aristotle (384–322 BC), whose views on animals and the natural world owe much to Plato's *Timaeus*,[71] which are to have the most influence in the whole Western history of the relationship between people and animals. In Sorabji's view, by Aristotle's denial of reason to animals, a crisis is provoked 'both for the philosophy of mind and for theories of morality'.[72] The Stoics take Aristotle's position further, and deny any justice to animals. They develop, to a high degree, the idea that animals are designed for human benefit – ideas which become embedded in Western Christianity to this day. Because, like Alcmaeon, Aristotle denies that animals can possess reason or belief, he has to expand the idea of 'perception'– which animals *do* possess – to include memory, experience and a form of thinking that allows animals to act voluntarily. He denies that animals have the power to exercise deliberate choice although, perversely, he holds that an animal can act in a way that implies moral responsibility, otherwise they would not be praised or blamed. Like Plato, he grants that animals – and even plants – possess souls, as the soul is no more than that which gives it life, and that animals have consciousness. But it is rationality, which he

alleges animals lack, on which so much hinges – to the exclusion of any other capacity, such as sentience. It is animals' lack
of rationality which precludes their right to any kind of justice.
Unusually, Aristotle allows a right to humans for which he stipulates no corresponding duty – the right to hunt and kill
animals.[73]

Finally, in this thumb-nail sketch of Aristotle, it is worth
noting that he, Socrates, and the Stoics, believe that all things,
including animals, are created for the sole sake of human
beings: 'as nature therefore makes nothing either imperfect
or in vain, it necessarily follows that she has made all these
things for men'.[74] This is taken up later by Cicero in his statement that 'the earth itself is for the sake of those possessing
reason, that is, for men and gods'.[75]

Among the inheritors of Aristotle's theories are the Nesto-
rian Christians who take them to Persia where they are
developed by Arab thinkers. These then reintroduce them
into the Europe of the Middle Ages where St Thomas Aquinas,
among others, adapt them until a modified form of Aristotelianism becomes the bedrock of Catholic philosophy.[76]

Meanwhile, the Stoics in Greece and Rome develop Aristotle's theories, particularly his refusal to allow animals any
form of justice. The Stoics grant justice and rights only to
those who belong to a community, the *oikeosis*, which is eventually extended to include all rational beings, that is, all human
beings. Any creature outside that community simply has no
share in justice or rights, and anything can be done to them
with impunity.[77] One particular Stoic, Chrysippus (280–207
BC), asserts that, with the exception of the universe, everything is made for the sake of something else, plants for
animals, animals for man, and man – a little portion of the
finished whole – is made to observe and imitate the universe.
Each animal has its role in serving man. The pig, for example,
has no reason for being except to provide meat, its soul
having been given to it simply in place of salt, to keep its flesh
from spoiling.[78] The uses of creatures harmful to people, such
as mice, moths, and snakes, were yet to be discovered.[79]

The necessity of belonging to a community reappears in the fourth century AD when the neoplatonist Iamblichus (*c*.250–330) suggests that there is indeed a community of belonging between the gods and animals – but that makes animals more fitted to be used for sacrifice.[80] St Augustine, too, is to make use of the theory of *oikeosis* in relation to membership of the Church – of which animals have no part and therefore may be killed at will.[81]

Another neoplatonist, Porphyry (AD 232–305), repeats Chrysippus's views with approval.[82] However, he attacks pagan animal sacrifice in his treatise *On Abstinence from Animal Food*. In it he reviews the arguments for sacrifice and meat-eating of the Epicureans, the Aristotelians, the Stoics and ordinary people, then responds to them, emphasizing the similarities animals have with people, even if their rationality is *less* than that of human beings. Nevertheless, while animals also have some human vices, such as sexual jealousy, they do not share the vice of ingratitude and disloyalty that humans show in killing the very creatures which plough people's fields and give them their milk and fleeces. While opposing meat-eating, he deals with the 'sliding', or *sorites*, argument, often used against vegetarians, that, if animals should not be killed, should not plants also be protected? Sorabji shows that this 'sliding' argument is found as early as from Solon of Athens (*c*.640–558 BC), who gives his own reason for keeping the plant-animal distinction by the fact that plants lack thought (*phronein*). Porphyry adds that plants also lack 'pain and terror' which animals do not.

As do so many others at the time, Porphyry believes in the transmigration of souls. However he denounces the ridiculous Platonist theory that, in order to have their souls released for reincarnation into people, animals actually *like* to be killed. In his treatises against Christianity, he questions Christ's apparent lack of concern in the fate of the Gadarene swine. His overt anti-Christian stance is a barrier for Christians in adopting his relatively moderate views on the treatment of animals, and provides material for Christians to denounce those ideas along with his others.

Another movement of influence in the centuries prior to Christianity is that of the Epicureans,[83] just mentioned, and their theory of justice as contract, which differs from one society to another. The Epicureans also deny justice to animals. Where Empedocles has argued for the extension of justice to animals, the treatise *Against Empedocles*, by Epicurus's successor Hermarchus (fl. 271 BC) denies the possibility on the grounds that, as they are not rational, animals cannot enter into contracts.[84] Now the task is to show how this smörgåsbord of ideas comes to influence Catholic theological theories of animals.

Notes

1 Empedocles held that, by killing animals, one could be killing one's reincarnated kin; similarly Pythagoras taught that vegetarianism deterred one from cannibalism; see Richard Sorabji, *Animal Minds and Human Morals: the origins of the Western debate* (London: Duckworth, 1993), p. 176.

2 Mary Douglas, 'The Forbidden Animals in Leviticus', *Journal for the Study of the Old Testament*, 59 (1993), p. 4.

3 Roland E. Murphy, 'Introduction to the Pentateuch', in *The New Jerome Biblical Commentary*, edited by R. Browne et al, (London: Geoffrey Chapman, 1990), p. 7.

4 The *ex nihilo* doctrine is supported also by 2 Maccabees 7:28 and re-echoed in the apocryphal Slavonic Enoch 24:2 and 4 Ezra: 38–5. It was also the orthodox view of Judaism until the third century AD, when Platonic ideas of pre-existent unformed matter (to which God gave form) began to predominate; see A. Altmann, 'A Note on the Rabbinic Doctrine of Creation', *The Journal of Jewish Studies*, 7. 3–4 (1956), pp. 195–206.

5 Richard Clifford, *Creation Accounts in the Ancient Near East and in the Bible* (Washington DC: The Catholic Biblical Association of America, 1994), p. 138.

6 Ibid., p. 139.

7 Paul Santmire, 'Beyond the Theology of Stewardship', *Environmental Stewardship*, edited by R. J. Berry (London: T&T Clark International, 2006), p. 262.

8 Claus Westermann, Genesis 1–11, London: SPCK, 1974 (German), 1984 (English), p. 221.

9 Gordon J. Wenham, *Genesis 1–15*, (World Biblical Commentary), Vol. 1

(Dallas, TX: Word Incorporated, 1987; Milton Keynes: Word (UK) edition, 1991), p. 67.

10 Apart from Sheol being a nebulous place of afterlife. The first real sense of personal redemption comes as late as 2 Maccabees 7:23. The hopes of the Day of the Lord, given expression, inter alia, in Isaiah 11, could have referred primarily to a state of future historical earthly blessedness, and only later, to an eschatological one.

11 Walter Kasper, *Jesus the Christ* (London: Burns & Oates, 1976), page 201.

12 Keith Ward, *Rational Theology and the Creativity of God* (London: Blackwell, 1982), page 223; cited in Andrew Linzey, *Animal Theology* (London: SCM, 1994), page 100.

13 *Animals on the Agenda*, edited by Andrew Linzey and Dorothy Yamamoto (London: SCM, 1998), page 119.

14 Santmire, 'Beyond the Theology of Stewardship', p. 263.

15 Lyn M. Bechtel, 'Rethinking the interpretation of Genesis 2:43–3:24', *A Feminist Companion to Genesis*, edited by Athalya Brenner (Sheffield Academic Press, 1993), p. 113. Her theory of maturation as against sin/guilt/Fall has the merit of a certain consistency within Genesis, but leaves subsequent redemption and Second Adam theology rootless.

16 Paul Evdokimov, 'Nature', *Scottish Journal of Theology* 18 (1965), pp. 9–10.

17 Robert Murray, *The Cosmic Covenant* (London: Sheed & Ward, 1992), p. 163ff. There are other cosmogonies, including those in Proverbs (3:19–20; 8:22–31); Psalms (8, echoing Genesis; 104); Isaiah (44:24–28) and Job (38–42) and innumerable references to God as Creator.

18 Murray, *The Cosmic Covenant* (1992), p. 163ff.

19 Mark I. Greenberg, 'Job', in *The Literary Guide to the Bible*, edited by Robert Alter and Frank Kermode (Cambridge, MA: Harvard UP, 1990), p. 298.

20 Greenberg, 'Job', p. 298.

21 Ibid.

22 W. P. Brown, *The Ethos of the Cosmos: the genesis of moral imagination in the Bible* (Grand Rapids: Eerdmans, 1999), p. 394; cited by Paul Santmire, 'Beyond the Theology of Stewardship', *Environmental Stewardship*, edited by R.J. Berry (London: T&T Clark International, 2006), p. 266.

23 James Barr, 'Man and Nature: the ecological controversy and the Old Testament', in the *Bulletin of the John Rylands Library*, 55 (1972), p. 31.

24 Examples include the blessing of man and woman in Genesis 1:26–30, repeated in 9:1–7; and the flood in chapters 6–9 being a reversal of the ordering of the waters in 1:6–10.

25 John Olley, 'Mixed Blessings for Animals: the contrasts of Genesis 9', in *The Earth Story and Genesis*, edited by Norman C. Habel and Shirley Wurst. (Sheffield Academic Press, 2000), p. 135.

26 B. W. Anderson, 'From Analysis to Synthesis: the interpretation of Genesis 1–11', *Journal of Biblical Literature*, 97 (1978), pp. 23–9.

27 In the NRSV and NIV, noticed by John Olley, 'Mixed Blesssings for Animals: the contrasts of Genesis 9', in *The Earth Story and Genesis*, p. 131.

28 Walter Brueggemann, *The Land: place as gift, promise and challenge in biblical faith* (Philadelphia: Fortress, 1977), p. 6.

29 Gordon J. Wenham, *Genesis 1–15* (World Biblical Commentary), Vol 1 (Dallas, TX: Word Incorporated, 1987; Milton Keynes: Word (UK) Edition, 1991), p. 195.

30 Mary Douglas, 'The Forbidden Animals in Leviticus', *Journal for the Study of the Old Testament*, 59 (1993) p. 22.

31 Ibid., pp. 3–23.

32 For example, Fr John Dear, SJ in his popular booklet *Christianity and vegetarianism: pursuing the nonviolence of Jesus* (Norfolk, VA: People for the Ethical Treatment of Animals, 2004).

33 The Gadarene swine of Matthew 8:28–34, Mark 5:1–20, Luke 8:26–39.

34 Norm Phelps, *The Dominion of Love: animal rights according to the Bible* (New York: Lantern, 2002), pp. 139–42.

35 This was influenced possibly by a passage in the *Testament of Naphtali* from the apocryphal *Testament of the Twelve Patriarchs*. In that, if the readers will 'do what is good . . . the devil will flee from you and the wild animals will be afraid of you' but for every man who 'does not do what is good' 'the devil will use him as his own peculiar instrument and every wild animal will gain the mastery over him'. *The Apocryphal Old Testament*, edited by H. F. D. Sparks (Oxford: Clarendon, 1985), pp. 571–2). Although only medieval copies exist, earlier fragments were discovered at Qumran, so the tradition could have been well known.

36 Fergus Kerr, OP, 'And was with the wild beasts', *The Ark*, 185 (Summer 2000), p. 35.

37 See Daniel J. Harrington, 'The Gospel according to Mark', in *The New Jerome Biblical Commentary*, edited by R. Browne et al, (London: Geoffrey Chapman, 1991), p. 599.

38 J. R. Edwards, *The Gospel according to St Mark* (Grand Rapids: Eerdmans, 2002), p. 41.

39 Fergus Kerr, OP, 'And was with the wild beasts', p. 35.

40 It is the oldest known to Robert Murray; see *The Cosmic Covenant* ((London: Sheed & Ward, 1992), p. 128.

41 Kerr, OP, 'And was with the wild beasts', p. 36.

42 It is worth noting that the garden of Eden in Genesis was not associated originally with 'a garden of God . . . or what is popularly known as paradise' until it was translated into Greek, when גן was rendered as παραδεισος; see Claus Westermann, *Genesis 1–11*, London: SPCK, 1974 (German), 1984 (English), p. 208.

43 Murray, *The Cosmic Covenant* (1992), p. 130.

44 See Murray (1992), Santmire (1985), and many others.

45 G. W. F. Lampe, 'The New Testament Doctrine of *Ktisis*', *The Scottish Journal of Theology*, 17 (1964), p. 451.

46 Leenhardt, in Lampe, 'The New Testament Doctrine of *Ktisis*', p. 458.

47 John Lightfoot, *A Commentary on the New Testament from the Hebraica; Matthew – I Corinthians*, Volume 4 (Grand Rapids: Baker Books, 1979), pp. 156–7.

48 Bultmann, Barth etc, see Santmire, 'Beyond the Theology of Stewardship', p. 202.

49 Lampe, 'The New Testament Doctrine of *Ktisis*', p. 451.

50 Ibid., p. 455.

51 Laurie J. Braaten, 'The Groaning Creation: the biblical background for Romans 8:22', *Biblical research: journal of the Chicago Society of Biblical Research*, Vol. L, 2005, pp. 19–39.

52 1 Corinthains 9:9:'It is written in the Law of Moses:*You must not put a muzzle on the ox when it is treading out the corn*. Is it about oxen that God is concerned, or is there not an obvious reference to ourselves? Clearly this is written for our sake to show that the ploughman ought to plough in expectation, and the thresher to thresh in the expectation of getting his share.'

53 James Gaffney, 'Can Catholic Morality make room for Animals?', in *Animals on the Agenda*, edited by Andrew Linzey and Dorothy Yamamoto (London: SCM, 1998), p. 102. Augustine continued this allegoricalizing, interpreting, for example, the young lions of Psalm 104:21 as spirits of wickedness; see Stephen R.L. Clark, 'Is Nature God's Will?', in *Animals on the Agenda* , edited by Linzey and Yamamoto.

54 St Augustine: 'We have heard the fact; [now] let us look into the mystery' [*In Jo*, tr. 50, n. 6 (PL, XXXV, 1760).]; cited in *Medieval exegesis, Vol.2: the four senses of Scripture*, by Henri de Lubac (Editions Montaigne, 1959), translated by E. M. Macierowski (Grand Rapids: Eerdmans; Edinburgh: T&T Clark, 2000), p. 83. In the same work is the following citation from Robert of Melun (1100–1165): 'By as much as (a doctrine) is the more evident in the literal sense, by so much is it the deeper in the mystical understanding', (*Sent. Praef.* (Martin, 32), p. 85.

55 I. Jakobovits, 'The Medical Treatment of Animals in Jewish Law', *The Journal of Jewish Studies*, 7.3–4 (1956), p. 208.

56 Ibid., p. 209.

57 Richard Schwartz, *Judaism and Vegetarianism* (New York: Lantern, 2001), p. 15.

58 Other possible 'suspects' include the earlier Anaxagoras, or his pupil Diogenes of Apollonia, in his work *On Nature*, and Aristotle prefers the earlier Hermotimus of Calzomenae, but Socrates is the best attested. See A. S. Pease, 'Caeli Enarrant', *Harvard Theological Review*, 34. 3 (1941), p. 163.

59 Pease, 'Caeli Enarrant', pp. 165–6. My emphasis.

60 However it is argued that Plato himself does not hold the dualistic view of two worlds, that of concepts and that of the senses. See A. E. Taylor (*Plato, the man and his work*, London: Methuen, 7th edn., 1960, p. 443 and n. 2) who lays that charge mainly at the Neo-Platonists. However, Carol Osborne detects a few passages in Plato's works of his Middle Period 'that seem to invite us to adopt some form of dualism'. Carol Osborne, *Dumb Beasts and Dead Philosophers* (Oxford: Clarendon, 2007), pp. 70–1.

61 Richard Sorabji, *Animal Minds and Human Morals: the origins of the Western debate* (London: Duckworth, 1993), p. 9.

62 See Sorabji, *Animal Minds and Human Morals* (1993), p. 8.

63 Ibid., p. 65.

64 Plato, *Republic* 430B, cited in Sorabji, *Animal Minds and Human Morals* (1993), p. 11.

65 Sorabji, *Animal Minds and Human Morals* (1993) p. 10.

66 See Timaeus, 90e1–9217–c1, cited in David Sedley, *Creationism and its Critics in Antiquity* (Berkeley, CA: University of California Press, 2007), p. 128ff.

67 See Carol Osborne, *Dumb Beasts and Dead Philosophers* (Oxford: Clarendon, 2007), p. 61.

68 David Sedley, *Creationism and its Critics in Antiquity*, pp. 98, 132.

69 Anthony Kenny, *Ancient Philosophy*, Volume 1 (Oxford: Clarendon, 2004), p. 64.

70 Carol Osborne, *Dumb Beasts and Dead Philosophers*, p. 31.

71 Anthony Kenny, *Ancient Philosophy*, Volume 1 (Oxford: Clarendon, 2004), p. 88.

72 Sorabji, (1993) p. 7, ff.

73 Aristotle, *Politics* 1.8, 1256b20–6; see Sorabji, (1993) p. 154.

74 Aristotle, *Politics* 1. 8.

75 Cicero, *ND* 2, 133; see Pease, 'Caeli Enarrant', p. 177.

76 C.W. Hume, *The Status of Animals in the Christian Religion* (London: Universities Federation for Animal Welfare, 1957), p. 23.

77 See Sorabji, *Animal Minds and Human Morals* (1993), chapter 10.

78 Mentioned by Cicero, *ND* 2, 160; see Pease, 'Caeli Enarrant', p. 177; also Sorabji, *Animal Minds and Human Morals* (1993), p. 199.

79 Plutarch *De Stoic. Repugn* 21, cited in Pease, 'Caeli Enarrant', p. 178.

80 Sorabji, *Animal Minds and Human Morals* (1993), p. 130.

81 Ibid., p. 131.

82 Porphyry, *De Abstin.* 3, 20; see Sorabji (1993), p. 182 ff.

83 Followers of Epicurus (341–270 BC).

84 See Sorabji, (1993), p. 162.

Chapter Three

The Theologians

Three streams run into the Catholic Church's river – the theological, the charismatic-monastic, and the magisterial-legal. In this and the following two chapters, these streams are represented by their key proponents, the theologians, the saints of the East and the West, and the teachers and law makers who work within the Church. Of course, sometimes these streams overflow, coalesce, or divert, but they help to make up the complexity and richness of the Church which runs on and absorbs them all.

The Greek ideas of the various schools are naturally assumed by Jewish and early Christian theologians, especially in the Eastern part of the Roman Empire. A midrash by a second-century rabbi, Simeon ben Eliezer, repeats the view that animals were created only to serve mankind – as mankind itself was created to serve God. This re-emerges in the twelfth century *Sefer HaHinnukh*.[1] On the other hand, third-century Judaism includes Rabbi Levi's teaching on the importance, as mentioned earlier, of the mitsvot, *tsa'ar be'alei chayim*, in which the inflicting of suffering to animals must be avoided.[2]

Christianity is just as ambivalent. Greek anthropocentrism is reflected in the writings of the Christian, Theophilus of Antioch (d. AD 181), who extols God for the creation of 'the divers species of quadrupeds, and birds, and reptiles, and fishes, ... [and] the instinct implanted in these animals to beget and rear offspring, *not for their own profit, but for the use of man'*.[3]

Lactantius However, another Christian apologist, also known as a Church Father, Lactantius, (*c*.260–*c*.317), tutor to the son of the Emperor Constantine, rejects the use of reason and many other claims as differentiators between animals and human beings. The only sort of reason which animals lack is pure or perfect reason, or wisdom, *sapientia*, the one by which humans can have the knowledge of God. This sort of reason has been given to human beings because of their immortal souls – not the other way round.[4]

The classical philosophers always enjoy playing with the permutations of the categories of the highly complex concept of reason, especially to differentiate human beings from animals. Lactantius allows animals three of the attributes normally considered to be exclusively human: spoken communication, foresight, and laughter.[5] Lactantius also draws heavily upon Isaiah 11's vision of the peaceable kingdom in his own view of a future golden age, when:

> The world itself will rejoice and the nature of all things will be glad, since the dominion of evil and impiety and crime will have been broken and cut off from it. Beasts will not feed on blood during this time nor birds on prey, but all things will be quiet and at rest. Lions and calves will stand together at the manger to feed; the wolf will not steal the sheep; the dog will not hunt; hawks and eagles will not do harm; a child will play with snakes.[6]

However, this inclusive Isaian vision finds no favours within the influential Gnostic movement with its seeds in pagan mystery cults. The dualist ideas of this syncretistic school permeate both Judaism and Christianity in the early centuries. It rejects the concrete present and admits into the community of the 'spiritual' only those who possess 'knowledge of the truth'. Mere 'carnals', unspiritually-minded people, and all animals, are denied any salvation. In various guises it re-appears throughout history. When conditions are especially hard in the world, the 'flight' into the sphere of the supernatural is all too tempting. The period of persecutions under the

Roman emperors is one which sees a particular growth in the movement. A major Gnostic creation myth involves the creation of the physical world by a divine power which is evil, not by the good divine power which, in their view, is concerned only about the spiritual.[7]

Irenaeus A formidable opponent of the second-century Gnostics is Irenaeus of Lyons (c.130–200), a pioneer of Catholic orthodoxy.[8] His view on creation is the earliest of such texts by the Church Fathers to be referred to in the *Catechism of the Catholic Church* (CCC).[9] In it he defends the view that the one, good, Trinitarian God is the creator of the world, physical and spiritual. The effect of his support for the material, corporeal reality of the millennium beyond the eschaton, is, however, reduced in the mid-third century by Dionysius, Bishop of Alexandria and former student of Origen, who turns it all into allegory. And when Irenaeus' work *Against the Heresies* is translated into Latin in the early fifth century, the translator omits references to this corporeality from the text.[10] However, Irenaeus' credentials are impeccable, his having been taught by Polycarp, who had, in turn, been taught by John the Apostle. Using biblical references, Irenaeus attacks the Gnostics for their negativity towards nature. For him, nature is 'good' and 'humanity's God-given home'.[11] Santmire admires Irenaeus' enlarged view that salvation history is the history of creation as a whole, with a beginning and an ending.[12] Creation moves temporarily through seven epochs or 'days' (corresponding to the 'seven days' of Genesis 1) and when it comes to an end, that fulfilment will be a new thing, not just a return to the beginning. Because of Christ's vocation being, according to Irenaeus, balanced between the fulfilment of creation on the one hand and the redemption of humanity on the other, eschatology is inclusive of *everything*: nothing of the good creation will be lost. Creation, in his theology, has not fallen – it retains its created goodness – but it has been cursed by Adam's sin, and so needs to be restored to full health. Even if it had not been

affected by Adam, it would still be moved, by the Divine
Logos, to fulfil its original destiny. This allows animals, too, to
partake of the glory of the eschaton.

Despite the declaration that 'man was not made for [the
creation's] sake, but creation for the sake of man',[13] Irenaeus
does not consider man's existence the *sole* purpose of
creation. The human person is central within the present
creation as representing the 'image of God' – the *imago Dei* –
with the act of glorifying God as the *telos* (ultimate end,
purpose) for the human being. This *imago Dei* can never be
destroyed, but the *similitudo Dei* can be impaired by sin.[14]
Martyrs and saints are rewarded by the resurrection of the
body, not just the ethereal spiritual after-life of the Gnostics.
This bodily resurrection is linked with the final restoration of
the whole creation to a new Eden, its 'primeval condition'.
Supported by Romans 8:20–1, Irenaeus describes the new
creation itself being placed under the dominion [this time] of
'the righteous', and stresses that it is really the earthly
creation transformed:

> For it is just that *in that very creation* in which they [the right-
> eous] toiled or were afflicted, being proved in every way by
> suffering, they should receive the reward of their suffering ...
> and that *in the creation* in which they endured servitude, in
> that they should reign. For God is rich in all things, and all
> things are His.[15]

This new Eden, 'the kingdom', is described as being the
creation 'set free', governed with true justice, fruitful and
fertile. In it, where saintly man now does no sin and therefore
rules as God intended, all creatures return to the vegetarian
diet of Genesis 1:29, and live with humans in peace, reminis-
cent both of Mark 1:12–13 and of Isaiah's vision of the
peaceable kingdom (Isaiah 11:5–9):

> ... and that all animals feeding [only] on the productions of
> the earth, should [in those days] become peaceful and harmo-
> nious among each other, and be in perfect subjection to man.[16]

Origen Origen (*c*.185–*c*.254) is a complex theologian, a giant figure in the Christian world of the third century, and a victim of Decian persecution. Where Irenaeus affirms nature and the body, Origen's 'dominating metaphor', in Santmire's terms,[17] is the 'spiritualising one of Ascent'. He is a proponent of the 'catechetical school' at Alexandria, [18] and his teaching is categorized as belonging to 'Middle Platonism', with belief in a chain of being proceeding from the utterly spiritual One (which is Good) at the zenith, down through spiritual and angelic realms towards the bottom of creation – the medium of matter – with, ultimately, the absence of being, or nonbeing, at the nadir. All living beings pre-existed at the highest, spiritual level in the state of Ideas, until some chose, individually and through free will, to degrade their existence by descending into first, soul, and then, matter. Origen's God creates 'the material-vital world as a kind of gracious act, to stop the fall of the rational spirits towards ultimate nonbeing'.[19] From their first spiritual existence, fallen rational souls need bodies of increasing levels of density: 'And when they reach the neighbourhood of the earth they are enclosed in grosser bodies, and last of all are tied to human flesh.'[20]

Origen's significance in church history is largely based on his refutation of the arguments of one antiChristian Platonist and syncretist, Celsus. One of Celsus' objections to Christianity is 'for asserting that God made all things for the sake of man'. He argues for the equality of status between human beings and animals on the grounds that 'from the history of animals, and from the sagacity manifested by them ... all things came into existence not more for the sake of man than of the irrational animals'.[21]

Origen suggests that Celsus contradicts the ancient academicians, who, 'not amiss, place man in the foremost rank, and rational nature in general before irrational animals, and who maintain that Providence created all things mainly on account of rational nature'.[22] Origen then uses the somewhat startling image of animals as the placenta – the necessary, but discardable, equipment in the formation of human babies: 'Rational beings, then, as being the principal ones, occupy the place, as it were, of children in the womb, while irrational and soulless beings hold that of the envelope which is created along with the child.'[23]

Celsus' (surprisingly modern) theory of creation is of a chance 'concurrence of atoms' – whereas Origen posits a generous Creator (Providence) who even 'provided food ... for the most savage animals', which animals have been created, not for their own sake or for that of the Creator's, but 'for the purpose of affording exercise to the rational creature'[24] – hunting presumably being the exercise. Celsus is accused by Origen of impiety for suggesting that God would arrange for human sustenance 'in no greater degree' than that of other creatures.[25] Celsus also argues animals' actual superiority in being provided with natural weapons with which to hunt prey, whereas people have to resort to manufacturing and using external weapons. He also suggests that, as humans are the prey of wild animals, it could be asked, 'Why were not *we* rather created on *their* account, since they hunt and devour us?'[26]

Origen uses his answer to this to give his most detailed account of the purposes of animals for the use of humans. He writes that, although smaller and weaker than many animals, it is human superior understanding that gives man mastery, enabling him to capture even the elephant. People subdue the tameable animals and kill them for food, and shut out or hunt down the wild ones. Dogs are trained for guarding homes and livestock, and oxen and beasts of burden employed for farming and transport. Wild, predatory animals have been provided 'in order to call into exercise the elements of the manly character that exists within us [by hunting]'.[27] All things have been made for the superior species. Even colonies of ants and hives of bees are for the purpose of 'putting rational beings to shame; so that, drawing on Proverbs (6:6–11), by looking upon ants, for instance, they might become more industrious and more thrifty in the management of their goods'.[28]

For Origen, animals possess not rationality but only natural instinct, although 'in some dumb animals there is found a more regular movement than in others, as in hunting-dogs or war-horses, so that they may *appear* to some to be moved by a kind of rational sense'.[29] This lack of rationality precludes animals from hosting a human reincarnated soul.[30] Nor can Origen accept Celsus' claim that human and animal souls are of the same nature, for the human soul is created in the image of God and it is impossible 'for a nature fashioned in the divine image to have its (original) features altogether obliterated, and to assume others, formed after I know not what likeness of irrational animals'.[31] Human reason is said to be the attribute which is has been created in the image of God.[32]

While Origen attacks Celsus, his own teachings are criticized by many later Christian authorities. For considering the body as a punishment for the sins of the soul, Emperor Justinian writes in 543 to Mennas, Patriarch of Constantinople, that 'It is clear that souls are not cast into bodies for the punishment of sins as they [the Origenists] foolishly claim, but rather that God fashioned body and soul simultaneously, creating man in his perfected entirety [that is, body and soul].'[33]

In the matter of transmigration, or metempsychosis, Theophilus, patriarch of Alexandria in AD 402 asks:

> What is the point of preaching that souls are repeatedly confined in bodies, only to be released again, and that we experience many deaths? Does he [Origen] not know that Christ came, not in order to free souls from bodies after their resurrection, or to clothe freed souls from bodies once again in bodies that they might come down from heavenly regions to be invested once again with flesh and blood? Rather, he came so that he might present our revived bodies with incorruptibility and eternal life.[34]

Although much of Origen's teaching was anathematized,[35] the area of his teaching concerning the animal creation was not, and so it continues to be a major influence throughout the early Christian Church. In a way, the teaching of the Church is 'set' now in his model (and that of the following two theologian-authorities) and many of the same arguments are used today as were employed by Origen against Celsus.

Augustine Gnosticism is still a movement of influence at the time of Augustine of Hippo (354–430) and its ideas lie behind the dualistic teachings of the founder of Manichaeism, whose beliefs the young Augustine espouses. However, as Santmire notes, Augustine's understanding of nature progresses during his life from Gnosticism's emphasis on the spiritual, to views closer to Irenaeus' more ecological emphasis on the bodily,[36] although he *does* emphasize the negative effects of original sin which leads to an anti-body, anti-world tendency in church teaching until recent times.[37] Later writers take from the works of both the younger and the older Augustine, according to their own agendas. De Lubac's magisterial book, *The Mystery of the Supernatural*,[38] shows how the understanding, or rather *mis*understanding, of Augustine's view of nature as a realm *extraneous* to that of the supernatural and where God's grace is seen as an extrinsic activity or interference, was interpreted right up to the 1960s in Catholic textbooks. His present-day influence is evidenced by the large number of references to Augustine's work in the 1994 CCC. [39]

When Augustine converts to Christianity (albeit with a Platonist focus) and leaves behind the ideas and practices of the Manichees, he dismisses the prevailing acceptance of a Demiurge in the creation process, an idea invented to help to distance God from earthly matter. He is also particularly contemptuous of the Manichees' abstinence from meat (too 'bodily' for them) and their repugnance at even personally 'killing' the vegetarian crops on which they live. In denouncing them in a treatise, written in AD 388, he adopts the Stoics' idea of *oikeiosis* to deny rights to any creature beyond the legal community. He considers Christ's apparent lack of concern for the Gadarene swine as wholly justified for, as animals lack reason, 'we had no community in justice (*societas iuris*)' with them. Exclusion from the *oikeiosis* prevents

even the painful deaths of animals from requiring any consideration by people: 'For we see and appreciate from their cries
that animals die with pain. But man disregards this in a beast,
with which, as having no rational soul, he is linked by no
community of law.'[40]

The concept of animals being outside the human – rational
– community reappears in the later work, *City of God*. The
question is raised of who is intended to be protected in the
biblical commandment 'Thou shalt not kill'. Augustine replies
that the prohibition cannot cover plants, which have no sensa-
tion or feelings, nor the 'irrational animals ... since they are
dissociated from us by their want of reason'. These are therefore 'subjected to us to kill or keep alive for our own uses; if
so, then it remains that we understand that commandment
simply of man'.[41] While Augustine here concedes that, unlike
plants, animals possess feelings, even that is no protection for
them. This very passage from *City of God* is used later by
Thomas Aquinas as mandating the killing of animals.[42] Sorabji
comments: 'We can see here the point at which the Stoic insistence on human reason as the prerequisite for receiving
justice became irrevocably embedded in the Christian tradition of the Latin West.'[43]

Augustine seals off any further discussion over whether
animals have reason or can appreciate their Creator: 'Let none
think that the dumb stone or dumb animal hath reason
wherewith to comprehend God. They who have thought this,
have erred far from the truth.'[44] Unlike Descartes, however, he
accepts that animals have memory and thus some form of
mind. Augustine writes: 'Beasts and birds also have a memory.
Otherwise they could not rediscover their dens and nests, and
much else they are habitually accustomed to. Habit could
have no influence on them in any respect except by
memory.'[45]

While Augustine's work has been accepted by the Church in
its entirety, that of his opponents has been equally entirely
rejected, whatever merits some of them might have had. One
of Augustine's theological detractors is the Celtic lay monk

Pelagius, influential in Rome in the early 380s and remembered solely for the heresy of 'pelagianism', the human
capacity for salvation apart from Christ's action. A dominant
feature in Pelagius' writings is the goodness of creation where
God's spirit dwells within animals, birds, and insects:

> There is no creature on earth in whom God is absent... When
> God pronounced that his creation was good, it was not only
> that his hand had fashioned every creature: it was that his
> breath had brought every creature to life ... The presence of
> God's spirit in all living things is what makes them beautiful:
> and if we look with God's eyes, nothing on the earth is ugly.[46]

Pelagius extends the boundaries of the community of God's
love to include all creation.[47] Indeed, when 'our love is
directed towards an animal or even a tree we are participating
in the fullness of God's love'.[48] None of this is inconsistent
with either biblical or Celtic spirituality, but is lost to the Tradition with much else that Pelagius stands for – including, for a
long time, the teaching of women to read the Scriptures.[49]

Augustine develops Origen's Chain of Being into a more
detailed hierarchy, which Aquinas will adopt. He describes an
ordered universe in which God has created attributes appropriate to each level, or order: sense, understanding and
immortality, for the angels; sense and understanding with
mortality, for humanity; bodily sense, but neither understanding, nor immortality, for animals: neither sense, nor
understanding, nor immortality, for herbs, trees and stones.
The beauty of each part and of the whole, 'praises' God in that
it evokes the desire in *people* to praise God for it.[50] However,
it is of a purely 'bestial' level to worship God only for 'temporal and earthly' gifts – it befits the righteous rather to look
upward and appreciate one's rationality and distinctiveness
'from the brutes'. Only then can 'all the earthly comforts' be
appreciated.[51] Nevertheless, it is a beautiful creation and the
older Augustine recites with delight its wonders which tell of
God's creative power.[52]

Material nature is, however, corruptible. In discussing the

passage in Romans 8 about the whole of creation subjected in futility to God, Augustine does not interpret *ktisis*, creation, as the world of nature – but only of fallen *human* nature. To him creation has not fallen, only humanity has. The curse in Genesis 3:17[53] refers only to human life, not beyond.[54] Nature itself is not of real concern to the Christian, for whom the real purpose is to attain salvation for the soul, the *imago Dei*.

Although fully Trinitarian in other respects, Augustine's doctrine of the human being's *imago Dei* concerns the domination of the body by the soul based on a view of God as singular, rather than Trinitarian; a 'psychological analogy' rather than a 'social analogy'.[55] The human being, in corresponding to a single Being of the triune God, is represented by a male individual.[56] The soul becomes the body's 'form' or determining principle (a Platonic concept, called by Aristotle, *entelechy*) and governs it in the way that God governs the world. The soul then is the part of the person that is related to God, corresponding to and resembling the divine nature, and therefore it constitutes 'the image of God'. As the soul has dominion and control over the body, so does the man over the woman, and the human over the animal. 'By proceeding from the unity of the Trinity in the divine being,' Augustine 'raised to divine dignity the human subject of reason, will and domination.'[57]

With this apotheosis of human reason, and Augustine's acknowledged desire to know solely 'the soul and God', he is awarded the first place in the Western tradition of a spirituality which rejects nature and espouses an 'other-worldliness'. Nature's connection with grace will become dangerously attenuated in the writings and teachings of such as Thomas à Kempis (1380–1471) and the French seventeenth- and eighteenth-century authors of devotional literature, such as Tanquerrey and Bossuet. In chapter 54, entitled 'On the Contrary Workings of Nature and Grace', of Thomas à Kempis' *Imitation of Christ*, the reader ('My Son'), is asked (by 'Christ') to 'carefully observe the impulses of nature and grace, for these are opposed one to another, and work in so subtle a manner that even a spiritual, holy and enlightened man can hardly distinguish them'. After several paragraphs excoriating nature in favour of grace, the final section describes grace as that which:

> raises man from earthly things to love the heavenly, and from worldly makes him spiritual. The more, therefore, that Nature is controlled and overcome, the richer is the grace bestowed, while man is daily renewed by fresh visitations after the likeness [image] of God.[58]

After Augustine, the 'barbarian' invasions and political upheavals in the Western Roman Empire put an end to the direct influence of classical philosophy until the Arab philosophers in the ninth century reintroduce Aristotelianism, mixed with neoPlatonism, into Europe.[59] In that ninth century too, Erigena (Johannes Scotus) translates from Greek the works of the neoPlatonist Dionysius the Areopagite, a source much quoted by one of Augustine's most favoured followers, Aquinas.

Aquinas There is no doubt of the Catholic Church's indebtedness to St Thomas Aquinas (1225–1274). In the 1879 encyclical, *Aeterni Patris* (Of the Eternal Father), Pope Leo XIII recommends that St Thomas' philosophy be made the basis of instruction in all schools run by the Church; and in 1950, in *Humani Generis* (Of the Human Race), Pope Pius XII commends it as the surest guide to doctrine and discourages departures from it. In 2003, the Prefect of the Congregation for Catholic Education remarks that Aquinas is more relevant than ever for his proposal for dialogue between faith and reason: 'The Angelic Doctor is the apostle of truth, the sure guide for harmony between faith and reason.' Compared with secular, religion-denying humanisms, the Cardinal promotes 'Thomist humanism' as today's 'ray of light in the night' and justifies such 'Christian humanism' as being that 'in which man is the centre of humanism, but not any man – rather, the one who [is] … the perfect man, which the Christian finds in the revelation of Christ'.[60] While several of Aquinas's teachings will be explored further in this book, particularly in the analysis of part of the *Catechism of the Catholic Church*, there are some major tenets of his teaching which need to be outlined here.

Although not the first to do so, Thomas places man at the centre of his entire world-view, demoting nature merely to an instrumentalist role in human salvation. This instrumentalism, particularly of animals, finds its extreme form later in Descartes and that philosopher's followers (whether they know it or not) in the factory-farms and the laboratories of today.[61] Descartes, according to Andrew Linzey 'carried the line of indifference to cruelty to animals (as not wrong in itself) already indicated by St Thomas, to its logical conclusion'.[62] Aquinas makes his argument for the human instrumental use of nature from Psalm 8:8, '[God has] made [the human being] lord over the works of [God's] hands, set all things under his feet, sheep and oxen, all these, yes, wild animals too ...'[63] All things are created for a purpose – their *telos*; for human beings it is to love God and return to him on death, for all else it is to serve man in this endeavour. (The subject of the *telos* of animals will be dealt with in Part Three.)

Cruelty to animals is directly addressed by Aquinas in the way described by a character in a novel by Nobel prize-winner, J. M. Coetzee: 'Because man alone is made in the image of God and partakes in the being of God, how we treat animals is of no importance except in so far as being cruel to animals may accustom us to being cruel to men.'[64] This is taken from passages in Aquinas; two in the *Summa Theologiae*[65] and one in the *Summa Contra Gentiles*. This latter gives the two reasons for refraining from cruelty to animals: one, so that the practice of it does not lead to acting cruelly to other people, as Coetzee's character mentions, and the second, 'because harm done to [domestic] animals turns to the temporal loss of man', as these are counted as a person's property. Cruelty to *wild* animals would fulfil only the first condition.[66] Coetzee's character asks what it was that Aquinas took to be the essential being of God, 'to which he will reply that the being of God is reason'.[67]

Although in many respects the inheritor of Aristotle, Aquinas also follows Plato and Augustine in holding that the superiority of reason over matter is paralleled in the free person by the superiority of the soul, the seat of reason, over the body – and with people over animals.[68] As Coetzee's character sums up: 'And the fact that animals, lacking reason, cannot understand the universe but have simply to follow its rules blindly, proves that, unlike man, they are part of it but not part of its being: that man is godlike, animals thinglike.'[69]

Animals are not the only thing-like creatures; in a passage of Aquinas that echoes pagan Roman jurisprudence, human slaves are in the same condition:

> Thus the intellectual nature alone is free, while every other creature is naturally subject to slavery. But under every government the freemen are provided for their own sakes, while of slaves this care is taken that they have being for the use of the free.[70]

Unlike Origen, Aquinas does not believe creation was designed as a repository for fallen souls.[71] While creation exists through a movement of the overflowing goodness of God, and is maintained in being by the immanent presence of God, yet God governs creation through the agency of a hierarchy of creatures,[72] whereby 'all corporeal things [are] ruled by angels'.[73]

Influenced by Dionysius the Areopagite, with his detailed hierarchy of the angelic world, Aquinas – known as the 'Angelic Doctor' – believes that angels are the highest created order of beings, whose pure spiritual existence is shared, in a degree, by the 'reasonable souls' of human beings. 'In a certain sense [the human person] contains all things' and in so far as the person has mastery over himself, 'in the same way he can have mastership over other things' – except for angels which, as beings of reason, can only ever be master, never subject.[74] Human beings have mastery over 'the sensitive powers' [animals] by command, whereas over 'natural powers' they make use of them without hindrance.[75]

To Aquinas, as to Augustine, nature did not fall when Adam fell: this world is good, even if it is violent[76] – and while only humanity fell, only humanity will be redeemed.[77] Before the Fall, the 'human creature' would have used natural objects in the way they had been designed to be used, so that 'poisonous animals would not have harmed him' – and only *after* the Fall were references made to animal products, and eventually (after the Flood), to meat eating.[78] Aquinas does not deny the significance of the human body, despite the high value he places on reason and the soul. He admits both that man's knowledge, including that of God, is obtained through the senses of the body, and that, after death, 'the natural condition of the human soul is to be united to the body'.[79] The whole created world would be renewed, as in Romans 8:19–25, as the bodily nature of redeemed man would require it.[80] While there would therefore be the conditions for the bodily existence of animals in the after-life, there would be no need for them to exist. Their service to the human race would be no longer required as the human person would have attained his *telos*.[81] So, as Santmire observes, 'The celebrated Thomistic principle that grace does not destroy nature, but perfects it, turns out to be narrowly anthropocentric ... for, in effect, grace does destroy the animals, the plants ... it only perfects spiritual creatures.'[82] The sequence in time for the nature of creation, is, for Aquinas, in three stages of perfection: the first perfection being the biblical seventh day, when God rested after bringing the universe into being; the second being the redemption of the human race, and the final perfection being the end of the whole universe, the perfect beatitude of the saints at the consummation of the world.[83] This is what Santmire calls an asymmetrical creation account – one where God's over-flowing goodness pours into all things to bring them into being and to maintain them, yet the return *to* God is not to be of *all* things, but only of the rational creatures.[84] (There will be more substantial reflections on Aquinas in later sections.)

Notes

1 Andrew Linzey and Dan Cohn-Sherbok, *After Noah: animals and the liberation of theology* (London: Mowbray, 1997), p. 6.

2 Ibid., p. 30.

3 Theophilus to Autolycus, 1. 6 [my emphasis]; trans. and eds Alexander Roberts and James Donaldson, also Ed. Philip Schaff, *Nicene and Post-Nicene Fathers of the Christian Church. Series I, Vol.2. The City of God, Christian Doctrine* (Edinburgh: T&T Clark, 1885).

4 Sorabji, *Animal Minds and Human Morals* (1993), p. 202

5 Ibid., pp. 90–2. The neoplatonists, following Aristotle's distinction between intuitive intellect (*nous*) or reason (*logos*), consider reason a function of the soul rather than of the intellect, which is the higher faculty, enabling philosophical reflection. Boethius (*c.* AD 480–524) continues this discussion, which is again taken up by Thomas Aquinas (ST 1, q, 79, a. 8) who disagrees that reason (*ratio*) is distinct from intellectual understanding (*intellectus*); see Sorabji, *Animal Minds and Human Morals* (1993), p. 75 n. 65).

6 Lactantius *Institutes* 7.24; cited in H. Paul Santmire, *The Travail of Nature: the ambiguous ecological promise of Christian theology* (Minnealopis: Fortress, 1985), p. 24.

7 Monika K. Hellwig, 'Gnosticism', *The Modern Catholic Encyclopedia*, edited by Michael Glazier and Monika Hellwig (Dublin: Gill & Macmillan, 1994), p. 347.

8 Andrew Wellburn, *The Beginnings of Christianity: Essene mystery, Gnostic revelation and the Christian vision* (London: Floris Books, 1991), p. 25.

9 *Catechism of the Catholic Church* (London: Geoffrey Chapman, 1994), paragraph 292, note 133. Henceforth the Catechism will be referred to throughout as CCC.

10 Robin Lane Fox, *Pagans and Christians in the Mediterranan World* (London: Penguin, 1988), p. 266.

11 H. Paul Santmire, *The Travail of Nature* (Philadelphia: Fortress Press, 1985), p. 35.

12 Ibid., p. 31ff.

13 Irenaeus, *Against the Heresies* 5. 29. 1; trans. and eds Alexander Roberts and James Donaldson, also ed. Philip Schaff, *The Ante-Nicene Fathers. Vol.1. The Apostolic Fathers with Justin Martyr and Irenaeus* (Edinburgh: T&T Clark, 1885).

14 Jürgen Moltmann, *God in Creation: an ecological doctrine of creation* (Munich and London: SCM, 1985), p. 230.

15 Irenaeus, *Against the Heresies* 5. 32. 1, trans. and eds Alexander Roberts and James Donaldson, also ed. Philip Schaff, *The Ante-Nicene Fathers. Vol.1. The Apostolic Fathers with Justin Martyr and Irenaeus* (Edinburgh: T&T Clark, 1885).

16 Irenaeus, *Against the Heresies* 5. 33. 3. Roberts, et al, *The Ante-Nicene Fathers.Vol.1.*

17 Santmire, *The Travail of Nature* (1985), chapter 3 *et passim.*

18 Many of his disciples went on to become influential bishops and effective evangelists, such as Gregory of Pontus, Bishop of Neocaesaria, Alexander of Cappadocia and Dionysus, Bishop of Alexandria.

19 Santmire, *The Travail of Nature* (1985), p. 49.

20 Origen, 'Loss or Falling Away', *On First Principles*, edited by G.W. Butterworth (Gloucester, MA: Peter Smith, 1973), pp. 40–1.

21 Origen, *Contra Celsum* 4. 74; Philip Schaff (1819–1893), *The Apostolic Fathers with Justin Martyr and Irenaeus* (Reprinted by Wm B Eerdmans, Grand Rapids, MI, 2001).

22 Origen, *Contra Celsum* 4. 74; trans. and eds Alexander Roberts and James Donaldson, also ed. Philip Schaff, *The Ante-Nicene Fathers. Vol. 4. The Fathers of the Third Century.* (Edinburgh: T&T Clark, 1885).

23 Origen, *Contra Celsum* 4.74.

24 Ibid., 4. 75.

25 Ibid., 4. 76.

26 Ibid., 4. 78.

27 Ibid.

28 Ibid., 4. 81.

29 Origen, *De Principiis* 3. 1. In one passage Origen suggests that human beings' claim to rationality is only one of degree compared with other animals. They [human beings] are 'rational animals possessing natural movements', but also possess the power of reason 'to a *greater extent* than other animals'; (see Roberts) but it seems to have been a slip in Origen's otherwise consistent views.

30 Origen, *Contra Celsum* 8. 30; but see *De Principiis*, 1. 4. 1; 1. 8. 4. Origen's belief in reincarnation differs from the Pythagorian belief in transmigration, and is known more accurately as 'metempsychosis'. The human soul is purified through successive bodies until it returns to the state of so loving God that its matter would be refined quite away, and God will be 'all in all' (1 Corinthains 15:28).

31 Origen, *Contra Celsum* 4. 83.

32 Ibid., 4.85.

33 Justinian, *Letter to Menna*, PG 86. 1, 951.

34 Jerome, *Letters* 98. 11; trans. and eds Alexander Roberts and James Donaldson, also ed. Philip Schaff, *Nicene and Post-Nicene Fathers of the Christian Church. Series II, Vol.6. Jerome.* (Edinburgh: T&T Clark, 1885).

35 His theories anathematized were those of pre-existence and reincarnation, christology and pneumatology.

36 Santmire, *The Travail of Nature* (1985) p. 55ff. The transition from Augustine's allegiance to the Manichees to that of Christian philosophy,

is well documented in Carol Harrison's *Augustine: Christian truth and fractured humanity* (Oxford: OUP, 2000). There she points out that against 'both Manichees and Platonists Augustine emphasizes the goodness of creation, including man's body (*De Natura boni liber unus*, 15–18) – based on the belief in the resurrection of the body' (p. 33), the body and the soul being 'united and yet not confused, within the one person of man' (p. 34). However, in her later book, *Rethinking Augustine's early theology: an argument for continuity* (Oxford: OUP, 2006) – as the title says – Harrison suggests that the Augustine of the early years is not 'another, recognisably different and alien person', from that of the Bishop of Hippo (p. vi).

37 Sean McDonagh, *The Death of Life: the horror of extinction* (Blackrock, Co. Dublin: Columba, 2005), pp. 60–3. Much of the anti-body tendency is both deeply embedded in the tradition he inherits and in that which succeeds him, rather than in Augustine's actual work. See Margaret Miles, *Augustine on the Body* (Missoula: Scholars Press, 1979) and *Fullness of Life* (Philadelphia: Westminster Press, 1981).

38 See H. De Lubac, *The Mystery of the Supernatural*, translated by Rosemary Sheed (New York: Herder and Herder, 1965).

39 There are ninety-two Augustinian references, with sixty-one of the next most prolific, Thomas Aquinas, compared with three from St Francis of Assisi and only twenty-three from all the women in the whole Catholic Tradition.

40 *De moribus ecclesiae catholicae et de moribus Manichaeorum*, 2. 17. 59, cited in Sorabji, *Animal Minds and Human Morals* (1993), 196.

41 Augustine, City of God 1: 20, trans. and eds Alexander Roberts and James Donaldson, also ed. Philip Schaff, *Nicene and Post-Nicene Fathers of the Christian Church. Series I, Vol.2. The City of God, Christian Doctrine* (Edinburgh:T&T Clark, 1885).

42 Aquinas, *Summa Theologiae* 2.1.q.102, a.6. All references to the Summa are those of the second and revised edition of 1920, literally translated by the English Dominicans.

43 Sorabji, *Animal Minds and Human Morals* (1993), p. 198.

44 Augustine, *Enarratio in Psalmos* 145.10, trans. and eds Alexander Roberts and James Donaldson, also ed. Philip Schaff, *Nicene and Post-Nicene Fathers of the Christian Church. Series I, Vol.7. Exposition on the psalms.* (Edinburgh: T&T Clark, 1885).

45 Augustine, *Confessions* 10. 7. 26, trans. and eds Alexander Roberts and James Donaldson, also ed. Philip Schaff, *Nicene and Post-Nicene Fathers of the Christian Church. Series I, Vol.1. Prolegomena.* (Edinburgh: T&T Clark, 1885).

46 Letter 71, *Letters of Pelagius*, edited by R. Van de Weyer (letter 71) (London: Arthur James, 1995); cited in McDonagh, *The Death of Life* (2005), p. 62.

47 McDonagh, *The Death of Life* (2005), p. 62.
48 Pelagius letter 71; cited in McDonagh, *The Death of Life* (2005), p. 62.
49 McDonagh, *The Death of Life* (2005), p. 63.
50 Augustine, *Enarratio in Psalmos* 36. 6, trans. and eds Alexander Roberts and James Donaldson, also ed. Philip Schaff, *Nicene and Post-Nicene Fathers of the Christian Church. Series I, Vol.7. Exposition on the psalms.* (Edinburgh: T&T Clark, 1885).
51 Augustine, *Enarratio in Psalmos* 36, 6; trans. and eds Alexander Roberts and James Donaldson, also ed. Philip Schaff, *Nicene and Post-Nicene Fathers of the Christian Church. Series I, Vol.7. Exposition on the psalms.* (Edinburgh:T&T Clark, 1885).
52 Augustine, *City of God* 12. 3. Roberts et al, *Nicene and Post-Nicene Fathers. Series 1, Vol.2.*
53 Genesis 3:17:'To the man he said ... Accursed be the soil because of you. / With suffering shall you get your food from it ...'.
54 Santmire, *The Travail of Nature* (1985), p. 66.
55 Jurgen Moltmann, *God in Creation: an ecological doctrine of creation* (Munich and London: SCM, 1985), pp. 234–5.
56 The woman is only 'the glory of the *man*' (quoting 1 Corinthians 11:7) and can be the image of God only in her being subordinated to her 'head', the man.
57 Moltmann, *God in Creation* (1985), p. 242.
58 Thomas à Kempis, *The Imitation of Christ*, translated by L. Sherley-Price (Harmondsworth: Penguin, 1952).
59 C.W. Hume, *The Status of Animals in the Christian Religion* (London: Universities Federation for Animal Welfare, 1957), p. 19.
60 Cardinal Zenon Grocholewski at the International Thomist Congress, 22 September 2003, Rome.
61 Descartes' notorious idea of animals being no more than mere machines or automata, in *Meditationes de prima philosophia* and *Principia philosophiae*, was not original to him. It had been previously expounded upon, in 1554, by a Spanish physician, Gomez Pereira in a bulky Latin volume, *Antoniana Margarita opus nempe physicis, medicis ac theologis non minus utile quam necessarium*; see E.P. Evans, *The Criminal Prosecution and Capital Punishment of Animals* (London: William Heinemann, 1906), p. 66.
62 Andrew Linzey, *Animal Rights: a Christian assessment* (London: SCM, 1976), p. 12.
63 Aquinas, *Summa Contra Gentiles* 2, 112.
64 The fictional character Elizabeth Costello, a novelist and lecturer, in J. M. Coetzee, *The Lives of Animals* (London: Profile, 2000), p. 24.
65 Aquinas, *Summa Theologiae* I-II, 3. 2. 112, and 102, 6 ad 8.
66 Aquinas, *Summa Contra Gentiles*, 1, 112. 2.
67 J. M. Coetzee, *The Lives of Animals* (London: Profile, 2000), p. 24.

68 Aquinas, *Summa Theologiae* 1, 96, 2.
69 Coetzee, *The Lives of Animals* (2000), p. 25.
70 Aquinas, *Summa Contra Gentiles* 2. 112. 2.
71 Aquinas, *Summa Theologiae* 1. 47. 2.
72 Ibid., 1. 103. 6.
73 Ibid., 1. 110. 1 and *Compendium of Theology* 127.
74 Ibid., 1. 96. 2.
75 Aquinas, *Summa Theologiae.*
76 Ibid., 1. 96. 1.
77 Ibid., 1. 73. 1.
78 Ibid., 1. 72. 1.
79 Aquinas *Compendium of Theology* 152.
80 Ibid., 151–3.
81 Aquinas, *Summa Theologiae* 1. 96. 1.
82 Santmire, *The Travail of Nature* (1985), p. 94.
83 Aquinas, *Summa Theologiae* 1. 73. 1.
84 Santmire, *The Travail of Nature* (1985), p. 93.

Chapter Four

The Saints of East and West

Apocryphal literature The eirenic reading of Mark 1:12–13 (mentioned on page 19) of Jesus being 'with the wild animals' – with the emphasis on the word 'with' – is highly developed in many of the apocryphal Christian writings from the second to the ninth centuries. From the first moment of Jesus' birth, he was 'with the animals'. In *The Gospel of Pseudo-Matthew* – which provides a consistent extra-canonical tradition ever since – the birth takes place with an ox and an ass in attendance, drawing on the reference in Isaiah where 'The ox knows its owner and the ass its master's crib' (Isaiah 1:3). Also at Christ's nativity, according to *The Protoevangelium of James*, the whole of creation stops 'dead' as if holding its breath, frozen in a moment of time, at the very moment of the birth. Andrew Linzey interprets this 'catalepsy of all creation' as showing that the birth of Jesus affects the entire created order; the one birth having cosmic significance.[1]

Some of the apocryphal stories anticipate the scene of Jesus in the wilderness by describing him as a child performing miracles on behalf of animals. One of the most well-known is from the (possibly) fifth-century *Infancy Gospel of Thomas* where the three-year-old Jesus revives a dead fish by breathing on it and returning it to the water, and the five-year-old boy moulds sparrows from soft clay and lets them fly off. Another from the same source is the creation of sparrows from mud, or earth dust, which then fly away. This work of the child Jesus parallels that of his Father in Genesis 2:11.

Behind some of the apocryphal accounts there may be a genuine motivation to encourage compassion (or 'mercy') to animals as appropriate to the Christian life, possibly borrowing from the Jewish religious duty of compassionate treatment, the *tsa'ar be'alei chayim*, especially to beasts of burden.[2] Also, the biblical injunction that compassion to animals even supersedes sabbath rules could be remembered.[3] Andrew Linzey provides an account from a Coptic manuscript (the provenance of which is not wholly proved) of Jesus healing a mule which had been beaten for having collapsed under a too-heavy load. The mule's owner is chided as he is dismissed: 'Now go on and beat it no more, that you also may find mercy.'[4]

Many of the stories serve as contemporary illustrations of biblical precedents, such as one in the third-century *Acts of Thomas*, where the eponymous hero meets a talking ass's colt who says: 'I am of that family which served Balaam, and to which also belonged that colt on which sat your Lord and Master. And now I have been sent to give you rest as you sit on me ...'[5] According to C. R. Matthews, 'the underlying message of the speaking animal narratives calls on the hearer to display, at least, the dignity and sensitivity to the divine displayed by these animals' and 'that readers are being asked to affirm that there is no life, be it human or animal, apart from God'.[6]

There is also an account in the second-century *Acts of Paul* of the apostle Paul engaging in dialogue with a lion, much as Balaam did with his ass.[7] The lion theme is most commonly accounted. In *The Gospel of Pseudo-Matthew*, the infant Jesus is adored by lions and panthers which accompany the Holy Family in the desert during their flight to Egypt. In fact the animals show them their way, and indicate their submission by bowing their heads, wagging their tails and worshipping the infant.[8] In another account, Jesus encounters a family of lions who run to meet him and worship him. Jesus sits in their cave, playing with the lion cubs, and rebukes his nervous parents and others, with:

> How much better are the beasts than you, seeing that they
> recognise their Lord and glorify him: while you men, who have

been made in the image and likeness of God, do not know him! Beasts know me and are tame; men see me and do not acknowledge me.' Then he tells the lions to 'Go in peace and hurt no-one, neither let man injure you ...'[9]

The reference to lions is deliberate. Lions and other big cats are the major agents of the bloody execution of the martyrs in the circuses. Perhaps the key to the interpretation of these stories is found in Daniel 6:2–29. Here God's angel 'closed the lions mouths' – recalled in 1 Maccabees 2:60: 'Daniel for his singleness of heart was rescued from the lion's jaw' and in Hebrews 11:33, which recites briefly the accomplishments of Old Testament heroes and prophets including one which 'stopped the mouth of lions'. Originally intended to provide solace and encouragement to Jews undergoing persecution, by the early Christian era the Daniel story serves the same purpose, only now the Daniel figure is a type of Christ. Later the Messiah's disciples could exist alongside even lions without being harmed. Legends even grow around the 'reluctance' of lions in the arenas to attack some condemned Christians, as noted by Ignatius of Antioch. After Constantine, when the persecutions cease, legends of martyrs unharmed in the arena by wild beasts become yet more fancifully embellished. The martyrs are even embraced and kissed by the animals, representing the saints having already entered a state of paradisiacal harmony and peace in the kingdom of Christ.[10]

In the tales of the Desert Fathers, lions and other fierce animals feature prominently. Their relationship with the saints is wholly peaceable, again providing epiphanies of the eschatological harmony, a restoration of the original harmony and peace of Eden.

The Desert Fathers The first of the Desert Fathers and the inspiration of the eremitical movement, St Paul the Hermit (*c.*228–341), is associated with one of the most outlandish of the animal legends. At his death, when St Antony is unable to dig a grave for the corpse of his friend, two lions discharge that duty for him by digging with their paws. Other animal legends around this saint evoke biblical precedent. A raven brings the cave-dwelling hermit a daily half-loaf of bread. Possibly this relates to the raven being a symbol of the life provided for by God.[11] Poisonous snakes, associated with the Tempter in the Garden of Eden[12] and the plague afflicting the Israelites,[13] hold no danger to the saint. In accordance with the promised sign associated with true believers,[14] Paul picks them up without coming to harm. When asked about this he replies: 'Excuse me, father, but when one has attained purity, everything is subject to him, as it was for Adam in paradise before he disobeyed the commandment.'[15]

Another Desert Father, the Syrian ascetic, Symeon, arranges for two lions to act as guides to a party of Jews who had lost their way.[16] There is also a lion story concerning St Gerasimus, a Palestinian monk of the fifth century. A lion's paw, with a thorn embedded, is treated by the monk. The grateful lion then becomes the monk's assistant, responsible for and protecting the monastery's donkey. The donkey is stolen and the lion (called 'Jordan') is falsely accused. At a later date, Jordan finds and frightens the thieves and returns the donkey to the monastery. There he lives until the saint's death, whereupon the lion refuses to eat, prostrates himself upon the grave of his friend and pines away.[17] By the Middle Ages, the name 'Gerasimus' had become confused by Italian scribes with 'Geronimo' the Italian version of the Latin 'Hieronymus' or Jerome, and the lion legend becomes associated with the biblical scholar – whose image in paintings, from the fourteenth century onwards, is always accompanied by a 'pet lion'.

St Macarius,[18] another cave-dwelling ascetic, is summoned by a hyena to attend to the blindness of her pup or pups. By prayer and, in one account, spitting in the eyes (an obvious reference to Jesus' action in Mark 8:23 and John 9:6–7), the saint restores sight to the pups. Palladius' account concludes with 'And what is surprising, if he who tamed the lions for Daniel, also gave understanding to the hyena?'[19] Other aspects of this saint's affinity with animals is in an account of his being suckled by an antelope, which saves his life on a long journey, and by his self-inflicted penance of staying for six months in a mosquito-infested swamp for having killed a midge.[20]

The prologue to the alphabetical collection of the *Apophthegmata*, the Fathers' sayings, gives a didactic motivation for them: 'They are meant to inspire and instruct those who want to imitate their heavenly lives, that they may make progress on the way that leads back to the kingdom of heaven.'[21] Stories of many of the Desert Fathers, similar to these, abound and have been well-known in the English-speaking world since 1934 when Helen Waddell published her popular *Beasts and Saints*. Some have a christological and eschatological focus. For example, an East Syriac saint of the seventh century, Isaac of Nineveh explains the effect of 'the humble man' when he approaches wild animals which then behave like pet dogs:

> They scent as coming from him the same fragrance that came from Adam before the transgression, the time when they were gathered together before him and he gave them names in paradise. This scent was taken away from us, but Christ has renewed it and given it back to us at his coming.[22]

The Celtic Tradition Celtic[23] Christian culture in its many forms was widespread throughout Britain but, after the Roman settlement ends, is found in higher concentrations in Ireland, Wales, Scotland, and Cornwall. Similar communities in France, or Gaul, are concentrated in Brittany. The early dating of Christianity among the British Celts is evidenced by their sending bishops to the Council of Arles in AD 314.[24] By the fifth century in Ireland it is known that of the three ethnic groups, one (the British) is Christian, as are some members of another (the Scotti).[25] Diocesan structures following the Roman model[26] were not working in this non-urban culture so, by the seventh century, bishops are replaced in influence by abbots of monasteries. These, such as at Iona in Scotland, Kells in Ireland, Lindisfarne in North East England, and St Illtud's in Wales, are based on Eastern Mediterranean models, but with a particularly distinctive social basis, and with learning and asceticism as their ideals.[27]

The conventional Celtic saint-and-animal legends follow the precedents set by the Eastern Mediterranean Desert Fathers. Despite their geographical remoteness, Celtic Christian communities have strong links with other cultures – with their Anglo-Saxon neighbours, with Vikings (disruptively), with Rome, and with Coptic and Orthodox Christians in the East. There are many explicit references to the influence of monks of the Middle East in the *Lives* of the early Welsh saints, and of the rigorous asceticism of the Eastern monastic ideal.[28] Even before the Cluniac reforms of the eleventh century, and the Norman invasions, which cause the integration of the Celtic style of monasticism within mainstream European models, the Celtic Church was not closed to foreign influences.

From the very many animal legends, just one each from Wales (St Melangell), Ireland (St Kevin) and England (St Cuthbert) will indicate their nature.

In a lonely spot St Melangell, a beautiful devout virgin, harbours a hunted hare beneath her hem. The hounds flee from the protected quarry and their master, instantly converted, donates the land to be used as a sanctuary and refuge (for people) in her honour. Melangell lives on there alone for many years, 'and the hares, which are little wild creatures, surrounded her every day of her life just as if they had been tame or domesticated animals'.[29]

In the story of St Kevin, the solitary saint stretches out his hands in prayer, whereupon a blackbird makes a nest in the palm of his hands, and lays an egg. The saint, much moved by this, does not withdraw his hands until the young hatches and flies off.[30]

St Cuthbert, in the *De Vita et Miraculis S. Cudberti* written by St Bede, prays all night while standing in the freezing North Sea and then again when on the beach. Two otters come ashore to lick his feet, dry them with their fur and warm them with their breath. They receive the saint's blessing and slip back into the water. The witness, one of the brothers, sees not 'a man on a beach with his pets', but rather:

> the face of Christ in a man so transfigured in prayer that the right order of creation was in him restored. For the story's chronicler, St Bede, St Cuthbert ... was the New Adam, once more at peace with all creation, naming the animals, who were the first servant and the first friend.[31]

There are many *pagan* animal legends of the Celts of an altogether different nature. The contrast between those of the saints and that, for example, of the Irish saga of Mac Dathó's Pig, could not be greater. In this story, Ailbe, the king of Leinster's famous dog, is bidden to choose between two rival groups of warriors. It picks 'the men of Connaught', who are then slaughtered, rather than the 'men of Ulster' who survive. Some of the pagan animal legends predate Christianity and reflect a pantheism condemned by later Christians. For example, the sixth-century Gildas writes of the pre-Christian past where 'the mountains and hills and rivers, once so pernicious, now useful for human needs, on which, in those days, a blind people heaped divine honours'.[32]

Particular animals are closely associated with paganism. Horses, particularly (actually small shaggy mountain ponies), hold a central role in pre-Christian Celtic culture. They are owned by gods or can be manifestations of gods. An image of the horse-goddess Macha – whose 'curse on the men of Ulster' is described in the heroic epic saga, the *Táin* – is found in Armagh cathedral. She is represented as a horse, the emblem of the sun-goddess.[33] Horse deities are particularly associated with the fertility of the land.[34] A truly white horse, as opposed to merely grey, holds particular significance in Ulster where the king's coronation includes the king's actual intercourse, or the mimicked action, with a white mare representing the goddess of the land. The mare is then sacrificed and the king sits in a bath of her blood, eating her flesh and sharing it with his nobles. This ceremony is reported to have continued until the twelfth century AD.[35]

There is very little in Christian legends concerning horses, probably because of their too-close association with paganism. The only notable exception is in one story of St Patrick (fl. mid-fifth century), when some workmen of a rich man let one of his horses graze on the land he has given to Patrick and his Christian community. Patrick is offended and the following morning the horse is found dead, and the enraged rich man also dies. At this, Patrick blesses some water, sprinkles it on both the horse and its owner, and brings both back from the dead, much to Patrick's great honour.[36] The horse in this story is a real, mortal, creature – the supernatural element is in Patrick's action. It is notable that the first reaction of Patrick to the presence of an animal on sacred land was outrage, although the later miracle reflects the more conventional view of Celtic saints and their relationship with animals. This is reinforced in another anecdote about Patrick, when he rescues a fawn which his companions wanted to kill, and tenderly carries it, with its mother following, to another valley where it is released.[37]

The Eastern Tradition *'Lex orandi, lex credendi'* is perhaps truer of the Eastern traditions than of others, and through the various liturgies of these traditions can the underlying theologies be deduced. According to John Zizioulas, an Orthodox Metropolitan bishop, as well as an academic, these ancient liturgies 'involve a sanctification of matter and of time'. Apart from the material eucharistic elements themselves, he points out how all human senses are employed in them, 'the eyes through the icons and the liturgical vestments; the ears through the hymns and psalmody; the nose through the smell of incense, and so on. In addition', he adds, 'prayer for "seasonal weather, for an abundance of the fruits of the earth", and so on, places the liturgy right in the middle of creation.'[38] In this way the earliest eucharistic prayers followed closely the Hebrew liturgical tradition which involved a blessing over the fruits of the earth. Until the Middle Ages, the concentration was on the *anaphora*, the lifting up, or offering of the gifts, more so even than on the anamnesis of the crucifixion, so that the name for the service

was called either the *Anaphora*, or the *Eucharistia*. A priesthood of sacrifice, rather than of one offering back to God his
own creation in thanksgiving, took over, as in the West.[39]

St Basil The influence of the Metropolitan of Caesarea, St Basil
the Great (*c*.330–379), on the Eastern Church is immense. His
Rule is particularly influential in the development of its monasticism and liturgy. Like Augustine, he sees the natural world as
revealing something of the beauty and power of God,[40] and each
created thing within it existing through the power of the Holy
Spirit.[41] But he goes far beyond Augustine in his empathetic
appreciation of the animal creation – predating St Francis of
Assisi in his language of kinship with animals – as is demonstrated in this prayer from the Russian liturgy, 'for a deeper
sense of fellowship with all living things', the first recorded
expression of shame for human cruelty to animals:

> *The Earth is the Lord's and the fulness thereof.* O God, enlarge
> within us the sense of fellowship with all living things, our
> brothers the animals to whom thou hast given the earth as
> their home in common with us. We remember with shame that
> in the past we have exercised the high dominion of man with
> ruthless cruelty, so that the voice of the earth. which should
> have gone up to thee in song, has been a groan of travail. May
> we realize that they live, not for us alone, but for themselves
> and for thee, and that they have the sweetness of life.[42]

His liturgy, still in use today in the Orthodox Tradition, contains
another prayer which speaks of God having saved both man and
beast,[43] 'We pray thee, O Lord, for the humble beasts . . . and for
the wild animals, whom thou hast made, strong and beautiful;
we supplicate for them thy great tenderness of heart, for thou
hast promised to save both man and beast . . .'[44]

Yet another, in the same liturgy, expresses inclusion of all
creation and brackets humans with animals:

> Remember O Lord, the air of heaven and the fruits of the
> earth, bless them. Remember, O Lord, the water of the rivers,

bless them, raise them to their measure according to your
grace. Remember, O Lord, the seeds, the herbs and the plants
of the field, bless them. Remember, O Lord, the safety of the
people and the beasts. [45]

Basil's homiletic writings[46] express a sympathetic treatment of
animals and the natural world in an unprecedented and
systematic way. His appreciation of animals leads him to go
beyond the focus of the classical philosophers' obsession with
rationality to consider animals' other qualities and attributes.
He recognizes that they lack reason – although 'the conduct
of storks comes very near intelligent reason'[47] – yet they are
none the less capable of emotion and feeling: 'How many
affections of the soul each one of them expresses by the voice
of nature! They express by cries their joy and sadness, recognition of what is familiar to them, the need of food, regret at
being separated from their companions, and numberless
emotions.'[48]

Rather than despising animals for their lack of reason, Basil
considers that their Creator has fully made up for that want in
other ways which equal those of the wisdom even of 'the
sages of the world', and also suggests that the virtues of dogs
surpass those of many people:

> The dog is not gifted with a share of reason; but with him
> instinct has the power of reason. The dog has learnt by nature
> the secret of elaborate inferences, which sages of the world,
> after long years of study, have hardly been able to disentangle.
> ... Does not the gratitude of the dog shame all who are
> ungrateful to their benefactors?[49]

In other respects too he contrasts the natural instincts of
animals with the wilful weaknesses of human behaviour; for
example, he compares the strong family bonds displayed by
lions and wolves with human sons insulting their parents, or
the father 'whose second marriage has made him forget his
first children'.[50] In his ninth Homily, 'The Creation of Terrestrial Animals', he explains that, 'Virtues exist in us also by
nature, and the soul has affinity with them not by education,

but by nature herself... Paul teaches us nothing new; he only tightens the links of nature.'

While avoiding the prevalent contemporary use of allegory,[51] as 'self-serving and fanciful', he does attribute anthropomorphic attitudes to animals, such as the cock being proud, the peacock vain, doves amorous, the partridge deceitful, and so on. Yet this attribution is as a result of observation, not imagination. As an opponent of Manicheaism, which he abjures as 'mad-minded', it is fitting that he should study and observe the natural world, and Homilies Eight and Nine are works of natural history as well as being spiritually didactic. It is in the natural world that God's power is revealed, particularly in the creation of animals:

> It is not in great animals only that we see unapproachable wisdom; no less wonders are seen in the smallest ... in the constitution of animals I am not more astonished at the size of the elephant, than at the mouse, who is feared by the elephant, or at the scorpion's delicate sting, which has been hollowed like a pipe by the supreme artificer to throw venom into the wounds it makes.[52]

At this point he answers the question of why God ever created predators and harmful creatures by suggesting that their purpose is much the same as a schoolmaster's rod and whip, used to discipline 'the restlessness of youth'.[53]

St Basil can empathize with and appreciate animal creation in ways far beyond most of his Christian predecessors, or even successors. Yet he is still heir to the dualist superiority of soul over body, and human over animal. In Homily Nine, in discussing the act of the creation of the human being, he suggests that the form – shape or outline – of animals indicates their status compared with the form of the human person: 'Cattle are terrestrial and bent towards the earth. Man, a celestial growth, rises superior to them as much by the mould of his bodily conformation as by the dignity of his soul.' Quadrupeds, he maintains, have heads facing the earth and their stomachs, and are interested only in providing for their stomachs, whereas the human person is upright, with eyes that look towards heaven. Therefore, he maintains, if a person degrades himself 'by the passions of the flesh, slave of th[e] belly, and th[e] lowest parts' then he approaches the condition of a reasonless animal and becomes as they are. Human persons, however, are 'to more noble cares', [to] "look for things that are in heaven, where Christ is",'[54] – which is the heavenly Jerusalem, 'thy true country'.[55]

Oriental Rite Catholic Churches While St Basil's positive approach to the natural world is reflected in the Orthodox liturgy, the Oriental rite Catholic Churches have responded to the subject in a variety of ways. In the Armenian liturgy, used by Catholic and Monophysite Churches, the choir at one point (during clergy vesting) sings a hymn, attributed to Vartapet Khatchandour (1205), in which the whole of creation is explicitly assumed to enjoy renewal:

> O eternal, unfathomable Mystery ... you created Adam in a most remarkable way, and made him lord over all your creatures, and in the garden of Eden you dressed him in glorious splendour. Through the sufferings of your only Son, *all creation has been renewed* and man has regained his lost heritage, which cannot be taken away from him now.[56]

Later, at the Prothesis, while the priest or bishop is kneeling at the altar and prays with extended arms, he says this prayer, attributed to St Gregory of Narek: '... *Every creature* which was created by you will be renewed at the resurrection, that day which is the last day of earthly existence and the beginning of our heavenly life ...'[57] Later again, at the pouring of wine into the chalice (*bashak*) the priest says: 'In memory of the life-giving Incarnation of our Lord Jesus Christ, from whose side blood flowed, which regenerated *all creation* and redeemed mankind.'[58]

A prayer of St Basil is recited in the Ethiopian liturgy as the priest enters the sanctuary and prostrates himself. In it, human dominion over animals is specified as being a reflection of God's rule over the world: 'O Lord, our God and Creator ... who made man through your wisdom and who made him prince over all creatures to rule them in *righteousness and truth* ...'[59] The prayer of absolution, at the end of the liturgy, includes the phrase: 'O good Lover of man and Lord *of all creation*',[60] while the prayer of Benediction includes a blessing on 'the winds of the sky' – while the priest gestures a blessing in the direction of the sky – as well as on 'the rains and fruits of the earth ...'[61]

The Coptic liturgy belongs to the Alexandrian tradition, as does the Ethiopian liturgy. However, here the emphasis is so spiritual that, at the conclusion of the reading of the Epistle, the people respond with: 'Do not love the world, nor things that are in it. The world and its attractions pass away, but he who does the will of God will live forever. Amen.'[62] There is one reference to Eden in the Coptic liturgy, but only in connection with mankind breaking the commandment. There are references in intercessions 'for favourable weather and fruitfulness of the earth' – appropriate in the agriculturally difficult environment of Egypt – but mention is made only of productive harvests.[63]

The Antiochene Syrian liturgy includes these phrases during the censing: 'O Creator of the world and Architect of the universe, we adore and praise you ... Mary has given *every creature* a taste of his wonderful sweetness ...'[64] Later a priest prays to God, 'Lord of *every created thing* ...'[65] and later again in the liturgy, 'O Lord God of spirits and *of flesh* ...'[66]

The Western Tradition While the Western Roman Empire suffers the collapse of order in the fifth and sixth centuries, and is subjected to political and social instability on a massive scale, Western Christianity is given fresh impetus by the rise of a new form of monasticism. St Benedict of Nursia[67] (c.480–550) breaks from the severely ascetic, eremitical model of the Desert Fathers to establish a network of communities of monks with an extra vow – one of stability. This stability, plus the novel inclusion of manual work – formerly

the task of slaves, not scholars – obliges the monks to cultivate
and care for the land in a sustainable way. From now on, the
land is less to be feared as an overwhelming wasteland or
forested wilderness, and more respected as a garden, something with which people co-operate with God in producing
fertility and fruitfulness.[68] Wild animals are fenced out, and
domesticated ones coerced into working, for traction or transport, or used for food. Later, especially in Britain, the
monasteries become large-scale breeders of sheep, fuelling
the lucrative wool industry. Animals are so taken for granted
that they are little referred to. The only reference to animals
by Benedict himself is found in his Rule, where – it is
presumed on ascetical grounds rather than animal welfare
ones – he commands that all, 'except for the sick who are very
weak … abstain entirely from eating the flesh of four-footed
animals'.[69]

   Not all goes well in the world beyond the monasteries, and
the centuries prior to the first millennium see such pestilence,
plague, famine and other disasters that people, such as Odo,
the second Abbot of Cluny (927–942),[70] are led to predict the
approach of the end of the world as a result of sin and God's
wrath. This pessimistic view of the created world persists into
the Middle Ages.[71] All the more remarkable, therefore, that St
Francis of Assisi, Hildegard of Bingen, Julian of Norwich,
Meister Eckhart and several other mystics and saints express
an exuberant, joyful appreciation of the natural world. Unfortunately, none of the last three mentioned significantly affects
the nature of the Tradition of the Catholic Church, particularly
in regards to the status of animals – unlike Francis.

St Francis of Assisi (1181–1226) Francesco Bernardone
(Francis of Assisi) is, for his time, radical in breaking from the
monastic tradition of scholarly stability. He and a small group
of like-minded followers are given papal approval in 1209 to
be itinerant preachers of penance. St Dominic de Guzman
receives papal permission in 1216 also to found an Order of
mendicant preachers. He soon sends his followers to the new

universities of Paris and Bologna, whereas Francis discourages the pursuit of scholarship as inimical to the life of absolute poverty: 'Friars of mine who are seduced by a desire for learning will find their hands empty in the day of trouble.'[72] In this, as in so much else, his wishes are to be contradicted as many of his followers will become among the most eminent of scholars, such as Alexander of Hales (d.1245), Bonaventure (d.1274), Roger Bacon (d.1294), John Duns Scotus (d.1308), and William of Ockham (d.1347). Franciscanism will develop as a broad school of theology to rival Dominicanism and Augustinianism in the medieval universities.

Francis' radicalism is novel, yet falls within the earlier tradition of the early Desert Fathers and the missionary Celtic saints with their severe asceticism and affinity with the natural world. The method of much of his teaching is prophetic action, in imitation of the Old Testament prophets and of the Jesus of the Gospels, rather than the use of words, particularly written words. Thus, much of what we know about Francis's views on nature and animals comes to us second-hand through his followers not long after his death. Thomas of Celano (1200–1255), a Franciscan friar, is his first, papally-appointed, biographer.[73] St Bonaventure is also commissioned to write the 'official' biography, the 'Legend', in 1260. Another body of work, the *Fioretti*, or *Little Flowers of Francis of Assisi*, a collection of popular 'wonder-stories' about life of Francis and his early companions, appear at the beginning of the fourteenth century, possibly from Latin originals, being a blend of an anonymous *Actus beati Francisci et sociorum eius* and of a *Floretum*, or 'garden of flowers', compiled by the Franciscan provincial, Ugolino of Montegiorgio (d.1348).[74] These are concerned to portray a hagiographical life of the saint rather than a historical or objective account, so that it is not possible to separate life from legend at this remove.

What the writings make clear, however, is that Francis views animals as part of creation as a whole, where everything created is, in a real sense, sacramental. For him everything that exists, since it comes from the heart of God, is a sign of

the holy, a sacrament of the Divine. Unlike some eco-
theologians of our day, for whom the created world itself is
divine, for Francis, the world displays and reveals the Divine,
but is utterly creaturely. God is revealed and encountered in
the mountains, the hills, the trees, the animals, and in
humans. In a sense, Francis is the first exponent of 'theos-
rights', or the movement for the 'democracy of all creatures',
where every creature in creation is given its fundamental
rights since it possesses those rights because it is a beloved
creation of God, and not because rational humanity imposes
them, or determines what those rights are. All such creatures,
animate or otherwise, are to be respected and cherished as
kin, sharing the same Divine paternal origin. They participate
in the expression of the reality of who God is and what God
has done, and Francis expresses this relationship in the famil-
ial relative terms of brother and sister. These terms signify a
relationship which for him is very real. When Francis, as
described by his biographer St Bonaventure, considered 'the
primordial source of all things,'[75] he was filled with even more
abundant piety, calling creatures, no matter how small, by the
name of brother or sister, because he knew that had the same
source as himself'.[76] Bonaventure himself declares that 'every
creature is by its nature a kind of effigy and likeness of the
eternal Wisdom'.[77] Troublingly, despite his compassionate
relationship with animals, there is no evidence to suggest that
Francis was a vegetarian, nor did he advocate abstinence from
eating meat, except in penitential terms. This inconsistency is
perhaps not something which would have occurred to a man
of his time.

The writings and legends of St Francis The well-known
composition of Francis, and the first work of Italian literature,
'The Canticle of Brother Sun', or 'Praise of the Creatures', with
its echoes of the Song of the Three Young Men (Daniel 3:17,
23, 51–90) and Psalm 148, first appears in a reference made by
Thomas of Celano in his *First Life*.[78] Before the first part,
verses one to nine, Francis tells companions, 'I wish to

compose a new hymn about the Lord's creatures, of which we make daily use, without which we cannot live, and with which the human race greatly offends its Creator.'[79] In the repeated phrase: 'May Thou be praised, my Lord, *for* sister ... [or brother]', there is some dispute as to whether the Italian *per* is to be translated as 'for', meaning that Francis means to praise God for having created the creatures; for the singer to praise God *on behalf of* the creatures; or whether he intends the creatures to praise God *themselves* (as in the Latin *propter*).[80] Whatever the case, the Canticle certainly provides the best example of Francis's theory of the kinship of all created beings.

Among the many animal legends associated with Francis are the following, recorded by Thomas of Celano,[81] and probably used as readings during Matins:

> Since this holy man attained the very summit of perfection and was filled with the *simplicity of the dove* (Matthew 10:16) he urged all creatures towards the love of the Creator. He used to preach to the birds, which heard him and allowed him to touch them; nor would they leave until he dismissed them.
>
> Once there were swallows chattering so much that they would not allow him to preach to the people; he told them to keep quiet and they immediately fell silent. The wild beasts harmed by others used to flee to him and they received the love of piety from him, finding in his presence solace amidst their trials.
>
> What love do you think he bore towards the salvation of human beings, since he was so compassionate towards even the lower creatures? For example, he often freed lambs and sheep from the threat of slaughter because of the graciousness he felt towards the simplicity of their nature; he even picked up worms out of the roadway so that they would not be harmed by passers-by.[82]

In another *Life of St Francis*, by Julian of Speyer (1232–1235), written to encourage younger brothers in their way of life, there is yet more detail of the preaching to the birds 'who sang in response', such as Francis beginning 'to accuse himself of great negligence before the brothers because he had previously neglected to preach to the birds'. From then onwards, whenever he advises people to offer praises, he 'also earnestly invited birds, beasts and all other creatures to do the same, calling them by the names of 'brothers' or 'sisters', to the praise of the Maker of all'.[83] In one recorded incident, a brother brings a live rabbit, having been caught in a snare, to Francis who is 'moved by great pity' and asks the animal 'Brother rabbit, come to me! Why did you allow yourself to be deceived like this?' On its release,

> the rabbit, as if confident, immediately ran to the man of God and *rested in his lap* (Luke 16:23) just like a tame animal. As often as it was placed on the ground by the blessed man so it could run away, it returned to him, not seeking any other freedom, until at last Francis commanded that it be carried away to a nearby woods by the brothers.[84]

A similar incident is reported with a fish which is returned alive to the water and which does not leave the neighbourhood of the saint until bidden to withdraw.[85] In another incident, Francis exchanges a borrowed cloak for two lambs, which he later returns to their first owner with strict instructions not to harm them.[86]

Apart from many more tales, and several very fanciful ones, Francis is also noted for having introduced the tradition of Christmas nativity scene 'cribs'. Three years before Francis dies, he instructs a religious-minded nobleman of Greccio, John, to assemble an ox and an ass with human actors in a stable, with a manger and so on, as a living tableau for the edification of the townspeople. It makes such an impression that even the hay from the manger is supposed to possess supernatural qualities, as it 'served both men and women from various perils and also proved health-giving when applied to stricken brute beasts'.[87] So important is the doctrine of the incarnation for Francis, that he insists on special provision being made for feeding birds and cattle on Christmas Day.[88]

The stories of Francis' concern for animals have been widely allegorized. This may be simply as a result of the early-medieval allegorizing tradition common to both biblical interpretation and beast fables. Or it could be to prevent derision towards their revered Founder, as his concern for real animals could be a source of embarrassment, particularly in an age of rationalism. One telling criticism of St Francis in that latter age is by the rationalist Voltaire (1649–1778) who calls the saint, 'A savage madman who ran around naked, spoke to animals [and] gave religious instruction to a wolf.'[89] One example of allegorizing concerns this fierce wolf, *il lupo*, of Gubbio, whom Francis tames and with whom he draws up an oral contract. The wolf would no longer predate upon the townspeople of Gubbio in return for their feeding him daily. It is suggested that 'Frate Lupo . . . was a man, perhaps a bandit by that name'.[90] It is also suggested, on a Franciscan website, that the wolf of Gubbio could be symbolic, 'to draw the moral of the need for the ministry of reconciliation'.[91]

Francis' scholarly followers draw their inspiration from him, but they pursue theological interests in christology and metaphysics rather than develop his compassionate response to the plight of animals.[92] The exception is St Anthony of Padua (*c*.1195–1231), a near-contemporary and friend of Francis who leaves an Augustinian monastery to join the Franciscans. Although a great Bible-based preacher, after his death he becomes remembered more for the numerous 'wonder works' attributed to him than for his scholarship.[93] Animal legends similar to those of Francis are among them, recorded in two Lives, one by the same Julian of Speyer (above). These include Anthony preaching to fish – when the inhabitants of Rimini are hostile, it is fish who line up in rows to hear him. Another time, Anthony exposes a monstrance (containing the sacrament of the Real Presence) before a hungry mule, who ignores nearby food to kneel before it. Both accounts have been allegorized as meaning that when people refuse to listen to the truth, or treat holy things contemptuously, animals will shame them by worthier actions.

Franciscanism There is, of course, much more to Francis'
teaching (by example) than that on animals – his elevation of
poverty as an ideal, his peace-making activities and his devotion to asceticism and the Passion of Christ. But why has so
little been advanced on the subject of animals by Franciscans
in the centuries since the death of the founder of the Order?
One answer could lie in the very instability of the Order from
the beginning, which prevents a smooth and systemic development of the founder's ideals. Francis gives up the running
of the Order several years before his death and, within twenty-
five years of it, his followers are caught up in bitter
controversy over Francis' teaching and the meaning of his
life.[94] A schism between the self-proclaimed *Spirituals* (claim-
ing to be the authentic heirs of Francis' zeal for poverty) and
the *Conventuals*, causes divisions which have never been
resolved.[95] To some commentators, the conflict lies between
the 'pure religion of the Spirit', represented by St Francis, and
the 'religion of authority', represented by the Order's protec-
tor, Cardinal Ugolino, later to become Pope Gregory IX, to the
extent that 'The original ideal of St Francis was progressively
diluted and finally smothered by the institutional Church.'[96]
The *Fioretti* emerge from the viewpoint of the Spirituals, and
the accounts of Thomas of Celano – especially when the
Second Life contradict some facts in the First – are discredited
by the Conventuals. Such schisms do little to advance causes.

The scholar and systematic thinker Bonaventure is elected
as Vicar General in 1257 in the hope of uniting the Order after
a long period of upheaval, and asked, by the General Council
of Narbonne in 1260, to compose the first codified General
Constitution and write the definitive Life of Francis. Bonaventure's friend, the Dominican Thomas Aquinas, considers the
plan admirable, 'Let us leave a saint to write of a saint', he is
reported to have said.[97] Six years later the Chapter orders all
previous Lives to be destroyed. Fortunately, this is done inef-
ficiently, by accident or design, and Celano's Lives survive.
However, the splits in the Order are not healed, and the Spirituals break away completely, only to diminish by the

fourteenth century, to be replaced by another movement in the following century, led by Bernadine of Siena, known as groups of the *Observants*. In 1517 Pope Leo X organizes the various Observant groups into one, with a Minister-General, and the Conventuals into a separate Order with a Master-General. By the nineteenth century there are several types of Observants – Discalced, Recollects and Reformed – with which Leo XIII forms the present Friars Minor. Today there are several bodies of Franciscans in both the Roman Catholic and Anglican Churches, and in the Roman Church they are divided into three Orders.[98]

With such instability, and the dominance of scholarship over Francis's doctrine of a simple and direct relationship with nature, the cause of animals finds no champion. The mantle of Francis largely falls on the anthropocentric St Bonaventure, who follows Francis at least in seeing the created world as reflecting the glory of God.[99] He believes that every creature is equally close to God, but that how that relationship exists depends on the creature's capacity to respond.[100] While he sees the Trinity as somehow permeating creation, Bonaventure's primary interest in the hierarchy of being is in the level *above* the animal – in other words, with humanity and with angels.[101] Animals, the 'irrational creatures', participate in the hierarchy of creation 'only mediately, through their relation to the rational'.[102] 'Since all things are created for humanity',[103] [and] 'It is true without any doubt that we are the end of all existing things, and all bodily things exist to serve humanity.'[104] The human creature, for Bonaventure, is where the hierarchy begins. He or she is the apex of creation, the last of the six-day creation sequence, and it is only the human creature who will participate in the 'return to the source, to God'.[105] Nature is necessary for the human being to operate within on earth, but then can be left behind at the end, the eschaton, when the purely spiritual takes over. Knowing that St Paul talks of the whole of nature being recreated, Bonaventure understands that to mean that the human being, as an embodiment, or microcosm of the whole of nature, takes up material nature into the human soul and it is that spiritual soul which ascends to God.[106] As Santmire sums up, 'For Bonaventure, in fact, there is no room for the world of animals, plants, and minerals in eternity. They are, in fact, left behind at lower rungs of the ladder of being, as humans ascend to perfect spiritual communion with God above.'[107]

St Francis is a towering figure, in some senses, in the tradition, probably being the only saint most people outside the Church have ever heard of, despite his kinship teaching being so comprehensively ignored by theologians. There are a few other saints, apart from the Celtic ones and Desert Fathers, who have made a contribution towards a positive attitude, if not a comprehensive theology, within Catholicism in relation to animals. Then there are theologians, followers of saintly Founders of religious Orders, whose contributions are anything but positive in relation to animals. Some of these will now be examined.

Saints of note and their followers Within the Dominican tradition there is the South American St Martin de Porres (1579–1639). As the illegitimate son of a Spanish father and a black African slave, at first he is accepted only as a lay helper or 'donato', but later allowed to make solemn profession as a Dominican Co-operator brother, while given the more unpleasant manual chores. However, he builds a reputation as one devoted to sick people, and compassionate to animals, with many accounts of acts of kindness to them – including keeping a cats' and dogs' sanctuary at his sister's house.[108] When householders complain about the ravages caused by rats and mice, Martin is reported to protest: 'What are they to do, the poor little beasts, if they are starving and they know that there is plenty of food in your houses?'[109] He suggests putting out food for them, to save them from burrowing holes in property. He is occasionally depicted holding a mouse in one hand and with dogs and cats about him.

St Philip Neri (1515–1595) is the only other named saint in CCC paragraph, n. 2416, which suggests that there should be kindness shown towards animals: 'We should recall the gentleness with which saints like St Francis of Assisi or St Philip Neri treated animals.' Better known as the founder of the Oratory movement, and a healer and confessor, he did embrace vegetarianism on the grounds of animal welfare, rather than on ascetical ones. Once, passing a butcher's shop, he says, 'If everyone were like me, they wouldn't kill animals.'[110] He does not confine his concern to animals, and once saves an ex-Dominican heretic from execution.[111] He also sets captive birds free, which, by their own choice, would not then leave him for many years. Animals are attracted to him – in the manner of some of the Celtic saints – such as a cardinal's small dog who refuses to leave Philip and whom Philip obliges some young noblemen followers to carry around for years.[112] Of Philip, John Henry Newman comments: 'Nothing was too high for him, nothing too low.'[113] At one time he is brought a young bird found in the chapel. 'Don't squeeze, don't hurt it,' Philip insists, 'Open the window and let it fly away.' But when it had done so, Philip worries whether he had done the right thing, 'It was so small; it won't know where to go.'[114]

Such small touches of humanity towards animals by saints are so rarely recorded. Philip insists on flies being shooed out of the window instead of being killed, of giving away a brace of live partridges donated for his meal, with instruction that they are not to be harmed. He expresses pity for animals on their way to slaughter, and releases captured mice into places of safety for them – all fairly commonplace acts today, but remarkable in their time. Maybe the very ordinariness of these actions is the reason for the selection of this saint in the Catechism. St Francis is perhaps rather intimidating as an example, as few people today come into contact with wolves, or would think of preaching to birds or fish, or (as in one legend) stay still while a bird nests on their shoulder. While these are rather extreme, there is nothing in the stories of St Philip Neri beyond the powers of anyone today.

These accounts exhaust the list of saints known to have

contributed significantly to a tradition of kindness to animals.
The following mention is of a saintly Founder of a greatly influential Order, but neither he nor it have a reputation for many
examples, written or enacted, of the compassionate treatment
of animals. A notable exception is the present-day Jesuit
theologian Robert Murray, whose 1992 book *The Cosmic
Covenant*, and other writings (such as the poem that ends
this book) shine like a light in the darkness.

There are just two references in the writings of St Ignatius
of Loyola (1491–1556) that refer to life other than human. The
first repeats the traditional negative formula that a creature,
i.e. anything created, has value only in as much as it is of help
to human beings in realizing their goal of heavenly perfection:

> Man is created to praise, reverence and serve God our Lord,
> and by this means to save his soul. The other things on the face
> of the earth are created for man in order to help him pursue
> the end for which he is created. It follows from this that one
> must use other created things in so far as they help towards
> one's end, and free oneself from them in so far as they provide
> obstacles to one's end. To do this we need to make ourselves
> indifferent to all created things ...[115]

The next, less significant, reference, also from the Spiritual
Exercises (which are much in use today in Ignatian spirituality) expresses amazement that the range of all beings – from
angels through the human saints to animals and the earth
itself – allows the individual sinful subject to continue in existence, and has not been a means of divine punishment (First
Week, Second Exercise).

What is of greater interest is the tradition which Ignatius of
Loyola founds, in which the members of the Society of Jesus
are encouraged to excel in secular scholarship and employ-
ment, the better to influence their milieu with Christian
values. Few, if any, have become concerned with animal
welfare, but two in particular are remarkable for the hostile
position they have taken in relation to animal creation. First,
though, are two minor Jesuit voices in the debate. The first of

these is the Fleming, Cornelius à Lapide (1516–1637), for whom the gulf between animals and humans is so great that some creatures, 'lice, flies, maggots and the like were not created directly by God but by spontaneous generation, as lice from sweat'.[116] The second minor voice expresses quite contrary views. The scientist, Pierre Gassendi, in his *Metaphysical Colloquy* of 1641, dismisses Descartes' conclusions as to the sentience and rationality of animals, ridiculing his illogical inconsistencies.[117]

The two remarkable hostile Jesuits are Père Bougeant and Fr Rickaby, in the eighteenth and early twentieth centuries respectively. Before the eighteenth century, the allegorical and internalized interpretation of the biblical expression: 'having dominion' over nature, was that of having control over unruly *human* nature. Now in the Enlightenment, this approach is being replaced by a new literalism. Scriptural sanction to 'having dominion' over the natural world is taken seriously, and now the means are increasingly available for effective exploitation of that world.[118] This Enlightenment, which begins to flourish in the seventeenth century, has its roots way back in the translations of Aristotle in the twelfth century, and is rapidly advanced by the invention of printing. It is characterized by the views of the early seventeenth-century philosopher, Francis Bacon (1561–1626). He justifies a new project for mastering the natural world by reference to science restoring what was lost in the Fall:

> For man by the Fall fell at the same time from his state of inno-
> cency and from his dominion over creation. Both of these
> losses however can even in this life be in some part repaired;
> the former by religion and faith, the latter by arts and sciences.
> For creation was not by the curse made altogether and for ever
> a rebel, but ... is now by various labours ... at length and in
> some measure subdued to the supplying of man with bread;
> that is to the uses of human life.[119]

The period is marked by an excessive anthropocentrism and by an unbiblical spiritualizing of religion, combined in certain 'refined' (middle and upper class) circles by a predilection for wit and clever philosophizing. The fashionable French Jesuit, Père Bougeant, develops, in his 1739 epistolary book, the disconcerting theory of the diabolic possession of animals.[120] His tone is facetious, but his intention is serious – or at least was taken to be so.[121]

He first argues, reasonably and like Gassendi, that the Cartesian theory that animals are mere unfeeling machines is untenable, basing his evidence on the behaviour of animals and the human treatment of them as sentient creatures. If an animal is a machine, like a timepiece, who, he questions, would stroke his watch as he does his poodle? He suggests that human beings infer from their own individual consciousness that other people are equally free and intelligent agents. They then apply the same reasoning to non-human animals which demonstrate expressions of feelings and emotions similar to those in people, proving therefore that 'there is within them a spiritual principle, which does not differ essentially from the human soul'.[122]

However, the soul of an animal would have to be either matter or spirit – and as matter is not capable of thinking (which animals do), and as animals' possession of spirit brings with it 'consequences [such as eternal life] *contrary* to the principles of religion' – so neither can be admitted.[123] In other words, animals are sentient and behave *like* people – and he deliberately pushes that similarity to an *absolute* identification with human behaviour, ignoring the uniquely human possession of free will – so animals' behaviour, as it can incur praise and blame, must also be worthy of the retribution of hell or the reward of heaven in the after-life, 'so that the pre-eminence of a man over a beast as an object of God's mercy or wrath is lost'.[124]

This would make animals a species of man, or men a species of animal 'both of which propositions are incompatible with the teachings of religion'. The fulcrum of his argument is based on the next stage of his reasoning. The only way in which these views can be reconciled is to affirm that animals

are endowed with intellectual sense and that they *do* have
immortal souls – but that they must be incarnations of evil
spirits, spirits of the fallen devils who, awaiting eternal damnation at the day of judgement, inhabit the world for the
temptation and tormenting of human souls.[125]

He foresees the objection to this suggestion (that animals
are incarnated devils) being the pleasure people take in
certain birds and animals, which they would not do, presumably, if these were satanic. He answers this by denying that
people love animals 'for their own sakes', but, as 'they are
altogether strangers to human society', their only service
could be 'of being useful and amusing. And what care we,
whether it be a Devil, or any other creature, that serves and
amuses us?' He accepts that he can live with 'little devils' as
easily as he can with the vast number of people 'of whom religion informs me, that a great number shall be damned'.[126]

Bougeant then describes the cruelties which animals are
subjected to, both by people and by nature – as being especially problematic, as they are 'as sensible as ourselves of pain
and death' – and questions how they could have been so
created by God.[127] The answer he gives is twofold, 'either that
God has taken delight in making beasts so vicious as they are;
or that they have, like man, original sin, which has perverted
their primitive nature'.[128] This leaves, so Bougeant has it, only
his theory:

> The souls of beasts are refractory spirits, which have made
> themselves guilty towards God. The sin in beasts is no original
> sin, it is a personal crime, which has corrupted and perverted
> their nature in its whole substance; hence all the vices and
> corruption we observe in them, though they can be no longer
> criminal; because God by irrevocably reprobating them, has at
> the same time divested them of their liberty.[129]

Part of the evil spirits' divine punishment is being incarnated
in such a 'degrading and humiliating' form. So, Bougeant
argues, the correct way to treat animals, being evil spirits in
flesh, is harshly. He explains that 'The Christian Church has

never deemed it a duty to take the lower animals under its protection or to inculcate ordinary natural kindness to them.' He applauds the relentless slaughter and extermination of wild beasts and birds in Catholic countries such as Italy and Spain, and even the suffering caused there, at the hands of their owners, of domestic animals such as donkeys, mules and horses. To treat animals in this way is to co-operate with God in punishing the devils of which animals are the visible and sentient forms. It is they who cry out when pain is inflicted. Bougeant, called by Evans, a 'crafty disciple of Loyola', is pleased to be provided with so many 'little devils' for his use and entertainment and finds nothing untoward in the prospect of the damnation of all animals, even cherished pets, as well as the majority of human beings.[130] He appeals to universal consent – the maxim *universitas non delinquit* – to justify his theory, on the basis that every culture, civilized or savage, regards or has regarded animals to be embodiments of evil spirits. He cites the title Baal-zebub, or Lord of the Flies, and the Christian depiction of Satan as cloven hoofed, as well as examples from folk-lore, to support this claim, seeing the origin of animal worship as a form of demonology. As death sets the human soul free, in animals it releases the devil-spirit to inhabit the egg or embryo of another creature, thus vivifying it, to resume its punished life in another body.

The second major Jesuit is an eminent canon lawyer in Victorian England, Fr Joseph Rickaby. In his manual of moral philosophy,[131] much used in English seminaries, he discusses the 'so-called' rights of animals. His central thesis is that animals, having no understanding and therefore not being persons, cannot have any rights. He goes further and states that, as they are mere chattels, or things, humans have no duties to them either, not of justice, nor of religion ('unless we are to worship them, like the Egyptians of old'); nor of 'fidelity, for they are incapable of accepting a promise'. He then asks whether humans have any duties of charity, and answers with a definitive no, giving as reason the distance between human and animal creation. Human ability to speak and to contemplate the Divine exonerates us from any more duties of charity, or of any kind, 'to the lower animals, as neither to stocks [*sic*] and stones'.[132]

However, Rickaby then mentions the duties that apply to persons in relation to animals. As an offence against the property of another, domestic animals must not be harmed. Nor must we 'break out into paroxysms of rage and impatience in dealing with them' as it would be a poor means of displaying human pre-eminence 'to torture poor brutes in malevolent glee at their pain and helplessness'. Quoting Aquinas,[133] such 'wanton cruelty' disposes people to be cruel to other people.[134] The same reason is to constrain actions which 'vex and annoy a brute beast for sport', and is 'unworthy of man'. However, there is no 'shadow of evil' involved in causing pain to animals *in* sport, where pain is not the purpose of, but is incidental to, the sport. As they are merely things and exist for human beings and not for themselves, 'we do right in using them unsparingly for our need and convenience, though not for our wantonness'. In fact, whatever 'conduces to the sustenance of man', as does the pursuit of science, allows us to inflict pain on animals. 'Nor are we bound to any anxious care to make this pain as little as may be.' For science – biology or medicine – where pain itself in animals is the subject of observation, there are no moral considerations which should prevent its infliction – with the slight caveat that the experimenter yet be 'mindful of mercy'.[135]

Rickaby concludes the section with the assurance that observing the rights and claims of other people (particularly the owners of animal property), control over one's emotions and reverence for the Creator will ensure 'a wise and humane treatment of the lower animals'. 'But,' he declares, 'to preach kindness to brutes as a primary obligation, and capital point of amendment in the conversion of a sinner, is to treat the symptom and leave unchecked the inward malady.'[136] With this teaching in the English Roman Catholic seminaries, is it to be wondered that the clergy have not pressed for a more humane treatment and theology of animals?

Monastic literature There are three genres of medieval monastic literature concerning animals: the bestiaries, the beast fables and the Lives of saints. The first two employ the instrumentalist principle that animals exist for the benefit of human beings – in these cases, spiritual benefit, animals being the subject of moral lessons. There is a biblical precept for learning from animals, as in Proverbs 6:6 and Job, 12:7–10a, and the medieval monks make use of the allegorical method, otherwise applied to biblical interpretation, taught in the universities from the eleventh to the fifteenth centuries.[137] One significant allegorical interpretation in the patristic and medieval period is made of the term 'dominion' as in Genesis 1:28, whereby the 'beasts' that were to be mastered were the passions and sinful impulses within the person, just as the domestic and peaceful animals in Eden had become fierce wild beasts after the Fall.[138] Origen, echoed later by John Chrysostom and even Augustine and Aquinas, had described the human person as a 'little world' containing 'herds of cattle', 'flocks of sheep and flocks of goats' and 'birds of the air'. In other words, these animals represent various aspects of the human psyche, and 'the directive to exercise dominion over the beasts was understood as an advocacy of self-control'.[139]

While certain animals carry benign, even spiritual meanings, there are others that fare less well. Wolves, foxes, bears, rats and snakes, for example, are all represented negatively – as 'evil', 'wicked', 'sly', 'dirty', and so on. This helps of course to desensitize those whose task it is to kill them. When human vices are projected onto an animal species, it becomes no sin to destroy the 'wicked'. Indeed, savagery itself is being 'conquered', even when the means of doing so are themselves savage and inhuman.

It is in the popular bestiaries where the development of animal imagery as a resource for teaching moral lessons reaches its zenith. As collections of animal allegories, they originate with a Greek work, the *Physiologus,* written between the second and fifth centuries AD. This consists of nearly fifty chapters about animals and birds (including such

imagined creatures as the unicorn and the phoenix), all
designed to convey Christian teaching. Each allegory begins
with a biblical quotation, followed by a fact (often of a highly
fictional nature), and concluding with a moral drawn from
human life.[140] There are many Greek copies, some highly
decorated, and translations in Latin from the sixth century.
After being condemned as heretical by Pope Gelasius in 469,
extra Christian moralizations are added to the *Physiologus,* so
the ban is lifted by Gregory the Great, who makes much use
of it. After much copying and expansion, the number of chapters grows from about 50 to 150 by the Middle Ages.

The *Physiologus* develops into the twelfth-century bestiaries
through other collections[141] of elaborate animal stories which
are given allegorical interpretation. The bestiaries tend to omit
the Scripture passage, expand the natural history (or fiction)
and provide an imaginative etymology for the names of the
animals.[142] In the thirteenth century, three encyclopaedic works
draw together all known animal lore material and make the
bestiaries yet more popular.[143] The didactic purpose of
bestiaries is to improve the minds of people 'that what they have
difficulty comprehending with their ears, they will perceive with
their eyes'.[144] Written in Latin they are designed for the clergy
and literate laity, although a much-copied set of sermons on
birds is to teach illiterate Augustinian lay brothers.[145] Six extant
bestiaries contain whole creation cycles, possibly following the
tradition of illustrated copies of St Ambrose's *Hexaemeron*.

Bestiaries become lavishly illustrated and the animal
imagery is reproduced in paintings, illuminated books of
Hours and of Scripture, church carvings and stained glass.
Animal symbolism is found, for example, on tomb effigies
which have lions, symbolic of virtue and strength, at the feet
of knights, and dogs, symbolic of fidelity and trust, at ladies'
feet. Some animals would be unknown in northern and
western Europe, such as lions and elephants, and some, like
griffons, unicorns and basilicks, completely fantastic. Most
illustrations, for example, of elephants, and descriptions of
their activities are wildly inaccurate,[146] although an elephant is

given to Henry III (1207–1272) from Louis IX, paraded
through the streets of London and kept in the Tower of
London for four years before it dies.

Every animal, bird, or natural element carries a moral
message or Christian allusion by representing emblematically
human virtues or vices; the camel, for example, representing
humility; sunrise, enlightenment; the fox, a hypocrite (often
depicted by secular writers as a friar) or the Devil.[147] The religious symbolism would be instantly recognizable; for
example, Christ represented by a lamb or a pelican;[148] sheep
are innocent laity, the followers of the Good Shepherd, while
goats are sinners.[149] One story has a lion sleeping with eyes
open representing Christ after the crucifixion, 'sleeping in the
body ... yet his Godhead was awake'.[150] Also lions cubs are
thought at the time to be born dead and after three days their
father (or mother, in some accounts) breathes on them and
brings them to life: 'just so did the Father omnipotent raise
our Lord Jesus Christ from the dead on the third day'.[151]

Beast fables feature animals, but here they talk or are
anthropomorphized in some way. The 'outer' story of the
fable concerns animals but the meaning (in parenthesis here)
is for the monks for whom it is written. An early fable, from a
French abbey, tells of an exiled swan (fallen human being)
flying across the ocean, who begins to fail in strength and
become battered by waves and winds. She is about to die
when dawn appears (Christ). She recovers and rejoices,
reaches dry land and encourages her fellows to assemble and
worship 'the great King'.[152]

In another fable, a calf escapes from its stall on Holy Satur-
day (a monk bored with monastery life, asks to be freed from
his vows) but falls into the clutches of a wolf who leads it to
his den. The wolf intends it for his festive Easter meal. The calf
begs for reprieve until the next day (paralleling Christ's
harrowing of hell). The calf's herd arrives to confront the
wolf, who convinces its allies – an otter and a hedgehog – that
it will prevail, unless the fox becomes involved. (A secondary
story explains how the fox and the wolf become bitter

enemies.) The wolf suffers several reversals before being killed as a result of the fox's cunning. The calf (and monk) gets a second chance and all go off to festivities.[153]

The use of animals to throw light on human behaviour is popular, particularly in English-language literature, from the Middle Ages to the present day. George Orwell's *Animal Farm* employs them to great effect, as does Nick Park in the animated *Creature Comfort* film stories. From the nineteenth century, most animal-character stories, such as the *Uncle Rufus* tales, the Beatrix Potter series, *Wind in the Willows* and the Winnie the Pooh stories, have been intended for a child readership. It may be that early exposure to personalized animals has formed the English-speaking cultures' tendency to be somewhat ostensibly kinder to animals than is the case in Mediterranean cultures that have not developed this tradition.

Whilst the bestiaries made popular reading, there develops alongside them an interest in animals for their own sakes. Cronin argues strongly[154] that many users of bestiaries are not without concern for the natural facts. A number of eminent theologians, including Aquinas, criticize their more fantastic features and St Bernard of Clairvaux in the mid-twelfth century denounces them as, 'those ridiculous monsters'.[155] Some real animals are deemed to be as fantastic as fictitious ones, as Bernard asks: 'To what purpose are those unclean apes, those fierce lions, those monstrous centaurs, those half-men, those striped tigers ...?'[156]

Aristotle's *De Animalibus* was translated in the twelfth century – representing animals and plants in an objective, non-symbolic way – leading to the slow development of real zoological science and the scientific approach to nature. The increasing knowledge of the biological world is seen at the time as a restoring of the complete knowledge of nature possessed by Adam before the Fall, and consequently lost. Dominion over nature is therefore now accomplished by comprehending, or the mental ordering, of creatures.[157]

One of the projects of the scientifically-influential Emperor Friedrich II of Hohenstaufen (1194–1250) is to review the stories in the bestiaries and dismiss those he can not verify. He is not interested in the moralizing motive for the stories, and compiles his own ornithological work[158] entirely from systematic observations and data recording. The encyclopaedic *De Animalibus*[159] and the thirteenth-century *De Proprietatibus*[160] both draw heavily on ancient sources, especially Aristotle, but contribute to the advance of the science by their objective approach to the natural world. The sixteenth century sees the first really modern-style zoological work[161] which is produced with only verifiable animals, including several new to Europe. By the seventeenth century, fictitious animals in bestiaries are strongly criticized, with Sir Thomas Browne writing, 'now herein methinks men much forget themselves, not well considering the absurdity of such assertions'.[162] And by the eighteenth century, the interest in mythical beasts has given way to an interest in science – with no consequent improvement in the treatment of animals.

Notes

1   Andrew Linzey, 'Jesus and Animals in Christian Apocalyptic Literature', *Modern Believing*, 48:1 (Jan 2007), p. 51.
2   Andrew Linzey and Dan Cohn-Sherbok, *After Noah: animals and the liberation of theology* (London: Mowbray, 1997), p. 66.
3   Matthew 12:10–12; Luke 15:15; 14: 5
4   Linzey and Cohn-Sherbok, *After Noah* (1997), p. 66.
5   Ibid., p. 67.
6   C. R. Matthew, 'Articulate Animals: a multivalent motif in the Apocryphal Acts of the Apostles', in *The Apocryphal Acts of the Apostles*, edited by F. Bovon, A. G. Brock and C. R. Matthews (Harvard UP 1999), p. 232; cited in Andrew Linzey, 'Jesus and Animals in Christian Apocalyptic Literature', *Modern Believing*, 48:1 (Jan 2007), p. 58.
7   Linzey and Cohn-Sherbok, *After Noah* (1997), p. 67.
8   'The Gospel of Pseudo-Matthew', in *The Apocryphal New Testament: a collection of Apocryphal Christian literature in an English translation based on M.R. James*, edited by J. K. Elliott (Oxford: Clarendon, 1993), pp. 94–5; cited in Linzey and Cohn-Sherbok, *After Noah* (1997), p. 65.
9   Pseudo-Matthew, 97–8, cited in Linzey and Cohn-Sherbok, *After Noah* (1997), p. 65.

10   William J. Short, 'Animals, a Christian approach', in *Modern Catholic Encyclopedia* (1994), p. 30.

11   Job 38: 41, 'Who makes provision for the raven when his squabs cry out to God and crane their necks in hunger', also Psalm 147:9, 'Who gives food to the cattle and to the young ravens when they cry?'

12   Genesis 3:1ff.

13   Until Moses raised the image of a snake on a standard, Numbers 21:6–9.

14   Mark 16:18, 'They will pick up snakes in their hands'.

15   Athanasius 63; cited by Murray, *The Cosmic Covenant* (1992), p. 146.

16   Theodoret of Cyrrhus, *A History of the Monks of Syria*, VI, 2; cited by Margaret Atkins in 'St Jerome and the Lion', *The Ark* 182 (Spring 1999), p. 12.

17   Margaret Atkins, 'St Jerome and the Lion', p. 12.

18   Macarius – either 'of Egypt', according to the Greek *Historia Monachorus*, or 'of Alexandria', in Palladius' *Lausiac History*.

19   Margaret Atkins, 'St Macarius and the Hyena', *The Ark* 193 (spring 2003), p. 11.

20   Atkins, 'St Macarius and the Hyena', p. 9.

21   Ibid.

22   Cited by Murray, *The Cosmic Covenant* (London: Sheed & Ward, 1992), p. 147.

23   The Greek term 'Celt' simply meant the people who live north of the Alps, 'beyond civilization', and was revived in the sixteenth century; see Oliver Davies, *Celtic Spirituality* (Classics of Western Spirituality) (New York: Paulist, 1999), p. 4.

24   This predates the arrival of St Augustine in Canterbury by some 283 years.

25   In 431 'a deacon of Auxerre called Palladius had been sent by Pope Celestinus *ad Scottos in Christum credentes* "to the Scotti who believe in Christ"'; see Terence P. McCaughey, *Memory and Redemption: Church, politics and prophetic theology in Ireland* (Dublin: Gill and Macmillan, 1993), p. 63. The third group are non-Christianized Hiberionaces living along the west coast.

26   Centred on 'sedes' or city-state 'seats'.

27   Oliver Davies, *Celtic Spirituality* (New York: Paulist, 1999), pp. 16–18.

28   Ibid., p. 22.

29   Ibid., p. 222.

30   Helen Waddell, *Beasts and Saints* (London: Darton, Longman and Todd, 1934, 1995), p. 121.

31   Benedicta Ward, *The Spirituality of St Cuthbert* (Oxford: Fairacres, 1992), p. 10.

32   *Gildas: the ruin of Britain and other works*, edited and translated by Michael Winterbottom (London: Phillimore, 1978), p. 17.

33 Occasionally she also represents the female aspect of the Godhead, or
    one of the three sisters of the triple Goddess, the Morrigan. Many mira-
    cles, mainly of fertility and of producing food, are attributed to the
    'Morrigan', who is also represented as a serpent. This, according to Jani
    Ni Mhorrigu explains the story of Patrick 'driving the serpent from
    Ireland' as the Christian Trinitarian God replaced the pagan female
    triple goddess. It was only after the rise of Christianity that the goddess
    became associated with a saint, Brigid of Kildare; see <www.inquirer.
    gn. apc. org/craft-two >.
34 White horses are found in chalk carvings on hillsides in England, some
    dating from pre-Christian times; for example, south of Wantage,
    Oxfordshire, is one in the district known as 'The Vale of the White
    Horse'.
35 Pope Gregory III had to instruct Boniface in 732 to insist on the avoid-
    ance of eating horseflesh in his missionary endeavours among the
    German tribes. Only in Hungary, where wild horses were plentiful, and
    in Ireland, was the ban ignored; see *Dictionary of the Middle Ages*, Vol.
    I, edited by Joseph Strayer (New York: Charles Scribner's Sons, 1982),
    pp. 299–300.
36 Davies, *Celtic Spirituality* (1999), p. 110.
37 Ibid., p. 111.
38 John Zizioulas, 'Priest of Creation', *Environmental Stewardship*
    (2006), p. 278. I shall return to Zizioulas and the Eastern Tradition in
    chapter four.
39 Zizioulas, 'Priest of Creation', *Environmental Stewardship* (2006),
    p. 278.
40 Paul Collins, *God's earth: religion as if matter really mattered* (Dublin:
    Gill and Macmillan, 1995), p. 11.
41 'There is indeed not one single gift which reaches creation without the
    Holy Spirit', St Basil, *De Spiritu Sancto*, para. 24 55; cited in Linzey and
    Cohn-Sherbok, *After Noah* (1997), p. 74.
42 St Basil, *Liturgy*; cited in Charles D. Niven, *History of the Humane
    Movement* (New York: Transatlantic Arts, 1967), p. 27.
43 See Psalm 36:6, 'Man and beast thou savest, O Lord' (RSV).
44 *Liturgy*, cited in Linzey and Cohn-Sherbok, *After Noah* (1997), p. 84;
    also Sorabji, *Animal Minds and Human Morals* (1993), p. 202.
45 *Liturgy*.
46 Particularly in his nine homilies on the Hexaemeron, the six days of
    creation in Genesis 1: 1–26.
47 St Basil, *Homily* 8.
48 Ibid.
49 Ibid.
50 Ibid.

51   'In which every element in a story is given another symbolic meaning
     in a one-to-one correspondence', Catherine Dooley, 'Liturgical Catech-
     esis according to the Catechism', *Introducing the Catechism of the
     Catholic Church*, edited by Brendan Walsh (London: SPCK, 1994, draft
     edition), p. 92.
52   St Basil, *Homily* 9.
53   Ibid.
54   Colossians 3:1.
55   St Basil, *Homily* 9.
56   Peter D. Day, *Eastern Christian Liturgies: Armenian, Coptic,
     Ethoiopian and Syrian Rites* (Shannon: Irish University Press, 1972),
     pp. 25–6; my emphasis.
57   Day, *Eastern Christian Liturgies* (1972), p. 30.
58   Ibid., p. 32.
59   Ibid., p. 113. My emphasis.
60   Ibid., p. 123. My emphasis.
61   Ibid., p. 139.
62   Ibid., p. 81.
63   Ibid., p. 93.
64   Ibid., p. 171.
65   Ibid., p. 176.
66   Ibid., p. 187.
67   According to the eminent microbiologist and environmentalist, René
     Dubos (1901–1981), St Benedict should be awarded the title of patron
     saint of those who believe that true conservation means 'developing
     human activities which favour a creative, harmonious relationship
     between man and nature', rather than, as St Francis, simply 'protecting
     nature against human misbehaviour'; see his article 'Franciscan Conser-
     vation versus Benedictine Stewardship', in *Environmental
     Stewardship* (2006), p. 56ff.
68   Santmire, *The Travail of Nature* (1985), pp. 78–9; also McDonagh, *The
     Death of Life* (2005), p. 65.
69   St Benedict, Rule 40; trans. Dom Boniface Verheyen, OSB, 1949.
70   Odo, in his *Occupati*; see Paul Collins, *God's Earth* (1995), p. 113.
71   See Paul Collins, *God's Earth* (1995), p. 113 ff.
72   St Francis, *Speculum Perfectionis* 69; cited in John R. H. Moorman,
     Richest of Poor Men: the spirituality of Francis of Assisi (London:
     Darton, Longman and Todd, 1977), p. 79
73   Commissioned by Gregory IX, the *First Life* appears in 1229, a supple-
     mentary *Second Life* in 1247 and, a few years later, the tract on the
     Miracles of St Francis.
74   *The Little Flowers of Saint Francis*, edited and translated by Dom Roger
     Hudleston (Springfield: Templegate, 1988), p. xivff. The earliest known

MS of the *Fioretti*, now preserved at Berlin, is dated 1390; the work was first printed at Vicenza in 1476, yet no English translation made until 1864.

75   For an expansion of the idea that this 'the primordial source of all things', is none other than the Logos doctrine, referring to the Word made flesh, see Andrew Linzey, *Animal Rites: liturgies of animal care* (London: SCM, 1999), p. 6.

76   Ibid., p. 6.

77   Ibid.

78   See 1 Celano 80–1, 109, 115; see also 2 Celano 213, 217.

79   The Assisi Compilation 83, 'Compiliatio Assisiensis' dagli Scritti di Fr Leone e Compagni su s. Francesco d'Assisi. Dal Ms. 1046 di Perugia. Il edizione integrale reveduta e correta con versione italiana a fronte e variazioni. (Biblioteca Francescana di Chiesa Nuova, 1992); cited in *Francis of Assisi: the saint*, edited by R.J. Armstrong, et al. Early Documents I (New York: New City Press, 1999), p. 113.

80   For a discussion of the use of *per* ('for') in this Canticle, see the translation from the Critical Latin Edition of *Die opuskula des hl. Franziskus von Assisi*, edited by Fr Kajetan Esser, OFM, Editiones Collegii S. Bonaventurae ad Claras aquas (Grottaferrata, Rome: 1976, neue textkritische edition), p. 159, n. 33.

81   Thomas of Celano also records this surprisingly negative note, from Francis' old age, about the created world, as if the signs of God were not good enough, as he really wants to experience the goal, God in Christ, towards whom the signs point: 'Because of his love for the Lord's name, he loathed the world and wished to be released (Phil 1:23) through the grace of martyrdom and to be with Christ'. From 'Legend for use in the choir', *Francis of Assisi: the saint*, edited by R. J. Armstrong, et al (1999), pp. 321–322.

82   Thomas of Celano, 'Legend for use in the choir', *Francis of Assisi: the saint*, edited by R. J. Armstrong, et al (1999), pp. 321–2.

83   *Francis of Assisi* (1999), p. 361ff.

84   Ibid.

85   Ibid., p. 398.

86   Ibid., p. 400.

87   Ibid.

88   Fr Cuthbert, OSFC, *The Romanticism of St Francis* (London: Longmans, Green & Co, 1924), p. 60.

89   See <www. franciscanfriarstor. com/stfrancis/stf_st_francis'_biographers_write>

90   Arthur Livingston, 'Introduction', in *The Little Flowers of Saint Francis*, edited and translated by Dom Roger Hudleston (Springfield: Templegate, 1988), p. xix.

91   See < www. franciscanfriarstor. com/poetry/index >

92 George Mercil, OFM, 'The Franciscan School', *The History of Franciscan Theology*, edited by Kenan Osborne (New York: The Franciscan Institute, St Bonaventure University, 1999), pp. 311–20.

93 John R. H. Moorman, *History of the Franciscan Order* (Oxford: Clarendon, 1968), p. 290.

94 C. H. Lawrence, *Medieval Monasticism* (London & New York: Longman, 1984), p. 197.

95 One example of division concerns the building of the magnificent basilica over the tomb of Francis in Assisi, which is taken by the Spirituals as a sign of the betrayal of the founder's ideals; see Lawrence, *Medieval Monasticism* (1984), p. 98.

96 Paul Sabatier, who published the first classic modern biography of St Francis in 1894; cited in Lawrence, *Medieval Monasticism* (1984).

97 Dominic Devas, *The Franciscan Order* (London: Burns Oates and Washbourne, 1930), p. 13.

98 The First Order (men only) is of the Conventuals and the Capuchins – the latter developing between 1525–1529 as a reform movement; the Second Order is that of Poor Clares (enclosed women); and the Third Order is split between Regular, of Friars Minor (men) and Sisters; and Secular, for lay men and women.

99 Santmire, *The Travail of Nature* (1985), p. 98.

100 Leonard J. Bowman, 'The Cosmic Exemplarism of Bonaventure', *Journal of Religion* 55: 2 (April 1975), pp. 181–998, cited in Santmire, *The Travail of Nature* (1985), p. 98.

101 Santmire, *The Travail of Nature* (1985), p. 100.

102 Zachary Hayes, *The Hidden Centre: spirituality and speculative Christology in St Bonaventure* (New York: Paulist, 1981), p. 160; cited in Santmire, *The Travail of Nature* (1985), p. 100.

103 Bonaventure, cited in *The History of Franciscan Theology*, edited by Kenan Osborne (1999), p. 63.

104 *The History of Franciscan Theology*, edited by Kenan Osborne (1999), p. 68.

105 Santmire, *The Travail of Nature* (1985), p. 101.

106 Ibid., p. 102.

107 Ibid.

108 Edward J. Van Merrienboer, OP, 'St Martin de Porres', *The Ark*, 198 (Autumn 1999), p. 24.

109 Edward J. Van Merrienboer, OP, 'St Martin de Porres', p. 24.

110 Meriol Trevor, 'Cats, dogs, mice, birds, flies and Padre Filippo', *The Ark* 182 (spring 1999), p. 16.

111 Paul Turks, *Philip Neri: the fire of joy* (Freiburg im Breisgau: Herder, 1986); translated by Daniel Utrecht (Edinburgh: T & T Clark, 1995), p. 109.

112 Turks, *Philip Neri* (1986, 1995), p. 51.

113 'The Mission of St Philip Neri,' in *Sermons preached on various occasions* (London: Longmans, Green, 1904), p. 239, cited in Turks, *Philip Neri* (1986, 1995), p. 109.

114 Meriol Trevor, 'Cats, dogs, mice, birds, flies and Padre Filippo', p. 16.

115 Beginning of the *Spiritual Exercises* 23. 2–3 (Exx 23. 2–3).

116 See Seamus Deane's notes in James Joyce, *A Portrait of the Artist as a Young Man* (London: Penguin, 1993) p. 324; cited by Rod Preece and David Fraser, 'The Status of Animals in Biblical and Christian Thought: a study in conflicting values', on the Society & Animals Forum website: < www. psyeta. org/sa/sa8. 3/fraser >

117 Pierre Gassendi, 'Metaphysical Colloquy, or Doubts and Rebuttals concerning the Metaphysics of Rene Descartes with his Replies (1641), Rebuttal to Meditation 2, Doubt 7', *The Selected Works of Piere Gassendi*, translated by Craig B. Bush (New York: Johnson Reprint Corp., 1972), pp. 197–8; cited by Rod Preece and David Fraser 'The Status of Animals in Biblical and Christian Thought: a study in conflicting values', on the Society & Animals Forum website: <www. psyeta. org/sa/sa8. 3/fraser>

118 Peter Harrison, 'Having Dominion: Genesis and the mastery of nature', *Environmental Stewardship* (2006), pp. 17–31.

119 Francis Bacon, *The Works of Francis Bacon*, IV, edited by J. Spedding, R. L. Ellis and D. Heath (London: Longman, 1857–74), p. 247f; cited in Peter Harrison, 'Having Dominion: Genesis and the mastery of nature', in *Environmental Stewardship* (2006), p. 24.

120 Guillaume-Hyacinthe Bougeant, *Amusement philosophique sur le langage des bestes et des oiseaux*, (Paris: Chez Gissey, 1739); cited in John Hildrop, *Free Thoughts upon the brute Creation, or, an examination of Fr Bougeant's philosophical amusements*, etc. (London: R. Minors, 1745, third edition), p. 4.

121 Hildrop reports a 'society talk' in which a 'learned Doctor' expresses the ideas which originated with Bougeant.

122 E. P. Evans, *The Criminal Prosecution and Capital Punishment of Animals* (London: Heinemann, 1906), p. 67.

123 Ibid., p. 67.

124 Ibid.

125 Ibid.

126 Bougeant, 11ff; cited in Hildrop, *Free Thoughts upon the brute Creation* (1745), p. 56ff.

127 Bougeant, 19; cited in Ibid., p. 60.

128 Ibid., p. 61.

129 Ibid., p. 62.

130 Evans, *The Criminal Prosecution and Capital Punishment of Animals* (1906), p. 83.

131 Joseph Rickaby, SJ, *Moral Philosophy: ethics, deontology and natural*

law (London: Longmans, Green & Co, [1890], 1918, 4th edition.

132 Rickaby, SJ, *Moral Philosophy* (1918 4th edition), Part III, chapter 5, Section II: Of the so-called Rights of Animals, par. 1.
For the term 'stocks and stones' see also Robert Browning's 'Guiseppe Caponsacchi', lines 1824–5: 'Why men – men and not boys – boys and not babes/ Babes and not beasts – beasts and not stocks and stones...' Book VI of *The Ring and the Book* (1868); see *Robert Browning's Poetical Works* (London: Smith, Elder & Co.,1904) Volume II, p. 142.

133 Aquinas, *Summa Theologiae*,1a 2ae, q. 102, art. 6, ad 8.

134 Rickaby, SJ, *Moral Philosophy* (1918, 4th edition), par. 2.

135 Ibid., par. 3.

136 Ibid., par. 4.

137 See D. W. Robertson, 'Historical Criticism', in *English Institute Essays*, edited by A. S. Downer (New York: Columbia UP, 1950), p. 13.

138 See Peter Harrison, 'Having Dominion: Genesis and the mastery of nature', *Environmental Stewardship*, edited by R. J. Berry (London: T&T Clark International, 2006), p. 19.

139 Harrison, 'Having Dominion', *Environmental Ethics* (2006), p. 19.

140 Hugh Feiss, OSB, 'Attitudes towards Animals in Medieval Monastic Literature: lessons for today', *The American Benedictine Review* 53: 1 (March 2002), pp. 27–41. See also 'Medieval bestiaries and the birth of zoology', by Aura Beckhšfer-Fialho on the website < www.antlionpit .com/aura >

141 Such as the late sixth-century *Etymologia* by Isidore of Seville (especially Book XII).

142 Feiss, OSB, 'Attitudes towards Animals in Medieval Monastic Literature', p. 29.

143 Bartolomaeus Anglicus, *De Proprietatibus Rerum*; Thomas of Cantempre, *De Apibus*, and Vincent de Beauvais, *Speculum Naturale*.

144 Aberdeen MS 24, f25v.

145 The *Aviarium*, by Hugh of Fouilloy (*c*.1132–1152).

146 For example, that elephants are jointless reptiles, sleep leaning against trees, and reproduce by both male and female eating in turn from a mandrake tree.

147 R. P. Miller, 'Allegory in The Canterbury Tales' in *Companion to Chaucer Studies*, edited by Beryl Rowland, (Oxford UP, 1979), p. 330.

148 The pelican is believed to feed her chicks, or restore them to life, with blood from her chest.

149 Matthew 25:33, 46.

150 See website <www.wheaton, edu/English/resources/medieval/animals/2>

151 See website < www.wheaton, edu/English/resources/medieval/animals/2>

152 J. Ziolkowski, *Talking Animals: medieval Latin beast poetry, 750–1150* (Philadelphia: University of Pennsylvania, 1993), p. 298.

153 From the eleventh-century *Ecbasis captivi*. See Feiss, 'Attitudes

towards Animals in Medieval Monastic Literature', p. 34.

154 G. Cronin, 'The Bestiary and the medieval mind: some complexities', *Modern Language Quarterly,* 2, (1941), pp. 191–8.

155 Cronin, 'The Bestiary and the medieval mind', p. 198.

156 Ibid.

157 Peter Harrison, 'Having Dominion: Genesis and the mastery of nature', in *Environmental Stewardship* (2006), p. 21.

158 *The art of falconry, being the De arte venandi cum avibus of Frederich II of Hohenstaufen,* edited and translated by Casey A. Wood and F. Marjorie Fyfe (Palo Alto, CA: Stanford UP, 1943).

159 Albertus Magnus, *De Animalibus;* see *Albertus Magnus on Animals: a medieval 'Summa Zoologica':* Vols 1–2 (Foundations of Natural History), edited by Kenneth F. Kitchell Jr & Irven Michael Resnick (Baltimore: John Hopkins UP, 1998).

160 Anglicus Bartholomaeus, *De Proprietatibus;* see *On the Properties of Things: John Trevisa's Translation of Bartholomaeus Anglicus De Proprietatibus Rerum: a critical edition,* 3 vols, general editor, M. C. Seymour (Oxford: Clarendon, 1975–89).

161 Konrad Gesner, the *Historia Animalium* (which includes the famous woodcut of Albrecht Dürer of a rhinoceros). 5 volumes bound in 3 (Zurich, C. Froschoverum, 1551–1558); see Caroline Aleid Gmelig-Nijboer, *Conrad Gesner's 'Historia animalium': an inventory of Renaissance zoology.* (Meppel: Krips Repro BV, 1977).

162 Thomas Browne, *Pseudodoxia Epidemica,* or *Vulgar Errors,* (1646), cited in *A Dictionary of Fabulous Beasts,* edited by Richard Barber and Anne Riches (London: Macmillan, 1971).

Chapter Five

Teachers and Lawmakers

The teaching office of the Roman Catholic Church is held by two magisterial groups, the theologians, and the prelates, or bishops, the latter of which also have powers of governance. The bishops exercise their powers particularly and, since the doctrine was defined in 1870, infallibly, either when assembled in ecumenical council with the pope as its head, or by the bishop of Rome, the pope, when speaking *ex cathedra*. Otherwise the 'ordinary' magisterium of the hierarchy is conducted in an authoritative, but non-infallible, manner by individual bishops, national conferences of bishops, and the pope. Govenance is largely practised juridically, through the implementation of Canon Law and, in earlier days, by the promulgation of penitentiaries. For example, in the so-called Roman Penitential of Halitgar, published in France around AD 830, clergy of every rank are banned from hunting, with the penance tariff set for one year for lower orders, two for deacons and three for priests.[1] This is no doubt to appease landowners who already contribute in tithes to the clergy.

While there has been no infallible papal or conciliar pronouncement concerning animals, and little mention of them in law, there is a significant papal bull, *De Salute Gregis,* proclaimed in 1567 by Pope (later, Saint) Pius V, against bullfighting. This Moorish custom for training horse-backed warriors develops into public spectacles in Spanish arenas and is imported into Rome in the reign of Alexander VI (1492–1503). Leo X is a spectator of one in 1519 in which three men are killed. Because of the risk to human life,[2] and referring to the Council of Trent's ban on duelling, Pius considers that deliberately courting death and injury by fighting with bulls 'and other wild [baited] beasts' is equally reprehensible. Therefore, 'as being contrary to Christian duty and charity' – which may relate to the treatment of the bulls as well as to the loss of human life – 'and desiring that these bloody and disreputable exhibitions of devils rather than of men should be abolished', he threatens all spectators, including all ranks of the clergy, with excommunication and anathema. He forbids soldiers or others from contending with bulls and deprives them, if slain in the arena, of Christian burial. And all debts, obligations and bets – 'even supposing they themselves wrongly imagine them to be held in honour of the Saints, or of any ecclesiastical anniversaries or festivals, which ought to be celebrated and honoured with godly praise, spiritual joy, and words of piety' – are declared void.[3]

For two decades, both clergy and laity in Spain are greatly disturbed by this ruling, and theologians argue desperately to justify the entertainment – saying, for example, that no saint has ever said bullfighting was a sin. Eventually King Philip II persuades the then pope, Gregory XIII, to raise the censures and penalties imposed by his predecessor. This he partly does in 1575, while leaving intact the prohibitions on clergy.[4] Some of the Spanish clergy, especially those of the University of Salamanca, refuse to acquiesce to this, so Philip again petitions a new pope, Clement VIII, who, in the bull *Suscepti Muneris* in 1597 lifts all former prohibitions apart from those attached to monks and mendicant friars. Part of his reason for relaxing the condemnation is for its element of training for fighting-men and also because of 'the avidity – which seems to be natural and almost insuperable – of the people for this sort of spectacle'.[5]

No argument is made at this time on the grounds of cruelty to animals, only of concern for the dangers to the people involved. However, there is evidence that there is, in time, some revulsion by Spanish clergy to cruelty to animals in another context, as reported by the chaplain of an official English expedition to Patagonia in the early 1740s. He describes the method by which Spanish and Indian hunters there kill cattle by severing the hamstring, leaving the animal in agony until they have disabled sufficient numbers, before returning to kill and skin them. Sometimes the animals are deliberately left until the following day so that the pain endured 'may burst the lymphaticks, and thereby facilitate the separation of the skin from the carcass'.[6] However, 'their Priests have loudly condemned this most barbarous practice, and have gone so far ... as to excommunicate those who follow it'.[7]

Bullfighting has continued off and on[8] until the present, despite intermittent church opposition, while the Church's arguments have tended recently towards including the animal-cruelty aspect. On the nineteenth-century importation of the bullfight into the Diocese of Nîmes the then bishop, Mgr Besson, in 1885, protests, referring to Pius V's prohibition as well as to Chrysostom and Augustine, but, 'as Spanish bishops' protests had been in vain, so it seems was that of Mgr Besson at Nîmes'.[9] In 1920 Benedict XV (r.1914–22) confirms Puis V's bull to be 'the mind of the Church' and

> is altogether in the spirit of our Holy Books, which call upon even wild animals to bless the good God, and wholly accords with the gentle law of Him Who has deigned to call Himself the Lamb of God ... And if, in spite of the spirit of humanity which the New Law encourages, human savagery falls away again in the promotion of bull-fights, there is no doubt that the Church continues, as she has done in the past, loudly to condemn these shameful and bloody spectacles.[10]

Unfortunately, there is a strand in Catholic papal tradition contrary to that of Benedict XV and Pius V, this time voiced by Pius IX (r.1846–78). The convenor of the 1870 First Vatican Council (in which he proclaimed the doctrine of papal infallibility), and author of the 1864 'Syllabus of Errors' against Modernism, he is adamant in his opposition to the founding

in Italy of a Society for the Protection of Animals.[11] He 'feared
the presence of such an organization would foster the theologically erroneous belief that human-beings have duties to
animals of other species'.[12] However, his equally ultramon-
tanist supporter, François-Auguste-Ferdinand Cardinal
Donnet (1795–1882), the Archbishop of Bordeaux, is outspo-
ken in his attempts to make people who 'are just and good to
each other ... also be just, good, and compassionate to the
animals'.[13] In a speech to a farmers' meeting, Donnet
welcomes the monthly circulars which are issued by the
Society for the Protection of Animals saying that, 'This ener-
getic start gives a hope that, from theory, the ideas of
compassion may pass into conduct, which is more powerful
than laws.' Referring to Pius's successor, Leo XIII (1878–1903),
agreeing to become patron of the French Society for the
Protection of Animals, Donnet goes on to announce that 'The
Church, by the voice of her Sovereign Pontiffs, has placed
herself at the head of the movement. It is for her to take the
lead whenever she can make herself heard.'[14]

To the French SPA, Leo's successor, Pope Pius X (r.1903–14),
sends an autographed blessing 'for all who protect from abuse
and cruelty the dumb servants given to us by God', and wishes
'prosperity and success to all workers in this field'.[15] On behalf
of this pope, his secretary, Cardinal Merry del Val, writes that
he is pleased to support 'so noble an undertaking, which has
the lofty object of caring for the lives and treatment of animals
and which at the same time endeavours to eradicate from the
hearts of men barbarous tendencies'.[16]

Even in the midst of the First World War, in 1915, Pope
Benedict XV[17] writes, in startlingly effusive terms, to the head
of the Italian Society for the Protection of Animals:

> His Holiness rejoices to know that the object of your Society is
> in perfect accord with the doctrine which the Church has
> always taught and the Saints have always followed, leaving us
> innumerable beautiful examples of compassion and tender-
> ness.

The fact that the Nations have not always followed the precepts of the Church and the example of the Saints moves the Sovereign Pontiff all the more to favour all that tends ... to foster respect for these other creatures of God, which Providence forbids us to exploit without concern and enjoins us to show wisdom in our use of them ...

Therefore the August Pontiff trusts that you will find faithful and efficient fellow-workers in the priests of God, since it is their duty to conform to the teaching of the Church and the example of the Saints.

It is for them nobly to train souls in sentiments of enlightened gentleness and fostering care and guidance, so that they may offer to the animals refuge from every suspicion of roughness, cruelty or barbarism, and lead men to understand from the beauty of creation something of the infinite perfection of the Creator.[18]

In the tradition of Pope Paul II (r.1464–71) who is known to have rescued and released birds intended for the table, and once paid for and released a she-goat to save its life,[19] Pius XII (r.1939–58), once rescued a wounded bullfinch in the Vatican grounds and nursed it back to health. He also refuses to meet representatives of the Spanish bullfight.[20] In an audience in November 1950 with the Duchess of Hamilton, who is representing two hundred animal welfare charities, he tells her that

The animal world, as all creation, is a manifestation of God's power, His wisdom and His goodness, and as such deserves our respect and our consideration. Any reckless desire to kill off animals, all unnecessary harshness and callous cruelty towards them are to be condemned ... The Catholic Church strives to influence individuals and pubic opinion to ensure the acceptance of these principles and their protection in daily life.[21]

In his pronouncement in the Holy Year of 1950, he mentions that 'cruelty to animals is sinful'.[22] He also appeals to the people of Rome to provide a feast for the animals within their reach to mark the feast of St Francis.[23] John XXIII (r.1958–63), addressing members of a conference of hydatidologists (specialists in tapeworm diseases, transmitted from sheep to dogs to people), reminds them that 'sheep and dogs also are God's creatures' and are not to be ill-treated in the course of their researches.[24] In 1967, Paul VI (r.1963–78) receives a delegation from the UK-based Catholic Study Circle for Animal Welfare[25] and replies to their petition for his support in effusively approving tones, telling them that their 'lofty goals ... reflect in a very beautiful way the gentle love which is an important fruit of Christian charity' and that what they seek to accomplish 'is in conformity with the ends which God had in creating this world...'.[26] However, in 1972, this pope becomes the first to receive in audience, and bless, a group of bullfighters.[27] Pope John Paul II (r.1978–2005) has written profusely on matters of ecological concern, with some, perhaps oblique, references to the welfare of animals.

Moving now from the pronouncements of the legislative magisterium to the legal praxis of Catholic people in their relation to animals, the following features are the most noteworthy.

Animals in the legal realm The way that the Catholic people of Christendom have viewed and treated animals springs both from their understanding of the status of animals in the created order, and from the practical necessities of living largely as rural peasants using animals for their livelihoods. As property of human beings, domesticated animals have always received some legal protection in proportion to their service to people. Dogs are of especial importance from earliest times because of their many services: guarding, hunting and herding. The taboo on eating dog-flesh is the earliest European food taboo, dating from the end of the Bronze Age.[28] In the story of Patrick's flight from Ireland after escaping from slavery, the boat he takes is one used for transporting dogs for sale in either England or Gaul, so valuable are they as commodities. Early Irish laws protect the lives of dogs by making their killers pay valuable compensation, measured by number of cattle required, as well as replacing the dog slain.[29] Throughout Europe, following the example of Scripture,[30] dogs and other animals are both protected and held to be capable of responsibility. The contract entered into by St Francis and the wolf of Gubbio,[31] and of the Irish St Moling and the fox[32] and many similar tales, are story-form examples of medieval jurisprudence. If animals are among those listed as having been taken by Noah into the ark (that is, those referred to subsequently in Scripture), they are included in the legal community, and their biblical 'rights' protected. One such right is that of reproduction, having been told by God in Genesis to 'be fruitful and multiply'.[33] Another is of subsistence, as God has given them 'all green foliage and herbs for nourishment'.[34]

One aspect of animal jurisprudence would be considered quite bizarre today, but is consistent with the medieval understanding of evil spirits and demonic possession. From the ninth century, Christian communities in Europe engage in the legal prosecution of animals considered to have 'offended' human beings or their livelihoods. The accused animals are classed in two groups – non-domestic animals, which are dealt with by ecclesiastical courts, in *Thierprocesse*,[35] and those cases where capital punishment is administered by secular tribunals, or *Thierstrafen,* upon pigs, cows, horses and other domestic animals, as a penalty for homicide. Biblical authority for the latter is found in Exodus 21:28, which states that oxen which kill people are to be stoned to death and their flesh not eaten.

Thierprocesse In some cases in the *Thierprocesse* category, infestations of insects, or attacks by animals, are considered to have been sent by God. Contrarily, in others, they are thought to have been sent by the Devil. The appropriate response to a visitation of divine justice is repentance and intercession, following the example of the people of Nineveh at Jonah's preaching.[36] After fulfilling their mission of bringing the people to repentance, the animals or insects would be sent to sanctuary land, allocated away from the original area, where they could live on in peace. However, the appropriate response to diabolical visitation or possession, to creatures *instigante sathana, per maleficium diabolicum*, is denunciation and exorcism, and even the excommunication of the creatures – however inappropriate. An early example of this took place in AD 880, as a plague of locusts afflicts Rome. A reward is offered for their extermination, but all attempts prove fruitless. The Church then turns to the full process of exorcism, with much sprinkling of holy water across the whole countryside.[37] The result of these ministrations is not known, but presumably something works for, in time, ecclesiastical courts sit frequently over many centuries to determine the cases for the expulsion of rats, mice, locusts, weevils and other such creatures (called 'vermin'), from orchards, vineyards, granaries and cultivated fields. Supernatural means are considered the only recourse for creatures beyond human control. Some members of the offending species are caught from time to time, and brought as representatives before the court for trial. At the local level, the priest from the pulpit would summons the creatures and then preside, as representative of the diocesan bishop, over a court to which there would be appointed proctors for the defence and prosecution.

Bartholomew Chassenée, an eminent medieval French expert of jurisprudence,[38] draws up methods of procedure:

> Animals should be tried by ecclesiastical tribunals, except in cases where the penalty involves the shedding of blood. An ecclesiastical judge is not competent *in causa sanguinis*, and can impose only canonical punishments, although he may have jurisdiction in temporal matters and punish crimes not involving a capital sentence.[39]

As in cases of heretics, there are also times when ecclesiastical courts hear cases and then hand the accused over to secular courts for formal condemnation involving sentences of death. In a curious note, the lawyer considers that animals should be looked upon as lay persons – but that if anyone thought they should have *ordinem clericatus* and be entitled to benefit of clergy, they were to show proof![40]

As an example of an ecclesiastical trial, Evans reports the proceedings in St Julien, France, before the Prince-Bishop of Maurienne, in 1587, against a second infestation of *charançons* (species of greenish weevils) which were ravaging the citizens' vineyards.[41] The first infestation receives the full treatment of Masses, processions and public prayers, especially for repentance and the proper payment of tithes, and appears to have been efficacious. Now, thirty years on, the new infestation warrants a full trial.

The advocate appointed for the insects argues from Genesis for the right to sustenance and so, he argues, the vineyards are theirs to eat by right and it is absurd to bring the weight of the law down upon irrational creatures which operate by natural law and instinct alone. He dismisses 'as neither true in fact nor pertinent to the case in hand' the claim that the lower animals are made subject to man and urges the townspeople instead to 'entreat the mercy of heaven' for their sins. The prosecution makes the traditional case that the animals are created to be subordinate to man and subservient to his use, and that they have no *raison d'être* other than to be under the dominion of human beings. A public meeting is called and a piece of land designated as a sanctuary for the *charançons*. While the legal proceedings continue, interrupted by acts of warfare and other distractions, and after some dispute as to whether the elected land is suitably nourishing for the insects, there must have been some closure, but the records at this point have not survived. Among many notable features of the case are the unchallenged right that animals of any sort should have the services of an advocate; that they are entitled to suitable subsistence, and that the Church is believed to possess the power to cause the transfer of insects from one location to another.[42]

In 1519, at Stelvio, in the Tyrol, field mice are arraigned before the local ecclesiastical court for eating excessively of food that does not belong to them. Their advocate's pleas fail but he obtains the right for them to be found a suitable alternative territory to which they are conducted with safe passage 'to protect them from the marauding cats of the local district'.[43] However, some caterpillars in the Diocese of Lausanne in 1478 are arraigned before a local magistrate for eating a large amount of cabbage but, as their kind were not passengers in Noah's ark, they are not afforded the protection given to the mice, that were.[44]

Thierstrafen There are many examples given by Evans of *Thierstrafen* in which animals, most often pigs – which so often live alongside their human owners – but also bulls, dogs and wolves, are condemned by the courts for having killed someone, usually an infant, and then executed by hanging or garrotting.[45] In 1457 in Savigny, a sow is found guilty of infanticide, and hanged by the neck. Her six piglets, accused of being accessories after the fact, are pardoned 'because of their extreme youth'.[46] A medieval Anglo-Saxon penitential stipulates that 'If bees kill a man, they ought also to be killed quickly', though – it adds, opportunistically – 'the honey may be eaten'.[47]

Centuries later, animals are still being punished for 'crimes', as Thomas reports that a bear which has killed a child is sentenced by James I (1566–1625) to being baited to death; a savage horse receiving similar treatment in 1682; and the frequent custom of hanging dogs found to have poached or killed sheep.[48] In Switzerland, in as late as 1906, a dog, which has 'co-operated' with its owner and two others in committing a murder, is condemned to death 'as chief culprit'. The three men receive sentences of only life imprisonment.

Bestiality incurs capital punishment for both beast and person (in accordance with Exodus 22:18), as at Tyburn, in 1679, when a woman and a dog are hanged together.[49] A great number of different Anglo-Saxon penitentiaries contain rules concerning bestiality, implying that it was a rather prevalent, if abhorred, activity and one in which the animals were somehow both culpable and morally sullied. 'Animals that are polluted by intercourse with men shall be killed, and their flesh thrown to dogs, but their offspring shall be for use, and their hides shall be taken. However, when there is uncertainty, they shall not be killed.'[50]

The absurdity of punishing animals as if they were capable of free will and rationality is apparent to Chassenée,[51] who distinguishes between preventative punishment – which is meant to apply in all cases of animals (an animal, once having killed, may do so again unless prevented) – and punitive treatment, which is only appropriate in cases of human beings. He uses the example of a layman being able to arrest a cleric in order to prevent a crime, but not able to once a crime has already been committed. Even an animal may restrain a person from wrong-doing, as in the case of Balaam's ass.[52] However, animals which harm other sentient creatures, *knowing* that to be wrong, are, according to Chassenée, guilty of criminal offences. He cites the community life of certain animals and insects being governed by natural law for the welfare of the group, any infringement of which is punished by members of the group. He insists that no penalty imposed by human beings on animals should be without process of law, using St Paul's declaration that 'sin is not imputed where there is no law'.[53] Without the observance of legal forms, the actions would be made ineffectual.

Thomas Aquinas questions the viability of cursing irrational creatures, on the basis that curses and blessings can only be pronounced on such as are susceptible of receiving evil or good.[54] However, there is biblical precedence for cursings or blessings on nonhumans. For example, God cursed the earth;[55] Jesus curses the barren fig-tree;[56] Job curses the day that he was born;[57] and David curses the rocks and mountains of Gilboa because they are bloodstained by 'the beauty of Israel'.[58] It would be blasphemous, according to Aquinas, to curse creatures employed by God for correction, and pointless to curse them as creatures *secundem se*, but as Chassenée explains, 'The anathema then is not to be pronounced against the animals as such, but should be hurled inferentially (*per*

modum conclusionis) at the devil, who makes use of irrational creatures to our detriment.'[59]

However Chassenée and intellectuals rationalize the practice, most people at the time believe that certain animals are
simply possessed by evil spirits and have to be destroyed. The
Jesuit Bougeant, as already reported, goes so far as to suggest
that all animals were evil spirits incarnated. Origen has
provided a precedent for belief in the possession of evil spirits
by animals, emphasizing as he does that the spirits of Christians are engaged in a battle against evil spirits.[60] His view of
animals is that they are as susceptible to diabolic possession
as are people, basing this on his understanding of the Jewish
separation of animals into clean and unclean. In this he holds
that Moses had observed the varying nature and 'the demons
which are kindred to each of the animals', judging such to be
unclean. 'Each species of demon, consequently, would seem
to possess a certain affinity with a certain species of animal ...
Observe, moreover, to what a pitch of wickedness the demons
proceed, so that they even assume the bodies of weasels in
order to reveal the future!'[61] In the most explicit of his statements in support of exorcism, he writes that

> so far are we from wishing to serve demons, that by the use of
> prayers and other means which we learn from Scripture, we
> drive them out of the souls of men, out of places where they
> have established themselves, and even sometimes from the
> bodies of animals; for even these creatures often suffer from
> injuries inflicted upon them by demons.[62]

As belief in witchcraft takes hold in Europe, so does belief that
the witches' companion or domestic animals, usually cats,
were 'familiars', specific and direct agents of Satan conspiring
with them in harmful practices. These are, of course, subject
to the same gruesome execution as their equally innocent
owners.

Notes

1 Clause 58, cited in *Medieval Handbooks of Penance: a translation of the principal libri poenitentiale and selection from related documents*, edited by J. T. McNeil and H. M. Gamer (New York and Oxford: Columbia UP, [1938], 1990), p. 307.

2 In an account by the friar Francisco de Alcocer in 1559, between 100–200 human deaths in the arena were reported every year; see Dr Pereda, SJ, *Los Toros ante la Iglesia y la Moral*, (1945); cited by F. J. Forgas, 'On Bull-fighting', *The Ark* 5 (December 1953), p. 73.

3 A. M. Grange, *The Church and Kindness to Animals* (London: Burns & Oates, 1906), pp. 3–5.

4 F. J. Forgas, 'On Bull-fighting', p. 72.

5 Ibid., p. 73.

6 Richard Walter, *A Voyage round the World by George Anson, Esq.* (London: Richard Walter,1748), p. 65.

7 Richard Walter, *A Voyage round the World by George Anson, Esq.* (1748), p. 65.

8 Charles IV in 1805 bans it completely, but Joseph Buonaparte restores it in 1808.

9 E. Eyre-Smith, 'De Salute Gregis', *The Ark* 51 (April 1954), p. 10.

10 Letter by Pietro Cardinal Gaspari in the name of the Pope, to the Toulon branch of the Society for the Protection of Animals; translated by E. Eyre-Smith, *The Ark*, 49 (August 1953), p. 50.

11 The *Ente Nazionale Protezione Animali* is founded, without papal approval, by Giuseppe Garibaldi in 1871.

12 James Gaffney, 'The Relevance of Animal Experimentation to Roman Catholic Ethical methodology', in *Animal Sacrifices: religious perspectives on the use of animals in science*, edited by Tom Regan (Philadelphia: Temple UP, 1986), p. 149.

13 Speech at an Agricultural meeting of the District of Blaye, Sant-Savin, 3 September 1866 (Report of the Society for the Protection of Animals); cited in Grange, *The Church and Kindness to Animals* (1906), p. 177.

14 Grange, *The Church and Kindness to Animals* (1906), pp. 178–9. See also Ambrose Agius, OSB, 'The Popes and Animal Welfare', *The Ark* 74 (December 1961), p. 100.

15 Ambrose Agius, 'The Popes and Animal Welfare', p. 101.

16 Ibid., p. 104.

17 Benedict XV (reigned 1914–22).

18 Ambrose Agius, 'The Popes and Animal Welfare', p. 104.

19 Ambrose Agius, *God's Animals* (London: The Catholic Study Circle for Animal Welfare, 1970), p. 52.

20 Agius, 'Pius XII loved animals', *The Ark* 69 (April 1960), p. 8.

21 J. Eyre-Smith, 'The Horse', *The Ark* 69 (April 1960), p. 14.

22 E. Eyre-Smith, letter in *The Ark*, 72 (April 1961), p. 33.

23 Ambrose Agius, *God's Animals* (1970), p. 50.

24 Ambrose Agius, 'Obituary [for Pope John XXIII]', *The Ark* 79 (August 1963), p. 188.

25 Since 2003 known as 'Catholic Concern for Animals'.

26 'The Reply of our Holy Father, Pope Paul VI', *The Ark*, 93 (April 1968), inside front cover.

27 See website: < www. all-creatures. org/murti/tsnhod-08 >

28 See the *Dictionary of the Middle Ages*, Vol. I, edited by Joseph Strayer (1982), p. 300.

29 The *Canones Hibernenses* (AD 675) stipulate, in Section V: 'A Synod of Wise Men: Concerning Dogs', par. 3: 'Concerning those who kill a dog that guards the flocks or stays in the house, wise men say: he who kills a dog that guards the flocks shall pay five cows for the dog and supply a dog of the same breed and restore whatever wild animals eat from the flock, by the end of the year', and again, par. 4: 'the constitution of the wise: He who kills a dog of the four doors – namely, [1] of the house where his master dwells, and [2] the fold of sheep, and [3] of the byres of the calves and [4] the oxen – shall pay ten cows and substitute a dog of the same breed that will do the dead one's services'; cited in *Medieval Handbooks of Penance*, edited McNeill and Gamer (1938, 1990), pp. 127–8.

30 Exodus 21:28 states that oxen which kill people are to be stoned to death and their flesh not eaten.

31 That the latter would refrain from eating the citizens in exchange for the regular provision of food.

32 That the fox should return a stolen book, dry and unharmed, having intended to eat it. It did return it and was then pardoned; see Helen Waddell, *Beasts and Saints* (London: Darton, Longman and Todd, [1934], 1995), pp. 96–7.

33 Genesis 1:22.

34 Genesis 1:30.

35 *Thierprocesse* and *Thierstrafen* are terms coined by Karl von Amira (Innsbruck, 1891); see E. P. Evans, *The Criminal Prosecution and Capital Punishment of Animals*, London: Heinemann, 1906), p. 2.

36 Jonah 3:4ff.

37 Evans, *The Criminal Prosecution and Captial Punishment of Animals* (1906), p. 3.

38 Bartholemew Chassenée, b. 1480, one of the greatest criminal lawyers of his century. A BBC film *The Hour of the Pig* (1993), starring Colin Firth as a character based on Bartholemew Chassenée, features the trial of a pig accused of murder.

39 Cons. Prim. IV #5; cited in Evans, *The Criminal Prosecution and Captial Punishment of Animals* (1906), p. 31.

40 Evans, *The Criminal Prosecution and Captial Punishment of Animals* (1906), p. 31.

41 From the appendix of *De l'origine de la forme et de l'esprit des juge-
    ments rendus au moyen-âge contre les animaux*, by Léon Ménebréa,
    Chambery, 1846, cited in Evans, (1906), p. 38ff.

42 Evans, (1906), p. 38ff.

43 Mark Elvins, OFMCap, 'Animal Rights', *The Ark*, 189 (Winter 2001), p. 11.

44 Mark Elvins, 'Animal Rights', p. 11.

45 Evans, *The Criminal Prosecution and Captial Punishment of Animals*
    (1906), Appendix F., pp. 313–34. In one example, in 1494, the Grand
    Mayor of the Church and Monastery of St Martin de Laon sentence a pig
    to be hanged and strangled for infanticide; in another, in 1621, the Law
    Faculty of the University of Leipsic (sic) condemn a cow to death for
    having killed a woman.

46 Evans, *The Criminal Prosecution and Captial Punishment of Animals*
    (1906), Appendix F., pp. 346–51.

47 *Penitentials of the Anglo-Saxon Church*: Penitential of Theodore, Arch-
    bishop of Canterbury, 668–690, in *Medieval Handbooks of Penance,*
    edited McNeill and Gamer (1938, 1990), pp. 207–8.

48 Keith Thomas, *Man and the Natural World: changing attitudes in
    England AD 1500–1800* (London: Penguin, 1983), p. 98.

49 Thomas, *Man and the Natural World* (1983), p. 98.

50 Ibid.

51 Evans, *The Criminal Prosecution and Captial Punishment of Animals*
    (1906), pp. 346–51.

52 Numbers 22:22–35.

53 Romans 5:13.

54 Aquinas, *Summa Theologiae*, 2. 2, Q. 72, art 2.

55 Genesis 3:17, 'because of you [Adam]'.

56 Mark 11:13.

57 Job 3:3.

58 2 Samuel 1:21.

59 Cited by Evans, *The Criminal Prosecution and Captial Punishment of
    Animals* (1906), p. 55.

60 Origen, *De Principiis* 3. 2. 6.

61 Origen, *Contra Celsum* 4. 93.

62 Ibid., 7. 67.

Chapter Six

The British Catholic Tradition

Does British tradition with regard to animals constitute a special case? According to an imaginary French visitor to London in the mid-twentieth century, 'Si les animaux avait un pape, leur Vatican serait a Londres!'[1] The nineteenth-century German philosopher Schopenhauer, responding to the news in 1839 that a Society for the Prevention of Cruelty to Animals had been introduced, writes loftily:

> We see this English nation of fine feelings distinguished above all others by a conspicuous sympathy for animals, which appears at every opportunity and has been strong enough to induce the English, in spite of the cold superstition which otherwise degrades them, to repair by legislation the gap that religion has left in their morality.[2]

It is a commonly-held perception that – whatever the facts of cruelty and indifference to the contrary – the English are 'animal lovers', even if only relative to other nationalities. In an authorized Catholic reference book of the 1960s, the opinion is given that 'In Anglo-Saxon countries ... in the matter of domesticated animals, sensibility has far outrun sense.'[3] If true, to what extent could the British Catholic tradition be responsible for it? Two major factors could contribute to a British Catholic input: a rich literary and imaginative culture, and the close association with the liberal Christian humanism characterized by Anglicanism.

Pre-Reformation Britain

Animals, essential in every aspect of pre-modern life, naturally feature in much ancient folklore and fiction. Despite the religious dualistic teaching that humans possess spiritual souls and animals do not, and despite rural people's daily dealing with animals destined to be prematurely killed, animals in the imaginative world could be knowledgeable, even wiser than humans.[4] In many of the medieval folk tales or 'fairy stories', animals are representatives, not of their real selves, but of 'non-rational and non-conscious aspects of human life, part of which links human beings to their animal heritage'.[5] In these stories, the animals play the part of the wiser creatures who serve the hero or heroine by providing advice – which is disregarded at a price. The hero, according to Haughton, is compassionate to 'the trapped bird, or listens to the advice of the faithful old horse'.[6]

In another story genre, animals are real but endowed with extraordinary gifts. The legend of the pig of Winwick, Lancashire, is an example. The pig, commemorated in a sculpture on the church tower, is involved in the siting of the church. While the church is first being built, each night the pig carries away the stones to another site. It has a reason, for the place to which the stones are being taken is the spot where Oswald, King of Northumberland, had been killed in battle. The church is accordingly built on the site chosen by the pig.[7]

Another example concerns the dog, Gelert. In the medieval Welsh legend, noble Llewellyn leaves his baby son to the care of the hound while he is called away. On his return, he finds the baby gone and Gelert's mouth dripping with blood. In anger, he kills the dog, then finds the baby alive and the corpse of a large wolf nearby. Obviously the faithful dog had saved the baby's life. The remorseful Llewellyn erects a monument to the dog and names the place where he was buried, Beddgelert, now a village. Similar stories with variations are found in Russia, Germany and France, having originated in India and been transported west to Europe and east to Tibet,

Mongolia and China.[8] The root consists of this: 'A man forms an alliance of friendship with a beast or bird. The dumb animal renders him a signal service. He misunderstands the act, and kills his preserver.'[9]

As the religious influence of monastic bestiaries and beast fables begins to decline by the fourteenth century, animal imagery and allegory continue as a feature within mainstream secular English literature. In the romance of *Sir Gawain and the Green Knight*, Gawain's resistance to the three seduction attempts by his hostess, Lady Bercilak, are mirrored by the three quarry animals being hunted by her husband. Gawain pretends to be asleep (a deer: shy and nervous), Gawain then escapes (a boar: which can defend itself); and finally, Gawain avoids succumbing to his hostess (a fox – an unusual quarry for those days – evades capture by its cunning). There can be another interpretation: the deer is the flesh, the boar is worldly pride, and the fox is the Devil – and to defeat the flesh, the world and the Devil are Gawain's real tests. Another feature common to heroic quest narratives is the relationship between the dangerous, wild outdoors where dwell hostile creatures, and the civilized, safe city or castle social environment – although the castle bedchamber is hardly safe for Gawain.[10]

Chaucer's treatment of animals is comprehensive, from glimpses of real life to beast fables as a literary device. From the description of the 'poor widow' in the Nun's Priest's Tale in the *Canterbury Tales*, we learn that a widow with no visible means of livelihood can nevertheless keep a family going with three 'hefty sows', three cows, a sheep and some hens. We further learn that the hens, while spending the day in a fenced yard, roost at night on a perch in the family hall-house. The actual tale concerns stock characters in animal allegory and, lest it be taken too literally as 'a foolish trifle of a fox, a cock, and a hen', the narrator, the priest-chaplain, exhorts his listeners to 'Take hold upon the moral.'[11] As a lay Christian poet, Chaucer has to express 'through figure and fable the doctrine which the priest [through his homilies] might present directly'.[12]

In the Prologue to the *Canterbury Tales*, we learn that
'hunters are not holy men' and, as the monk-pilgrim stables
several horses, it is assumed that some monks are not above
breaking the veto on clergy hunting. The character also owns
greyhounds for coursing. The fur trim of his sleeves also
invites censure, but presumably more for the abuse of poverty
than for the misuse of animals. The description of the Prioress
invites the reader to be amused – if somewhat contemptuous
('she certainly was very entertaining' in her 'straining to coun-
terfeit a courtly kind of grace'). That 'she had little dogs she
would be feeding/ with roasted flesh, or milk, or fine white
bread' is to help us to realize that she has misplaced her affections and is treating animals to a better diet than most people
would enjoy. To further the mockery, she is described as
weeping bitterly if one of her little dogs 'were dead/ or
someone took a stick and made it smart' for she 'was all sentiment and tender heart'. However, by being 'so charitably
solicitous/ she used to weep if she but saw a mouse caught in
a trap'[13] she shows how her 'sympathies could be extended
outwards from pets to other animals'[14] – which Chesterton,
with characteristic wit, considers makes her 'an exceedingly
English lady'.[15]

In the long poem, *The Parlement of Foules*, Chaucer uses
the popular medieval device of a parliament of animals in an
extended allegory of a dream vision.

After Chaucer, a real pilgrim, the Englishwoman Margery
Kempe (*c*.1373–*c*.1440) is moved by suffering, animal and
otherwise, despite the harshness of fifteenth-century life.

> When she saw a crucifix, or if she saw a man had a wound, or
> a beast, whichever it were, or if a man beat a child before her
> or hit a horse or other beast with a whip, if she saw or heard it,
> she thought of Our Lord being beaten or wounded, just as she
> saw it in the man or in the beast . . .[16]

In the fifteenth century it is also considered a mark of saintly
eccentricity for one of royal blood to reject hunting on the
grounds of cruelty. The contemporary biographer of the

austere, serious-minded King Henry VI (1421–1471), John
Blacman, 'portrays a king at odds with the mores of his
court'[17] for his dislike of sport, and especial distaste for
hunting. The king does not care 'to see the creature, when
taken, cruelly defiled with slaughter ... [for] the king was of a
retiring disposition, detesting cruelty and readily forgiving
injury'.[18] While the footnote in Lovatt suggests that Blacman is
not entirely accurate, as Henry is known to have hunted on
various occasions, it remains noteworthy that his biographer
thinks it would enhance the reputation of his subject thus to
describe him.

In 1516, Sir (later, Saint) Thomas More, a man of great
integrity and scholarship, creates an impressive work of social
satire, the fable *Utopia*, ('nowhere'). It is made clear that he
thinks that all forms of cruelty are uncivilized and, in the ideal
world, delegates the killing of cattle to 'slaves' on the grounds
that the Utopians 'think that pity and goodness, which are
among the best of those affections that are born with us, are
much impaired by the butchering of animals'.[19] Any hunting
for food animals is also left to the butcher-slaves, considering
that to be among their 'basest' chores. The free citizens themselves eschew all hunting (and gambling), for they cannot
understand that there is any pleasure to be taken 'in seeing
dogs run after a hare, more than of seeing one dog run after
another' – for, in their view, 'if the pleasure lies in seeing the
hare killed and torn by the dogs, this ought rather to stir pity,
that a weak, harmless and fearful hare should be devoured by
strong, fierce, and cruel dogs'. The Utopians look on hunting
and 'the desire of the bloodshed, even of beasts, as a mark of
a mind that is already corrupted with cruelty, or that at least
by the frequent returns of so brutal a pleasure must degener-
ate into it'.[20] With religious freedom in this fictional ideal
society, there are some Utopians who disbelieve in the immortality of human souls, but there are some who 'run far to the
other extreme', and think that 'The souls of beasts are immortal, though far inferior to the dignity of the human soul, and
not capable of so great a happiness.' This idea is 'neither

thought an ill nor unreasonable opinion, and therefore is not at all discouraged'.[21]

The beast fable is still in literary service in Elizabethan England, only now serving political rather than religious purposes. The young courtier Sir Philip Sidney (1554–1586) writes an extended poem to his sister, the Countess of Pembroke, in which an animal fable signifies the writer's support for a strong aristocracy as a bulwark against tyranny. 'Man', elected king among the creatures, and allowed the privilege of being the only speaking animal, soon becomes tyrannical, fomenting factions, expelling the stronger animals and enslaving the weaker. Starting by taking their wool and feathers, he progresses to killing for food and sport. Then the poet warns man to 'rage not beyond thy neede' and not to glory in tyranny, for 'Thou art of blood; joy not to make things bleede: /Thou fearest death; think they are loth to die.'[22]

Post-Reformation Catholics in Britain

William Shakespeare's father was a recusant Catholic, and it is likely that the son was too – or at least is influenced by his family's faith. There are two passages in his plays that indicate that he is sympathetic towards the kind treatment of animals and, in the first, that he is opposed to the use of animals in experiments. This is where Cymbeline's queen asks the physician, Cornelius, for some drugs which bring about a painfully slow but inevitably fatal condition. She suggests that she should try them out 'on such creatures as / We count not worth the hanging – but none human'. Cornelius is shocked: 'Your Highness/ Shall from this practice but make hard your heart; / Besides, the seeing these effects will be / Both noisome and infectious.'[23] In *As You Like It*, Duke Senior (an admirable character) suggests a deer hunt, but then regrets it: 'And yet it irks me the poor dappled fools, / Being native burghers of this desert city, /Should, in their own confines, with forked heads / Have their round haunches gor'd.'[24] Then one of the attendant lords describes a similar sentiment in

Jaques [sic] (a character of exaggerated affections), whom they recently observed watching the agonized death of a hunted stag and 'weeping and commentating on the sobbing deer'.[25]

With the enforced decline of Catholicism in post-Tudor Britain, there is little to report on the writings or influence of British Catholics until the restoration of the hierarchy in 1850. Meanwhile, the concept of anthropocentrism itself is being challenged by one of the greatest English Protestant naturalists John Ray (1627–1705), who notes that it is 'vulgarly received' that 'all this visible world was created for Man', adding that 'Wise Men now think otherwise'.[26] Even the Anglican Archbishop of Dublin, William King (1650–1729), states that anthropocentrism is a view beset by 'inextricable difficulties',[27] thus indicating one of the responses to the Copernican revolution and the onset of Cartesian science. Other responses are far less benign, such as the rise of Cartesian dualism leading to the total instrumentalizing of all non-human nature.

However, even in the 'blackout' of Catholic culture in Britain there is a little illumination. In one of the manuals popular in seventeenth-century England to guide parents in the upbringing of their children there is one written in 1699 by a Catholic, Obadiah Walker, which contains the following: 'A child that delights in tormenting, and vexing either Beasts or Men ... is of an evil, perfidious, and bestial Nature'.[28] This echoes Locke's insistence in his 1693 *Thoughts Concerning Education* that, as humans and animals are so closely linked in the chain of being, children should be brought up to abhor the mistreatment of 'sensible' creatures.

The Catholic poet Alexander Pope (1688–1744) in *Essay on Man* (1734) pursues the idea of the interdependence of species on the chain of being: 'Vast chain of being, which from God began ...' [later he calls it 'the chain of love / Combining all below and all above'] and goes on:

> Nothing is foreign; parts relate to whole;
> One all-extending, all-preserving, soul

> Connects each being, greatest with the least;
> Made beast in aid of man, and man of beast;
> All serv'd all serving: nothing stands alone;
> The chain holds on, and where it ends unknown.

He condemns most forcefully the betrayal of animals by people who hold that animals are created for their human benefit; addressing man: 'Had God, thou fool! Work'd solely for *thy* good, / *Thy* joy, *thy* pastime, *thy* attire, *thy* food?' (my emphasis). Later in the poem he describes the innocence of Eden, when: 'Man walk'd with beast, joint tenant of the shade; / The same his table, and the same his bed; / No murder clothed him, and no murder fed.'[29] Pope's sympathy towards animals is outstanding in this poem, but in another piece of writing, his use of animals is purely allegorical. In chapter six of *Peri Bathous, or Martinus Scriblerus*, his treatise on 'the art of sinking in poetry' he compares contemporary authors with different species of animals.[30]

The eighteenth century sees both the flourishing of the scientific Enlightenment in England, and the emergence of an awareness among some theologians that human beings have not been given a mandate to abuse the animal creation. John Hildrop, an Anglican rector, responds with ill-concealed contempt to the Jesuit Fr Bougeant – who 'has done no credit to his order' – and his theory of evil-spirits within animals. In possibly the first ever book devoted to the theology of animals, he also criticizes Cartesian mechanistic theory:

> how mean, how trifling, how unworthy of God, how repugnant to Scripture, is the philosophy of those, who suppose [animals] to be either animated by Evil Spirits, or else allowing them no spiritual principle of motion or action, suppose them to be mere machines, to have no more sense or perception than a clock, or a watch ...[31]

Far from despising animals, Hildrop maintains that some animals are more commendable than are some people, especially those who use their superior power of speech only to:

'show how little the real difference is (shape only excepted) betwixt a sagacious, good-natured, governable, useful animal, which we agree to call a brute; and a wrong-headed, vicious, ungovernable, mischievous brute, whom we agree to call a man'.[32] Hildrop also takes on 'the Great Mr Locke', and suggests that he does not go far enough in his *Essay on Human Understanding*,[33] when he 'allows that brutes have ideas, and that they reason, though they are not capable of comparing and comprehending these ideas, and reasoning abstractly, as we do' for the process of interpreting sense-experience is the same. He challenges the philosopher with the classic question: 'Why does he take so much pains to persuade himself and us, that rationality in brutes must proceed from a quite different cause, from what it does in ourselves? What is he afraid of? What would be the terrible consequences of such a concession?'[34]

The reactions of Alexander Pope[35] and John Hildrop to René Descartes' (1591–1650) justification of vivisection on animals by their being, in his theory, mere machines or automata,[36] are not unique. Other English writers who also express their revulsion at the use of live animals in experiments include Jonathan Swift (1667–1745), Joseph Addison (1672–1719), Henry Fielding (1707–1754), Samuel Johnson (1708–1784), Thomas Carlyle (1795–1881), Alfred Lord Tennyson (1809–1892), Robert Browning (1812–1889)[37], John Ruskin (1819–1900) (who resigns his Chair at Oxford because of it), Christina Rossetti (1830–1894), Thomas Hardy (1840–1928) and C. S. Lewis (1898–1963).[38] Robert Louis Stevenson strenuously opposes experiments on guinea pigs, even though the experiments are designed to provide a cure for a disease from which he suffers.[39] Not only writers, but scientists and many of the public too express their repugnance of Descartes' methods. In 1648 Henry More, Newton's mentor, writes to Descartes to protest about his 'cutthroat' idea which 'snatches life and sensibility away from all the animals'.[40] Also in 1686, chemist Robert Boyle notes that many people's 'veneration' of nature impedes the use of animals in this way as 'something impious to attempt'.[41]

Hildrop also proposes that animals possess immortal souls, indeed he cannot comprehend by 'what authority we have to strike out of the system of immortality so great a part of the creation, without an absolute and evident necessity'.[42] His view on this echoes that of one of the first clergymen to teach the immortality of animal souls, Bishop Joseph Butler (1692–1752), who writes 'Neither can we find anything in the whole analogy of Nature to afford even the slightest presumption that animals ever lose their living powers, much less that they lose them by death.'[43] Other theologians subscribe to the same view[44] as do many of the Romantics, including William Wordsworth (1770–1850), Coleridge (1772–1834) and Robert Southey (1774–1843).[45] Anne Brontë, another writer in the Romantic school, writes movingly in *Agnes Grey* of the cruelty to birds considered normal behaviour at the time, and justified by the doctrine that 'the creatures were all created for our convenience' – one theory which she feels 'admitted some doubt'.[46]

It is this feeling expressed by so many of the prominent English writers of the nineteenth century that prompts legislation, the first in the world, to be passed (after several unsuccessful attempts, and facing much initial scoffing and scorning) to protect some animals from cruelty. Richard Martin, an Irish Protestant MP, enables the Act to Prevent the Cruel and Improper Treatment of Cattle (which includes sheep and horses) in 1822. This is extended to domestic animals by the 1835 bill. Cruelty is still prevalent, and the law needs to be monitored, so in 1824 the Anglican clergyman Arthur Broome founds a 'Society for the Prevention of Cruelty to Animals' (later to be given royal patronage by a very supportive Queen Victoria). Founded to be run on exclusively Christian grounds, and to be open only to Christians, in 1832 it disgracefully obliges its second Secretary, Lewis Gompertz, a Jew, to resign.[47]

However, an intellectual revolution concerning humans and animals burst into the nineteenth century, the ramifications of which are still felt today, particularly in the United States.

While there was already a discussion of evolutionary theory before Darwin, such as Robert Chambers' (anonymously published) popular 1844 *Vestiges of Natural History of Creation*, Charles Darwin's *On the Origin of Species by means of Natural Selection* in 1859 is really the catalyst. The general Christian reaction at the time is expressed in this outburst by the Anglican Bishop of Oxford, Samuel Wilberforce,[48] in an anonymous review of Darwin's *Origin* book in 1860:

> Man's derived supremacy over the earth; man's power of artic-
> ulate speech; man's gift of reason; man's freedom and
> responsibility; man's fall and man's redemption; the incarna-
> tion of the Eternal Son; the indwelling of the Eternal Spirit, –
> all are equally and utterly irreconcilable with the degrading
> notion of the brute origin of him who was created in the image
> of God, and redeemed by the Eternal Son assuming to himself
> his nature.[49]

Thus the apparent threat to humankind's supremacy is met by a defensive restatement of an extreme anthropocentrism that will become standard Christian parlance for many years. While some, such as science-writer Mary Somerville,[50] rejoice in the implied end of anthropocentrism and that nature's beauty would now be seen as for nature's sake, not man's, some Darwinians pushed their theory beyond that which could be accepted by churchmen: the biologist Ernst Haekel[51] uses it as a resource for monism, and microbiologist John Tyndall[52] in his 'Belfast address' of 1874, as one for anticlericalism.[53] Monism, which makes no difference at all between species, and grants no hierarchy, puts the flea on a dog's back on equal consideration with the dog. In the midst of the ferment, a Catholic convert, St George Jackson Mirvart, 1827–1900, professor of comparative anatomy at St Mary's medical school, London, supports Darwinian natural selection, arguing that organic change, by whatever mechanism, is perfectly compat-ible with Catholicism,[54] and that the Darwinism versus religion debate was based on a misunderstanding.[55] In response to the statement, typical of the anthropocentrism of the time, by Sir

William Hamilton that 'Nature conceals God and man reveals Him'[56] Mirvart disagrees, preferring to say that

> physical nature reveals to us one side, one aspect of the Deity, while the moral and religious worlds bring us in contact with another, and, at first, to our apprehension, a very different one. The difference and discrepancy, however, which are at first perceived, is soon found to proceed not from reason but from a want of flexibility in the imagination.[57]

His attempts to reconcile scientific Darwinism with Christianity are appreciated by Cardinal John Henry Newman,[58] but unfortunately, in later life, Mirvart incurs the displeasure of the church authorities for his views on hell and infallibility, and is excommunicated shortly before his death in 1900.[59]

The current situation? Mirvart would have approved of the Church's current accommodating position, which maintains a teleological creationism while endorsing the basic tenets of Darwinism. Cardinal Christoph Schönborn, the Editor-in-chief of the CCC, has declared that he sees no difficulty 'in joining belief in the Creator with the theory of evolution, but under the prerequisite that the borders of scientific theory are maintained'. He describes attending a symposium in Rome in 1985 under the title 'Christian Faith and the Theory of Evolution', at which he contributed a paper. It was presided over by the present Pope, then Cardinal Ratzinger, and the then Pope, John Paul II, gave the participants an audience at the conclusion, saying that:

> Rightly comprehended, faith in creation or a correctly understood teaching of evolution does not create obstacles. Evolution in fact presupposes creation; creation situates itself in the light of evolution as an event which extends itself through time – as a continual creation – in which God becomes visible to the eyes of the believer as 'creator of heaven and earth'.[60]

John Henry Newman (1801–1890), deserves further mention. He is one of two influential English Catholic churchmen to make a remarkable contribution to the cause of animal welfare in the nineteenth century. Eighteen years after the 1829 Act of Catholic Emancipation, and three years before becoming a Roman Catholic, Newman (later Cardinal), as Anglican Vicar of Oxford's University church, preaches movingly about cruelties exercized on animals:

> At one time it is the wanton deed of barbarous and angry owners who ill treat their cattle or beasts of burden; and at another it is the cold blooded and calculating act of men of Science, who make experiments on animals, perhaps merely from a sort of curiosity.

In a daring comparison between the suffering of animals and that of Christ's suffering on the Cross, he concludes that:

> there is something so very dreadful, so satanic in tormenting those who have never harmed us, and who cannot defend themselves, who are utterly in our power, who have weapons neither of offence nor defence, that none but very hardened persons can endure the thought of it.[61]

The second Cardinal Archbishop of Westminster since the restoration of the hierarchy, himself a former Anglican, Edward Cardinal Manning (1808–1892), joins with Miss Frances Power Cobb and a few others in the 1870s to protest against the practice of vivisection and in 1875 they form the Victoria Street Society (from 1897 known as the National Anti-Vivisection Society).[62] After a Deputation to the Home Office by Manning, the Earl of Shaftesbury and other eminent dignitaries, partial success is achieved with the Cruelty to Animals Act of 1876 which controls vivisection by limiting it to the granting of Home Office licences. Manning, Vice-President of the Society until 1891, in company with other distinguished clerical and lay opponents of vivisection, makes frequent speeches against the 'detestable practice' which he considers 'immoral in itself',[63] including the following:

> this I do protest, that there is not a religious instinct in nature, nor a religion of nature, nor is there a word in revelation,

either in the Old Testament or the New Testament, nor is there to be found in the great theology which I do represent, nor in any Act of the Church of which I am a member; nor in the lives and utterances of any one of those great servants of that Church who stand as examples, nor is there an authoritative utterance anywhere to be found in favour of vivisection.[64]

In the 1920s a group of lay and clerical English Catholics meet to discuss animal welfare issues. They form the Catholic Study Circle for Animal Welfare officially in 1935 with a bishop as ecclesiastical adviser and a mandate from the then Archbishop of Westminster, Cardinal Bourne, to be devoted to researching and promoting Catholic teaching on animals, and to be involved in other organizations of a practical nature. The first official meeting is chaired by the editor of *The Tablet*, Ernest Oldmeadow, with committee-member Prior Kuypers, OSB of Ealing being elected to the Council of the RSPCA.[65] The society produces a thrice-yearly bulletin, *The Ark*, from 1937, which is sent to members and readers now in fifty-two countries. Several branches or 'daughter' organizations are founded in all parts of Britain and the world, some of which survive with new names. It has been the instrument for many public, national and local acts of worship for animals and some with animals present, and provided some media coverage. It has always received support from the hierarchy of England and Wales, and blessings from each successive pope, although its influence in affecting Catholic culture and church policy has yet to be assessed. However, as the first Catholic society anywhere dedicated to animal welfare it reflects the consciousness of the nation which produces both the first anti-cruelty legislation and the first society for the prevention of cruelty to animals.

Are Catholics more or less likely than any other Britons to support animal welfare? No comprehensive survey, comparing British Catholics' views on animals with those of other Britons, has ever been carried out. A major study of adolescent development and offending, the Edinburgh Study of Youth Transitions and Crime, conducted by researchers from

Edinburgh University, reports that while young people aged thirteen to fifteen attending Catholic schools were 'slightly less likely to be involved in animal cruelty', there was 'no difference between them and people from other schools at ages 16 and 17'.[66]

Part One of this book has demonstrated that, although there have been many and varied influences and views about animals, there has not been a consistent and univocal theology on animals to date. A compendium of doctrine and teachings has been published and circulating since the 1990s, the *Catechism of the Catholic Church* – so perhaps such a theology can be found within it.

Notes

1 Pierre Daninos, *Le Secret du Major Thompson* (Paris: Hachette, 1956), p. 99. ('If the animals had a pope – their Vatican would be in London.')

2 Arthur Schopenhauer, *On the Four-fold Root of the Principle of Sufficient Reason* (1839), ch.5, §§.26–8; cited in Sorabji, *Animal Minds and Human Morals* (1993), p. 210.

3 'J. M.', 'Animals in Theology', in *A Catholic Dictionary of Theology*, edited by H. Francis Davis, et al., Vol. One (London: Thomas Nelson and Sons, 1962), p. 98. Interestingly, in the Bibliography in this section is the statement that 'There is little that deals with this precise topic in modern times.'

4 Rosemary Haughton, *Tales from Eternity: the world of faerie and the spritual search* (London: George Allen and Unwin, 1973), p. 55.

5 Haughton, *Tales from Eternity* (1973), p. 51.

6 Ibid.

7 'C', 'Animal Legends', *The Ark*, 45 (April 1952), p. 27.

8 Sabine Baring-Gould, *Curious Myths of the Middle Ages* (London: Longmans, Green & Co, 1901), p. 138ff.

9 Ibid., pp. 140–1.

10 See < www.wheaton, edu/English/resources/medieval/animals:2 >

11 Chaucer's *Canterbury Tales*, translated by Nevill Coghill (Harmondsworth, Middx: Penguin, 1960), p. 249.

12 R. P. Miller, 'Allegory in The Canterbury Tales' in *Companion to Chaucer Studies*, edited by Beryl Rowland, (Oxford UP, 1979), p. 124.

13 Chaucer's *Canterbury Tales*, translated by Nevill Coghill (Harmondsworth, Middx: Penguin, 1960), p. 23.

14 Keith Thomas, *Man and the Natural World: changing attitudes in*

England AD 1500–1800 (London: Penguin, 1983), p. 120.

15 G. K. Chesterton, *Chaucer* (London: Faber and Faber, 1934), p. 199.

16 *The Book of Margery Kempe*, translated by B. A. Windeatt (London: Penguin, 1985), p. 104.

17 R. Lovatt, 'John Blacman: biographer of Henry VI', in *The Writing of History in the Middle Ages*, edited by R. H. C. Davies et al. (Oxford: Clarendon, 1981), pp. 415–16.

18 R. Lovatt, 'John Blacman: biographer of Henry VI', (1981), p. 439.

19 Thomas More, 'Of the travelling of the Utopians' in *Utopia*, 'Book II: Of their Traffic'; cited in Liam Brophy, 'No Animal Torture in Utopia', *The Ark*, 106 (April 1972), p. 15; see also *Ideal Commonwealths*, (New York: P. F. Collier & Son, The Colonial Press edition, 1901).

20 Thomas More 'Of the travelling of the Utopians', p. 15.

21 Ibid.

22 Sir Philip Sidney, from The Third Eclogues, 66, *Poems from the Countess of Pembroke's Arcadia (The Old Arcadia)* lines 150–1; in *The Poems of Sir Philip Sidney,* edited by W. A. Wrangler (Oxford: Clarendon, 1962), p. 412n.

23 Shakespeare, *Cymbeline*, Act I, sc. 5, lines 19ff.

24 Shakespeare, *As You Like It*, Act 2, sc. 1, lines 22ff.

25 Ibid., line 66.

26 John Ray; cited by Peter Harrison 'Having Dominion: Genesis and the mastery of nature', in *Environmental Stewardship* (2006), p. 27.

27 Ibid., p. 28.

28 Obadiah Walker, *Of Education, especially of young gentlemen* (London: Richard Wellington, 1699, 6th Edition), p. 192.

29 Pope, *Epistle on Man*, I: 8; III; *Alexander Pope*, edited by P. Rogers (Oxford UP, 1993), p. 22ff.

30 *Alexander Pope*, edited by P. Rogers (Oxford UP, 1993), p. 633.

31 Hildrop, *Free Thoughts upon the brute Creation* (1745), p. 4.

32 Ibid., p. 73.

33 John Locke, *Essay on Human Understanding*, lib. 2. cap. 11; cited in Hildrop *Free Thoughts upon the brute Creation* (1745), pp. 14–16.

34 Ibid.

35 See also article by Alexander Pope, *The Guardian*, 61 (21 May 1713).

36 See previous note 163.

37 Robert Browning wrote two anti-vivisection poems ('Tray' (1879) and 'Arcades Ambo' (1889) and remarked further that he would 'rather submit to the worst of deaths, so far as pain goes, than have a single dog or cat tortured on the pretence of sparing me a twinge or two'; see website for citation: www.ivu.org/people/quotes/experim.html

38 Joseph Addison, *The Spectator*, 120, (18 July 1711); Samuel Johnson, *The Idler*, 17 (5 August 1758); for Tennyson, Browning, Carlyle, Ruskin and Christina Rossetti, see Jan Marsh, *Christina Rossetti: A Literary*

Biography (London: Jonathan Cape, 1994), p. 433 ff. C. S. Lewis discussed the issue in *That Hideous Strength* (1945) and wrote a leaflet, *c*.1950, for the National Anti-Vivisection Society. For the latter, see Richard D. Ryder, *Animal Revolution: changing attitudes towards speciesism* (Oxford: Basil Blackwell, 1989), pp. 10–11.

39 Cited on their website by Rod Preece and David Fraser , 'The Status of Animals in Biblical and Christian Thought: A Study in Colliding Values', *Society & Animals Journal of Human-Animal Studies* < www.psyeta.org/sa/sa8.3/fraser.s >

40 See Gary Steiner, *Descartes on the Moral Status of Animals* (Archiv für Geschichte der Philosophie, 80, 3, 1998), pp. 268–291; cited on the Preece and Fraser website: < www.psyeta.org/sa/sa8.3/fraser.shtml>

41 Robert Boyle, 'A Free Inquiry into the Vulgarly Receiv'd Notion of Nature'; cited by Peter J. Bowler, *Norton History of the Environmental Sciences* (New York; W. W. Norton, 1993), p. 89; cited on the Preece and Fraser website: < www.psyeta.org/sa/sa8.3/fraser.s >

42 Hildrop, *Free Thoughts upon the brute Creation* (1745), p. 73.

43 Joseph Butler, *The Analogy of Religion*, 1736, see the website <www.all-creatures.org/murti/tsnhod-08>

44 Including the Revd John George Wood (1827–89) in *My Feathered Friends* and *Man and Beast: here and hereafter*, and Elijah D. Buckner in the latter's 1903 book *The Immortality of Animals*; cited on the website: < www. all-creatures. org/murti/tsnhod-08 >

45 S. T. Coleridge, A Lay Sermon (1817) in *The Collected Works of Samuel Taylor Coleridge: Lay Sermons*, edited by R. J. White (London: Routledge & Kegan Paul, 1972), p. 183, n. 6; Robert Southey, 'On the Death of a Favourite Old Spaniel', in *Poems* (Bristol: John Cottle, 1797); cited on the Preece and Fraser website: < www.psyeta.org/sa/sa8.3/fraser.s >

46 Anne Brontë, *Agnes Grey* (London: Penguin [1847], 1988), p. 123.

47 See Mark Gold, *Animal Century: a celebration of changing attitudes to animals* (Charlbury, Oxon: Jon Carpenter, 1998), p. 203.

48 This is the Bishop Wilberforce whose debate in 1860 with the Darwinian scientist T. H. Huxley in a meeting in Oxford of the British Association for the Advancement of Science is considered to have been won by Huxley. Wilberforce had asked: 'Did Huxley prefer to be descended from an ape on his grandmother's or grandfather's side?' In 1994 the debate was replayed in Edinburgh between atheist evolutionary Professor Richard Dawkins and the then Archbishop of York, John Habgood. *The Daily Telegraph* reported it (9 September 1994) under the headline: 'Apes have souls too, says primate' – which shows some progress!

49 Samuel Wilberforce, review in the *Quarterly Review*, 108 (1860), pp. 257–8.

50 Mary Somerville (1780–1872), after whom Someville College, Oxford, was named.

51 Ernst Haekel (1834–1919), was a German biologist.

52 John Tyndall (1820–1893), was an Irish natural philosopher and professor of physics.

53 From a talk given at Blackfriars, 7 March 2005, by Dr John Brooke, Director of the Ramsey Centre for Science and Religion, Oxford.

54 See John Brooke and Geoffrey Cantor, *Reconstructing nature: the engagement of science and religion* (Edinburgh: T&T Clark, [1998], paperback 2000), p. 259.

55 Brooke and Cantor, *Reconstructing nature: the engagement of science and religion*, p. 262.

56 Sir William Hamilton, 'Lectures on Metaphysics and Logic', Vol I, Lecture ii, p. 40, cited in Brooke and Cantor, *Reconstructing nature* (1998, 2000) p. 307.

57 St George Mivart FRS, *On the Genesis of Species*, London and New York: Macmillan and Co, 1871; cited in Brooke and Cantor, *Reconstructing nature* (1998, 2000), p. 370.

58 See *The Letters and Diaries of John Henry Newman*, edited by C.S. Dessain et al, in 31 Vols, (Oxford: OUP, 1961–1977), xxv, p. 446; cited in Brooke and Cantor, *Reconstructing nature* (1998, 2000) p. 259.

59 Mirvart also opposes Pope Leo XIII's 1893 encyclical *Providentissimus Deus* on the study of Holy Scripture, which had the effect of discouraging the scientific biblical criticism which Mirvart had championed. See Brooke and Cantor, *Reconstructing nature* (1998, 2000), p. 259.

60 From the lecture by Cardinal Christoph Schönborn, 'Borders Are Neither Recognized nor Respected' given on 2 October 2005, in St Stephan's Cathedral, Vienna, on creation and evolution. The lecture was meant, in part, to clear up misunderstandings that arose from an article he had written in the previous 7 July issue of the *New York Times*; from zenitenglish@zenit.org email: 12 December 2005, ZE05121221.

61 From the sermon preached on Good Friday 1842, *Parochial and Plain Sermons* VII, 10 (London & New York: Longmans, Green, 1875).

62 From which the British Union for the Abolition of Vivisection broke away in 1898 to pursue, with Miss Cobb, a totalist policy as distinct from the gradualist approach of NAVS.

63 Speech at the AGM of the Victoria Street Society, 25 June 1881. See Cardinal Manning, 'Speeches against Vivisection', *The Ark* 130 (August 1980), p. 47ff.

64 Speech at the house of Lord Shaftesbury, 21 June 1882, 'Speeches against Vivisection', *The Ark* 130 (August 1980), p. 49.

65 See Ambrose Agius, 'Building "The Ark"', *The Ark*, 75 (April 1962), p. 8ff.

66 Private email from Susan McVie, Senior Research Fellow at Edinburgh University, School of Law, and co-director of the Edinburgh Study.

Part Two

Animals in the Catechism

Chapter Seven

Introducing the *Catechism of the Catholic Church*

The first part of this book shows just how varied the Catholic tradition has been in respect of created matter as a whole, and of the place of animals in particular. From St Francis' theology of kinship of all creation, on the one hand, to the Jesuit Fr Rickaby for whom animals deserve no more consideration than do 'stocks and stones', on the other, animal theology in the Roman Catholic Tradition has received no definitive magisterial teaching. There has been very little published at any level to advance a 'Catholic' point of view about animals at all.[1] For example, none of the catechisms available in Britain, major or minor, prior to the *Catechism of the Catholic Church*[2] (henceforth, CCC), refers specifically to the treatment of animals, apart from *The New Catechism*, by Bishop James Bellord, designed for children, and published in London by the Catholic Truth Society in 1901. In a section, in question and answer format, about the Fifth Commandment (Thou shalt not kill) is the following straightforward statement:

> Q. Is cruelty to animals a sin?
> A. Yes, a very cowardly and disgraceful sin.

As catechisms are the traditional means by which the Roman Catholic Church has propagated its core doctrines, it is appropriate to turn to the most recent and authoritative of the catechisms to see if the Church has finally provided a coherent and univocal teaching on animal theology.

A brief account of the history of catechisms may be helpful here. Prior to the CCC there have been a number of summaries, or compendia of doctrine, including the two towering 'Summas' of St Thomas Aquinas,[3] and the humbler *Lay Folks' Catechism* of Archbishop John Thoresby of York in 1357 – the first time that the noun 'catechism' was used to describe a book of instruction in the faith. The first 'major' catechism (the CCC is the second) was a product of the Council of Trent when, in 1562, Charles (St) Borromeo proposed a 'formulary and method for teaching the rudiments of the faith'. Published in Latin and Italian in 1566,[4] it was known in English as *The Roman Catechism*, or *The Catechism of the Council of Trent*. This major catechism formed the basis of all other, 'minor', catechisms until the CCC.

In October 1985 at an Extraordinary Synod (of bishops) to mark the twentieth anniversary of the ending of the Second Vatican Council and to celebrate its achievements, it was proposed that a commission of cardinals should prepare a draft of a Conciliar Catechism to be promulgated after due consultation with other bishops. It was argued that national catechisms were no longer adequate, and an authoritative and universal summary of the Church's faith was needed. It was to be 'a catechism or compendium of the whole of Catholic doctrine, of both faith and morals, which would be "a point of reference" for catechetical materials produced in various regions'.[5] Its aim was to be an organic synthesis of current church teaching and not an instrument for defining any new dogma.

After much consultation and at least one draft, the approved version, written in French, was published on 11 October 1992 with Pope John Paul II's apostolic constitution *Fidei Depositum,* situating this document within the ordinary papal magisterium. It was subsequently translated and published in other language editions – the English edition being one of the last, appearing only in 1994.[6] Later, on 15 August 1997, a Latin *editio typica* was promulgated, and on 8

September 1997, a second edition English translation was produced to harmonize the English text with this official Latin text. The Latin text, and thus the revised English one, made certain significant changes, mainly to the admissibility of capital punishment, and, inter alia, to paragraph 2417, which will be examined later. The precedent has been set that changes can be made to the text, although the American Archbishop William J. Levada, who later takes the place of Cardinal Ratzinger as Prefect of the Congregation for the Doctrine of the Faith, finds the idea of change somewhat troublesome.[7]

The CCC contains teachings that carry differing degrees of authority and consequently requiring differing degrees of adherence.[8] This principle was made explicit in the Second Vatican Council's decree on Ecumenism: 'In Catholic doctrine there exists an order or "hierarchy" of truths, since they vary in their relation to the foundation of the Christian faith.'[9] While the CCC makes no distinction between any of the teachings, as to do so is 'the work of theology, not catechesis, and would not be appropriate for the catechism',[10] the bishops of England and Wales suggest that readers 'need to be aware of the difference between, for example, statements carrying papal authority or the authority of a Council of the Church or a Synod, and quotations taken from the writings of saints or theologians'.[11] The co-ordinating editor of the project, Fr (now Cardinal) Christoph Schönborn, OP, explains the principle protecting the hierarchy of truths as one of organizing the material via three criteria:

1. the mystery of the Blessed Trinity as the centre of the hierarchy of truths;
2. the Christocentric approach; and
3. the fourfold plan ('Four Pillars') of the *Catechism*, 'intrinsically expressing a principle of organic structure'.[12]

It is necessary in this book, therefore, to assess where in the 'hierarchy' of truths fall the CCC's teachings regarding animals, particularly in view of any changes that might be

made to them. As church teaching develops, there will be the
need for new editions with changes and amendments. Change
is inevitable for, despite the claim, in CCC. n. 5, of being 'a
sure norm for teaching the faith', this Catechism is heir to the
Roman Catechism which was itself discovered to contain a
significant error.[13] With the prospect of changes, a coherent
and compassionate theology of animals could be defined and
included in future editions.

One notable aspect of the CCC is its use of Scripture. The
biblical texts used to support the teachings are approached
both literally and typologically, despite the problems of typol-
ogy even in the patristic era.[14] The CCC avoids both biblical
criticism and biblical scholarship – deliberately, according to
Francis J. Buckley, and comprehensively, according to Luke
Timothy Johnson.[15]

Animals in the text

The structure of the *Catechism of the Catholic Church*, based
on the model of the sixteenth-century Roman catechisms,
comprises the 'four pillars' of creed, sacraments, commandments, and prayer. The main section that specifically refers to
animals is found in the four paragraphs 2415 to 2418 within
the third part (the 'Third Pillar'): the Commandments, under
the heading 'Respect for the integrity of creation'. These four
paragraphs greatly amplify the two paragraphs (below) which
most closely approximate them in the (unpublished) 1989
Provisional Text. In that document they appeared under the
heading 'The proper use of natural resources' and were drawn
largely from the 1987 Apostolic Letter *Solicitudo rei socialis*
(SRS), nn.26, 34:

> 3717 a) The proper extent and limits that ought to be
> respected in the use of natural resources are part of true devel-
> opment. Man today must not compromise the future for man
> tomorrow by disposing, without let or hindrance, of mineral,
> vegetable and animal resources which are creation's common
> patrimony.

3718 b) Improving the quality of life, particularly in urban areas, must ensure that the risks and dangers of accident or of contamination resulting from an industrial production concerned more with output than the environment, are properly controlled.

The amplification of these two paragraphs in the final edition indicates the extent of the work and thought involved by the redactors in producing the CCC.

The four CCC paragraphs obviously neither exhaust the subject, nor can they be understood apart from consideration of the theme of Creation within the CCC as a whole.

The treatment of particular moral questions in the second half of this section [which includes the four relevant paragraphs] should always be placed in the context established in the first half, where principles about conscience, freedom, law, human dignity and other matters are explained. These are as important as the later treatment of separate issues.[16]

The Third Book of the CCC is entitled 'Life in Christ' and deals with the moral life and the virtues, before turning, in its Section Two, to the Ten Commandments. In the treatment of the seventh commandment ('Thou Shalt Not Steal') are the specifically animal-oriented paragraphs. In the previous major *Roman Catechism*, the commentary on this Commandment was primarily a defence of private property, with a consequent classification of the terms of theft, and concluding with an exhortation to give alms to the poor, for the sake of charity. There was no reference to animals, as they were subsumed under the category of property.

On this seventh commandment, in the CCC, are hung six specific themes. The first is the universal destination of created goods, which means that the right to private property is not absolute, as everything in creation is really intended – and this is the crux of the matter – for the good of the whole of mankind. As the Dominican scholar, Aidan Nichols, extrapolates from this social teaching, 'For the Church, there can be no theft where refusal of what is sought by another is "contrary to reason and the universal destination of goods", for example, for those desperate for food, shelter, clothes.'[17]

The second is 'Respect for Persons and Their Goods', divided into 'Respect for the goods of others' and 'Respect for the integrity of creation' – this latter being the heading for the four paragraphs relating to animals. According to J. L. Nash, 'The CCC is one of the first catechetical documents to emerge from Rome that expresses this new moral imperative [that] the human dominion over the created world, referred to in Genesis, is not absolute (par. 2415). There is need for a "religious respect for creation's integrity".'[18] (The other four themes are not relevant for this book).

Respect for the integrity of creation

The subheading 'Respect for the integrity of creation' repeats part of the title given to the World Council of Churches' European Ecumenical Assembly in Basel, Switzerland in 1989: 'Justice, Peace and the Integrity of Creation'. The Roman Catholic Church was by then committed *solely* to the twin concerns of justice and peace, although more is being done and said recently on the environment, if only for the sake of the human species. Concern for animals is invisible, as the anthropocentric agenda holds sway. The year after the WCC Assembly, at an Earth Day Gathering in Central Park, New York City, Cardinal O'Connor comments disparagingly on people who worry about saving whales, adding, with a flourish: 'The earth was made for man, not man for the earth.' In 1995, Pope John Paul II, despite his environmentally-themed 1990 Peace Day address, writes: 'Everything in creation is ordered to man and everything is made subject to him.'[19]

It is also of interest that the whole issue of animals and the environment in the CCC is dealt with in the context of the command against *theft*. From whom is what being stolen? 'In one sense it is true that by exploiting excessively the earth's resources we are stealing from future generations as well as those currently living on the planet who must live with the consequences of foul air and water – even if they do not share in the benefits'.[20] A previous paragraph, n. 2402, expresses many of the same ideas as are in n. 2415, while spelling out more clearly the 'Common Good' (of humanity) that is the end for which the earth's fruits are intended:

> In the beginning God entrusted the earth and its resources to the common stewardship of mankind to take care of them, master them by labour, and enjoy their fruits. The goods of creation are destined for the whole human race. However, the earth is divided up among men to assure the security of their lives, endangered by poverty and threatened by violence. The appropriation of property is legitimate for guaranteeing the freedom and dignity of persons and for helping each of them to meet his basic needs and the needs of those in his charge. It should allow for a natural solidarity to develop between men.

This reading, however, does not exhaust the range of possible meanings. There is also the sense in which, as all belongs ultimately to God, it is from God that theft is committed by abuse of his creation: 'Animals are God's creatures', it says in n. 2416. Can it not also be taken to imply that the lives of animals, 'by [whose] *mere existence*' God is blessed and given glory (n.2416) have value in themselves and thus to deprive them of life or liberty is to steal from them also?

Each sentence of the crucial four paragraphs is given a preliminary examination here. In Part Three, certain themes and ideas from them will be revisited. Sentence numbering is added to facilitate cross-referencing.

Notes

1 Although, in explaining why he is sometimes accused of being hard on Roman Catholics, Andrew Linzey declares that 'unlike Anglicans ... they don't just have an awful tradition [with respect to animals], they go on repeating and defending that tradition in one moral textbook after another'; cited in Christopher Bartlett, 'A Conversation with Andrew Linzey: on Christianity and animals', *The Animals' Agenda*, IX, 4 (April 1989), p. 22.

2 *Catechism of the Catholic Church* [note, no definite article] (London: Geoffrey Chapman, 1994; 2nd revised edition, 1997).
3 The *Summa contra Gentiles* and the *Summa Theologiae*.
4 As *Catechismus ex decreto Concilii Tridentini ad parochos Pii V*.
5 Bishops' Conference of England and Wales, 'Guildelines for the Use of the CCC', *Briefing*, 24 (26 May 1994), p. 3.
6 It had been delayed because of Vatican objections to the use of gender-inclusive language in the originally-proposed edition. In the finally-approved English edition, all references to 'man' in the original French text have been reinserted, and even more added.
7 His concern is that 'some teachings of the church may be considered "changeable" because they have not been infallibly proclaimed'. He explains that, 'whether a teaching may change in the future is not a necessary, but only an accidental quality of a teaching which may be called "non-fallible"'. He worries that, in a catechism such as the CCC, 'the suggestion that something may "change" could be understood as a teaching which is unreliable to believe or put into practice' which would be the opposite of what the Church wishes to propose. Archbishop William J. Levada, 'The New Catechism: an overview', United States Conference of Catholic Bishops, Office for the Catechism; see website < www.usccb.org/catechism/resource/lev94art.htm >
8 'The question of what authority the individual doctrines of the Church possess in themselves is a complex theological issue. For centuries theologians assigned theological "notes" to the formulation of church doctrines, by which they indicated whether a particular teaching was "of divine faith", "defined infallibly", "theologically certain", "Catholic doctrine", "near to the faith" and the like.' Archbishop William J. Levada, 'The New Catechism: an overview'.
9 *Unitatis Redintegratio*, n. 11.
10 Levada, 'The New Catechism: an overview'.
11 Bishops' Conference of England and Wales, 'Guildelines'; *Briefing*, 24 (26 May 1994), p. 6.
12 Christopher Schönborn, 'Major Themes and Underlying Principles of the CCC, *The Living Light*, (Fall 1993), p. 57.
13 This concerned the nature of the validity of the sacrament of confirmation. It stated that confirmation is valid by anointing only, without mentioning the necessity of the laying on of hands.
14 See Catherine Dooley, 'Liturgical Catechesis according to the Catechism', *Introducing the Catechism of the Catholic Church*, edited by Brendan Walsh, draft edition (London: SPCK 1994), p. 92.
15 Francis J. Buckley, 'What to Do with the New Catechism', *Church*, 9 (Summer 1993), p. 50; and Luke Timothy Johnson comments, 'The second thing which impressed me as a biblical scholar is how completely this catechism ignores the results of critical biblical scholar-

ship', in *Commonweal*, 120 (7 May 1993), cited in Dooley, 'Liturgical Catechesis according to the Catechism', p. 172.

16 Bishops' Conference of England and Wales, 'Guildelines', p. 11.

17 Aidan Nichols, *The Service of Glory* (Edinburgh: T&T Clark, 1997), p. 215.

18 J. L. Nash, 'Catechisis for Justice and Peace in the Catechism', *Introducing the Catechism of the Catholic Church: traditional themes and contemporary issues*, edited by B. L. Marthaler (New Jersey: Paulist Press, 1994), p. 116.

19 John Paul II, *The Gospel of Life*, 1995; cited (as is the O'Connor quotation) by Larry Rasmussen in 'Symbols to Live By', *Environmental Stewardship*, edited by R. J. Berry (London: T&T Clark International, 2006), p. 174.

20 J. L. Nash, 'Catechesis for Justice and Peace in the Catechism', p. 116.

Chapter Eight

Paragraph 2415: The integrity of creation

n. 2415. 1. The seventh commandment enjoins respect for the integrity of creation. 2. Animals, like plants and inanimate beings, are by nature destined for the common good of past, present, and future humanity [Cf. Gen 1:28–31]. 3. Use of the mineral, vegetable, and animal resources of the universe cannot be divorced from respect for moral imperatives. 4. Man's dominion over inanimate and other living beings granted by the Creator is not absolute; it is limited by concern for the quality of life of his neighbour, including generations to come; it requires a religious respect for the integrity of creation [Cf. CA 37–38].

2415:1. The seventh commandment enjoins respect for the integrity of creation

This statement implies that creation itself, for itself alone, deserves consideration in its entirety and 'in an unimpaired state'.[1] However, in juxtaposition with the next sentence ('Animals, like plants and inanimate beings, are by nature destined for... humanity') it might be inferred that creation is to be respected *only* for the benefit of the human species. In this it echoes part of an earlier paragraph, n. 299, which links the two sentences into one: 'Because creation comes forth from God's goodness, it shares in that goodness – "And God saw that it was good ... very good" [Cf. Gen 1:4, 10, 12, 18, 21,

31] – for God willed creation as a gift addressed to man, an inheritance destined for and entrusted to him.'

Again, in that earlier paragraph, n. 299, the CCC gives: 'The universe, created in and by the eternal Word ... is destined for and addressed to man ...'.

At the same time, and in that same paragraph, n. 299, there is the claim that the Church has frequently defended the integrity of creation: 'On many occasions the Church has had to defend the goodness of creation, including that of the physical world.'[2] This is elaborated in n. 339, repeating the biblical affirmation of created goodness of each creature,[3] and supported by a passage from the Concilliar document *Gaudium et Spes*,

> By the very nature of creation, material being is endowed with its own stability, truth and excellence, its own order and laws' [*GS* 36 n. 1]. Each of the various creatures, willed in its own being, reflects in its own way a ray of God's infinite wisdom and goodness.

The following, final, sentence of this CCC paragraph, n. 299, gives both clear instruction for respecting the integrity of creation – and then draws the inevitably anthropocentric conclusion: 'Man must therefore respect the particular goodness of every creature, to avoid any disordered use of things which would be in contempt of the Creator and would bring disastrous consequences for *human beings* and their environment' (My emphasis).

In true Thomistic tradition, there is no category for sin or wrong against creation itself. Peter Singer notes that Aquinas 'divides sins into those against God, those against oneself and those against one's neighbour. So the limits of morality ... exclude nonhumans. There is no category for sins against them'.[4] However, it could be argued that, as all creatures are created and loved by God and have been drawn into covenantal relationship with him (Genesis 9:9–15), sins against God also entail or imply sins against his creatures. The phrase in the paragraph just cited indicates that abuse of creation 'would be in contempt of the Creator', and therefore be a sin against God.

In practice, how does the Church officially interpret this 'integrity of creation'? In 2000, the Pontifical Academy for Life is reported to have asked 'whether it is licit for man to intervene in creation by means of cross-species transplants' and answers it by drawing on CCC nn. 342 and 343:

> 342. The hierarchy of creatures is expressed by the order of the 'six days', from the less perfect to the more perfect. God loves all his creatures [cf. Psalm 145:9] and takes care of each one, even the sparrow. Nevertheless, Jesus said: 'You are of more value than many sparrows', or again: 'Of how much more value is a man than a sheep!' [Cf. Luke 12:6–7; Matt 12:12.]
>
> 343. Man is the summit of the Creator's work, as the inspired account expresses by clearly distinguishing the creation of man from that of the other creatures. [Cf. Gen.1:26]

Their answer is, unsurprisingly, that 'there is a clear hierarchy in creation, with the human person being placed at the summit of all created beings', and that, while that does not allow humans 'the right to abuse other creatures in a capricious way', it does mean that 'there is a natural order in which it is licit for us to make use of what is created to help us in our lives'.[5] They go on to say that using animals as a source of organs 'does not contravene the order of creation, but is a reasonable use of the power God has given us over creation'. They deny the validity of the charge that to use animals is 'speciesism, a kind of tyranny' by saying that man, being created in the image of God, gives him 'a superior dignity to that of other creatures'. And that 'Sacrificing the lives of animals to provide organs for humans is licit as it satisfies a legitimate human good.'[6]

These Academicians do not address the issue of transspecies genetic engineering. This activity, as with trans-species organ transplantations, could be construed as trespassing against the divine law and intention for that creature, thereby abusing its 'integrity'. The injunction in Leviticus 19:19 – 'You are not to mate your cattle with those of another kind; you are not to sow two kinds of grain in your field; you are not to wear a garment made of two kinds of fabric' – can be interpreted as prohibiting whatever infringes the 'integrity' of both animal and plant life, that is, whatever fails to respect what is 'given' in creation. This would logically preclude all forms of artificial genetic engineering and trans-species organ transplantation.

2415:2. Animals, like plants and inanimate beings, are by nature destined for the common good of past, present, and future humanity [Cf. Gen.1: 28–31]

This statement is concerned with identifying the category of people who should benefit from the resources of nature; namely, every member of the human race. The passage from Genesis given as a footnote reference to support this is: 'be masters ... of all living things' (Gen.1:28). The truer translation from Hebrew would be 'be masters *under God*', and that has implications which are unfortunately rarely drawn out in the usual reading. The following verse in the Genesis text indeed gives plants as God's gift of food for mankind, 'seed-bearing plants ... and trees with seed-bearing fruit'. So plants (and, presumably, inanimate beings) are 'destined for the good of humanity'. But 'mastery' of animals and birds – to the extent of killing them for food – is not endorsed in this original text. Indeed even the animals are not allowed to kill each other at this prelapsarian stage, for they too had only vegetation to eat, as the next verse states (v. 30). This point does not seem to have been picked up in this or in the other 'animal' paragraphs of the CCC.

In this, as in other passages, the CCC maintains the radical distinction between people and animals, based on the understanding of the human soul being 'rational' whereas animals' souls (while being superior to those of plants) are not rational. [This subject will be revisited at length]. Hence, according to Augustine, Aquinas and other authorities discussed in the first part of this book, the absence of reason would 'rule out ... any possibility that animals can experience true happiness, namely the love of God, or true misery, namely its absence'.[7] An earlier paragraph in the CCC, n. 293, speaks of 'both orders of creatures, the spiritual and the corporeal', of which the spiritual is understood as comprising the angels and the human intellect (n.311 mentions 'angels and men, as intelligent and free creatures'), and the corporeal being the animals and human bodies. In other words, the human being is the bridge between the two orders, whereas animals fall entirely into the 'corporeal' order.[8]

Another passage in the CCC restates the idea of the dual aspect of humanity: 'The human person, created in the image of God, is a being at once corporeal and spiritual' (n.362). This is a more biblical concept. Body and soul are not simply two factors existing alongside or in each other, but form an indivisible whole. A person – or an animal – is wholly body and wholly soul and both are at all times the whole being. In other words we do not only 'have' a body, or 'have' a soul – we are both body *and* soul. The Hebrew language does not talk of the two as separate entities; it is the hellenistic culture in which the categories are separated into the three-fold composite of body, soul and spirit. The spiritual and eternal soul, that which 'animates' the body, so says the CCC (nn. 394, 396) is created immediately by God, and is not 'produced' by the parents. This is given in the context of the human person but there is nothing about it which suggests it is exclusive, so long as a creature is 'animated'. In Genesis (1:21, 24), God creates 'every living creature'. The Hebrew words (transliterated) are *chay* (living) and *nephesh* (soul). *Nephesh* is mentioned over four hundred times in the Old Testament signifying soul. The words *chay nephesh* are used from Genesis 1:20, when the waters are filled with living creatures. The close translation from Hebrew is: 'And God said: Let the waters swarm [with] the swarmers [having] a soul of life ...' and in the next verse: 'And God created the great sea animals, and all that creeps, [having] a living soul ..."⁹ In verse 30, God provides food – purely vegetarian – to every living thing, in which, the Hebrew adds, '[is] a living soul'. There is a definite separation here between 'every green plant', which of course are living things, and every creature possessed of a 'living soul'. In Genesis chapter two, the second, and older Creation account, the first human being was created from dust, then God 'blew into his nostrils [the] breath of life and man became a living soul', a *chay nephesh*. Here we have the real sense of *nephesh*, or soul, as a being animated by the breath of life. This reminds us of the glorious invocation of Psalm 150, where 'everything that breathes' is to praise the Lord.

Pope John Paul II declares in a public audience in 1990 that 'also the animals possess a soul and men must love and feel solidarity with our smaller brethren' and goes on to state that all animals are 'fruit of the creative action of the Holy Spirit and merit respect' and that they are 'as near to God as men are'. After quoting from Psalm 104, he concludes that 'all living creatures depend on the living spirit/breath of God that not only creates but also sustains and renews the face of the earth'.¹⁰

According to the Genesis account, the distinction, or alienation, between human and animal, and within species¹¹ is a result of the Fall. These alienations, or 'privations of good relations',¹² are descriptions of, not prescriptions for, a postlapsarian world. Human alienation, according to John Paul II in *Evangelium Vitae*, n. 2, is from the 'truth of creation', and one major consequence of this is the instrumentalization of nature.

Christian tradition, on the other hand, posits the healing of divisions and the restoration of harmony at and by the Incarnation (although the fullness of this is to be experienced only at the last times, the *eschaton* – which topic will be dealt with under n. 2416). In the words of the Solemn Blessing at Christmas Midnight Mass, 'When the Word became man, earth was joined to heaven.' As evidenced by the lives and legends of the Desert Fathers – who anticipated the peaceable kingdom –

divisions within the orders and species are ultimately reconciled. Hence it is through Christ that spiritual and corporeal
both find their apotheosis, the rational/spiritual *and* the
material, the human *and* the animal. The radical distinction
between man and animals is transcended in Jesus Christ, who
is one in flesh with all that is fleshly, and true God. The words
of Pope John Paul II have a vital significance in bringing out
this theological point, so often overlooked, and providing a
basis for a radically new respect for animals:

> The Incarnation of God the Son signifies the taking up into
> unity with God not only of human nature, but in this human
> nature, in a sense, of everything that is 'flesh': the whole of
> humanity, the entire visible and material world. The Incarna-
> tion, then, also has a cosmic significance, a cosmic dimension.
> The 'first-born of all creation', becoming incarnate in the indi-
> vidual humanity of Christ, unites himself in some way with the
> entire reality of man, which is also 'flesh'–and in this reality
> with all 'flesh', with the whole of creation.[13]

To view all created things as 'destined' for man depends on
seeing things created for a purpose; having a knowledge of
the 'ends', or 'telos', for each order of creation. In Aquinas's
words: 'There is no sin in using a thing for the purpose for
which it is. Now the order of things is such that the imperfect
are for the perfect...'[14] In his teaching not only is there a hierarchical order—imperfect to more perfect – but each
successive order is created for the sake of the one above it. At
the top is the perfection which is God alone, pure spirit and
prime mover. All others are creatures, descending from the
spiritual to the material, angels to stones, from the more
perfect to the less perfect.

As the claim that the whole of creation is 'destined' for
mankind is so pervasive in the CCC, it is worth looking in
more detail at the arguments of Aquinas on which it is based.
He gives his argument for the subjection of animals to man in
three parts:

His first point is 'from the order observed by nature', where he sees the 'imperfect' are for the use of the 'perfect' – 'as the plants make use of the earth for their nourishment, and animals make use of plants, and man makes use of both plants and animals.[15] This answer is irrefutable, but is descriptive, rather than prescriptive. In this part of the Summa, the actual uses to which man puts plants and animals are not mentioned, although in his next sentence, using Aristotle, Aquinas justifies the hunting of wild animals as a 'natural right' of man. Humans being hunted by wild animals, though, he considers is 'against justice ... For animals of this kind attack man that they may feed on his body, and not from some motive of justice, the consideration of which belongs to reason alone'.[16] It seems to run counter to logic to suggest that hunting by instinct for necessity is 'against justice', while hunting by choice, whether for food, sport, or protection, is somehow 'just'.

The second proof for Aquinas is 'the order of Divine Providence which always governs inferior things by the superior'. Two objections might be made to the unqualified use of this argument in relation to animals. The first is that whilst a hierarchical order may be descriptively accurate, it by no means follows that the lower order exists for the benefit of the one higher to it: man, for example, is not ordered for the angels, but for God alone. So it could be said that animals are not ordered for man but for God alone. It could also be argued that the inanimate (the minerals, for example) are ordered for the animate, but that within the category of the animate there can be the subdivision of the sentient and the non-sentient, where the non-sentient (plants) are ordered to the sentient (animals and man). It could also be argued that between all the orders there is a mutuality which transcends the hierarchical uses. For example, the cycle of death and decay of animals (human and non-human) and plants nourishes the minerals which in turn give the sustenance of life to the animals and plants.

The second objection which might be made is taken from the economy of salvation. This is crucial for a Christian perspective for, far from the 'lower' *serving* the 'higher' we have the example of the condescension (*katabasis*) and self-emptying (*kenosis*) of Christ himself who, though 'his state was divine, yet he did not cling to his equality with God but emptied Himself to assume the condition of a slave, and became as men are; and being as all men are, he was humbler yet...' (Philippians 1:4,6–8a).[17] An example of a higher order acting on behalf of the order lower to it, is that of the angels, the next one 'up', acting on behalf of people (faith in which is supported by the numerous prayers to 'St Michael the Archangel', and others). The activities of all angels are purely beneficent (Guardian Angels, etc), with the sole exception of the 'Fallen Angels', Satan and his crew. The model therefore for man's treatment of animals should surely be that of the 'good' angels, not that of Satan.

The third argument of Aquinas is 'proved from the property of man and of animals'. This differentiates the 'participated prudence of natural instinct' possessed by animals, with the 'universal prudence as regards all practical matters' enjoyed by man. The examples he gives illustrate this opinion: the 'fact that cranes follow their leader, and bees obey their queen' indicate that for animals to follow human beings is a form of instinct.[18] The fact that animals concern themselves with the 'here and now', whereas human beings engage in what is 'essential and universal' shows, for Aquinas, that the subjugation of animals to man is entirely natural.

To take issue with this third argument we would have to question whether what is 'right' *always* follows from what is 'in accordance with nature'.[19] While Aquinas does not accept that creation is fallen, the CCC affirms it in n. 400, drawing from Romans 8:21 to say that 'Because of man, creation is now subject 'to its bondage to decay', and from Genesis 3:17,19 that 'Harmony with creation is broken: visible creation has become alien and hostile to man.'

There are many natural instincts in animals which would not be considered as suitable moral exemplars for man – for example, the practice of a male lion to kill the progeny of other males in his pack, or the tendency of mother mammals of certain species to consume their own offspring if resources are scarce. It is also in accordance with the laws of nature for the strong to dominate the weak, to the extent of killing them. However, that tendency is precisely the reason for human beings to set up safeguards in laws and moral principles. Obviously, whoever has the capacity to comprehend the 'essential and universal' is in a position of power over creatures whose 'prudence' encompasses a much more limited intellectual field. So the weak, in this case, animals, need the protection of laws and moral principles to prevent human beings from exercising this bullying property. The major moral tenets of Christianity, given expression in the Beatitudes and the Magnificat, for example, run counter to the 'natural' tendency, this 'law of the jungle', so that to be 'in accordance with nature' is not an infallible guide for Christian praxis.

The point of whether animals fulfil their *telos*, or function – the point and purpose of their being – by their service to man, is given short shrift by Stephen R. L. Clark:

> There is a further point consequent upon the proper understanding of the argument from 'function': those who believe that animals are defined by extrinsic teleology, by their use to man, must imagine, given that fulfilment of one's nature is one's good, that it is to a pig's benefit to be killed and eaten: that is what he is *for*, that he fulfils his 'function' (see Porphyry (I) III 20). The absurdity of supposing that such treatment can be a direct benefit to the animal itself may weaken the temptation to imagine that such extrinsic functionality is sound.[20]

The Thomist-based argument of all creatures being destined for man does not take into account the paragraph in the CCC which allows that 'there is a solidarity among all creatures arising from the fact that all have the same creator and are all ordered to His glory' (n. 344). This is followed in n. 344 by an extract from the 'Canticle of the Creatures' by St Francis of Assisi. All creatures, and that includes all animals, have as their goal, their *telos*, God, and the purpose for their being is to give glory to God. St

Bonaventure is quoted (n. 293) as explaining 'that God created all things "not to increase his glory, but to show it forth and to communicate it"'. All creation, according to the letter to the Romans 8:18–25, is groaning in the birthing process of becoming free from chaos, decadence, sin. 'Creation has not yet reached perfection' (n. 310) but 'still retains the hope', in the words of Romans 8:21, 'when it will enjoy the same freedom and glory as the children of God'. Meanwhile, the worship of God is to be the purpose of creation, as paragraph n. 347 states: 'Creation was fashioned with a view to the sabbath and therefore for the worship and adoration of God. Worship is inscribed in the order of creation [Cf. Gen. 1:14].'

According to the Dominican Scripture scholar, Celine Mangan, the traditional 'dominion' reading of the Genesis account of creation has led to a distortion of the place of man in the overall schema. Rabbinic tradition also regards the classical Christian reading as a distortion, as 'the sabbath and not the creation of humans, is the crown and climax of the creation story itself'.[21] The account is read in the CCC as having a hierarchical structure,[22] with creation 'waiting with bated breath for the emergence of humankind on the sixth day as the high point of creation'.[23] However, Sr Mangan detects a chiastic structure in the seven-day account, where verses are paired: day one (light) with day four (sun, moon, stars); day two (sky, separation of waters) with day five (birds, fish and sea creatures); day three (earth, vegetation) with day six (animals, humans) – culminating in day seven: Sabbath rest. As she observes, 'In such a model humankind takes its place within the circle of creation, not at its peak.'[24] The goal of creation is not the creation of man but Sabbath rest. This is actually stated in the CCC, n. 347, 'Creation was fashioned with a view to sabbath and therefore for the worship and adoration of God.' But with the standard traditional reading the impression is given that, with the dominion of the earth given to man, God's involvement with creation could even be redundant. That is not borne out in Scripture, where, from Noah in Genesis 9:12ff. to Hosea 2:2, human sin causes new covenants to be made – with the whole of creation. The history of the people of God is also the history of the relationship of God with his creation.

2415:3. Use of the mineral, vegetable, and animal resources of the universe cannot be divorced from respect for moral imperatives

This sentence introduces the control of mankind's use of animals by 'moral imperatives' – in other words by considerations other than the financial, the expedient, the culturally conformist, etc. It could almost be read as a rejection of the Thomist approach whereby everything is for man's use, 'full stop'. The word 'imperatives' expresses further obligation than what one simply 'should' do, to what one really 'must' do – or *not* do. In an earlier paragraph in the CCC, n. 373:

> In God's plan man and woman have the vocation of 'subduing' the earth [Gen. 1:28] as stewards of God. This sovereignty is not to be an arbitrary and destructive domination. God calls man and woman, made in the image of the Creator 'who loves everything that exists' [Wis. 11:24], to share in his providence towards other creatures; hence their responsibility for the world God has entrusted to them.

The image of 'stewardship' is a crucial qualification in the process of 'subduing' the earth, with its reminder of true ownership being other than man's. The topic will be revisited more fully in chapter twelve.

2415:4. Man's dominion over inanimate and other living beings granted by the Creator is not absolute; it is limited by concern for the quality of life of his neighbour, including generations to come; it requires a religious respect for the integrity of creation[25]

By saying that dominion is limited it implies that there is something about dominion which needs to be limited; that unlimited, or absolute dominion would be wrong. What might the writers of the CCC think dominion is about? It is obvious that in much of Christian tradition it has been interpreted as a divine mandate to use nature entirely for the benefit of human beings. However, can it not mean, as Berkman puts it 'that God has chosen humanity to be an image of God's own rule in the world'[26]? This implies that people are to act as God's deputies – with the caveat: 'Of course, how Christians are to rule over animals is directly connected with how humans understand God to be ruling over them.' ('Dominion' will be more fully addressed in the examination of n. 2417).

The use of the word 'religious' for the respect required towards creation conveys a sense of the obligations owed by human beings to God, so acknowledging the serious level of the respect required. To cause animals 'to suffer or die need-lessly' (n. 2418) 'is the epitome of disregard, the very opposite of respect for their integrity. Therefore it is in violation of one of the moral imperatives limiting man's dominion over nature.'[27] Karol Wojtila, in his 1960 book *Love and responsi-bility*, endorses the limits of the uses made of animals: 'In his treatment of animals in particular, since they are beings endowed with feeling and sensitive to pain, man is required to ensure that the use of these creatures is never attended by suffering or physical torture.'[28] In an endnote he adds that 'Moral obligations are imposed on the person as subject of action not only by other persons ... but also by non-personal beings by reason of their specific value, and in particular by living creatures especially those capable of suffering.'[29]

Notes

1 Definition of 'integrity', *The Chambers Dictionary* (Edinburgh: Chambers Harrap, 2003).

2 [Cited in the text: Denzinger-Schonmetzer, *Enchiridion Symbolorum* (1965), 286; 455–63; 800; 1333; 3002]. This statement is given further analysis in the following section, under the treatment of n. 2416.

3 'Each creature possesses its own particular goodness and perfection. For each one of the works of the "six days" it is said: "And God saw that

it was good".'

4 Peter Singer, *Animal Liberation: a new ethic for our treatment of animals* (London: Jonathan Cape, 1976), p. 212.

5 Vatican internet news agency, < http://www.zenit.org/ >, 24 November 2000.

6 Ibid.

7 Gillian Clark, 'The Fathers and the Animals: the rule of reason?', *Animals on the Agenda*, edited by Andrew Linzey and Dorothy Yamamoto (London: SCM Press, 1998), p. 76.

8 This concept of 'orders' derives from the Fourth Lateran Council of 1215 and was revived in the First Vatican Council document, *Dei Filius* I.

9 From *The Interlinear Hebrew-Aramaic Old Testament*, Vol I of 'The Interlinear Hebrew-Greek-English Bible', edited by Jay P. Green Sr, (Peabody, Mass.:Hendrickson, 2nd edn 1985), p. 2. The words in square brackets are not used in Hebrew, but are understood.

10 Public Audience address on the Holy Spirit, 19 January 1990, reported in an article by Mimmo Pacifici in *Gente*, (February 1990); translated in leaflet form by the Catholic Study Circle for Animal Welfare.

11 For example, between man and woman (blaming each other for eating the forbidden fruit); between brother and brother (Cain killing Abel); between man and the environment (expelled from the Garden and having to toil); between man and animal/ animal and animal (killing and predation) , above all the alienation between man and God.

12 John Berkmann, 'Is the Consistent Ethic of Life Consistent without a Concern for animals?', *Animals on the Agenda*, edited by Andrew Linzey and Dorothy Yamamoto (London: SCM Press, 1998), p. 242.

13 John Paul II, Encyclical *Dominum et Vivifanctum* (1986), n. 50; see website < www.vatican.va/edocs/ENGO142/_PF.htm >

14 *Summa Theologiae*. II, II, Q64., art.1.

15 *Summa Theologiae* P.I. Q.96, Art.1.

16 *Summa Theologiae*. II, IIQ 159, art.2

17 For a fuller treatment of this theme, see Andrew Linzey, *Christianity and the Rights of Animals*, (London: SPCK, 1987), p. 43ff, and in much else of his work.

18 Aquinas' reply to Objection 4 of the question in *Summa Theologiae*. II, IIQ 159, art.2.

19 A fuller discussion of the natural fallacy (deriving 'ought' from 'is'), and of natural law, will be found in Part Three.

20 Stephen R. L. Clark, *The Moral Status of Animals* (Oxford: Clarendon Press, 1997), p. 58.

21 Larry Rasmussen, 'Symbols to Live by', *Environmental Stewardship*, edited by R. J. Berry (T&T Clark International, 2006), p. 176.

22 Note n. 342: 'The hierarchy of creatures is expressed by the order of the "six days" from the less perfect to the more perfect.'

23 Celine Mangan, 'The Bible: salvation or creation history?', *Priests &
    People*, 14. 2 (February 2000), p. 56.

24 Celine Mangan, 'The Bible: salvation or creation history?' p. 57.

25 Cf. *Centesimus Annus* 37–8.

26 John Berkman, 'Prophetically Pro-Life: John Paul II's gospel of life and
    evangelical concern for animals', *Josephinum Journal of Theology*, 6.1
    (1999), p. 56.

27 Andrew Tardiff, 'A Catholic Case for Vegetarianism', *Faith and Philoso-
    phy*, 15.2 (1998), p. 219.

28 Karol Wojtila, *Love and responsibility*, translated by H.T. Willetts. (First
    published in Polish, *Milosc I Odpowiedzialnosc*, Krakow: Wydawnicto,
    Zualosc, 1960, Revised edition, first published in English, London:
    William Collins Sons and Co., 1981; this edition, London: Fount Paper-
    backs, 1982), p. 25.

29 Karol Wojtila, *Love and responsibility*, p. 289.

Chapter Nine

Paragraph 2416: Animals are God's creatures

n. 2416. 1. Animals are God's creatures. 2. He surrounds them with his providential care. 3. By their mere existence they bless him and give him glory.[Cf. Mt 6:26; Dan 3:79–81.] 4. Thus men owe them kindness. 5. We should recall the gentleness with which saints like St. Francis of Assisi or St. Philip Neri treated animals.

2416:1. Animals are God's creatures

This statement carries two potential meanings (though not of the same importance) depending on the emphases given to certain words. One meaning becomes apparent when the stress is laid on the word 'creatures', as it implies that animals cannot themselves be divinized. Included with nature as a whole, animals are, to some extent, divinized today by some followers of the Gaia or Living Earth philosophies. Their views, considered extreme by most Christians, serve as a 'counter-example to the neo-Darwinian notion that providence plays no part in things, and also to the merely anthropocentric fantasy that it is our advantage that such a providence provides'.[1] This touches on a concern about which the Church was exercised until recently: metempsychosis, or belief in the transmigration of souls. In a Catholic Truth Society pamphlet published as late as 1960, the writer considers that 'The Church must be cautious because there are many heresies concerning animals, based chiefly on Metempsychosis and animal-worship.'[2] A lengthy section devoted to this heresy is to be found in the 1911 *Catholic Encyclopedia* (Volume X), but none at all in its 1994 successor, *The Modern Catholic Encyclopedia*.

When, however, the word 'God' is emphasized, the statement appears to negate the argument that animals are made for man, that they are exclusively 'man's' creatures. It is consistent with the 1992 statement of the US Catholic Conference, 'Renewing the Earth' which says that 'It is appropriate that we treat other creatures and the natural world not just as means to human fulfilment but also as God's creatures, possessing an independent value, worthy of our respect and care.'[3] Accepting this 'independent value' is something of a breakthrough in Catholic literature concerning animals. (The question of whether much notice is taken by the Vatican of North American pronouncements is, however, doubtful.) Asserting animals' 'independent value' helps to avoid the purely instrumentalist approach in which animals and nature as a whole are reduced to mere 'matter' to be used and abused at will. Avoidance of instrumentalism is also a safeguard for human life, which could be vulnerable to exploitation similar to that suffered now by animals. If the possession of the quality of 'reason' or 'intellect' is the criterion differentiating people with rights from animals without, it is a short step for humans without full possession of those qualities to be exploited. If, however, the capacity to suffer, to feel stress or pain – which is common to all animals with nervous systems – is the inhibitor for activity concerning the human or nonhuman creature, then not only are animals safeguarded, but so also are human beings in (nearly) all stages of development.

However, this CCC sentence has to be taken in the light of the more Thomist passages in the CCC, where animals are part of the gift which God is considered to have made to man. Thomism seems to provide the familiar language into which the CCC lapses, despite the contradictions this sets up. For example, n. 299 again:

For God willed creation as a gift addressed to man, an inheritance destined for and entrusted to him. On many occasions the Church has had to defend the goodness of creation, including that of the physical world.

The defences of the 'goodness of creation' presumably include those undertaken in the early Church against, for example, the anti-material doctrines of docetist gnosticism; and the belief of the Manichees, against which Augustine argues, that creation was the product of an evil creator.

The 'goodness' of creation is itself a thorny question. In the words of the short poem by Walter de la Mare, 'The Spotted Flycatcher':

> Grey on grey post, this silent little bird
> Swoops on its prey – prey neither seen nor heard!
> A click of bill; a flicker, and back again!
> Sighs Nature an *Alas*! Or merely, *Amen*?[4]

We can see much in creation, in nature, which does not seem to be good at all – for example, predation, death and decay. This has led to a range of theological opinion, as Hauerwas and Berkman remark, 'In Christian theology, the last thing creation does is to serve as an explanation.'[5] Views range from predation, death and decay being the consequence of a cosmic fall, or of the fall of the first man and woman; to acceptance of predation, death and decay as the way it is being God's mysterious will. Hauerwas and Berkman urge that a Christian understanding of creation does not privilege Genesis 1 and 2 but rather that these chapters must be read in the light of redemption in Christ, Romans 8:19–21 and Isaiah 11, 'where the original creation is understood in relation to the present bondage of creation and the dawning eschatology of the new creation'.[6]

For Alistair S. Gunn:

> the divine 'plan' . . . is certainly not designed to reduce suffering or to protect rights . . . the Christian, noting that God saw

that the creation was good, and accepting that parts of the plan
(such as suffering) may turn out to be good after all, has a
reason for considering the interests of animals and the
integrity of ecosystems which the secularist lacks.[7]

The CCC asks (n. 309) why, if God created 'the ordered and
good world [and] cares for all his creatures' does the 'evil' of
predation, death and decay exist? It is a question to which the
CCC does not give an answer, but suggests that the process of
salvation itself, with its notions of sin, covenants, redemption
– the whole Christian message, as n. 309 concludes – is bound
up with it. The CCC rather humbly leaves the mysteries of
Providence to full disclosure at 'the end', when 'we see God
face to face', as n. 314 says, quoting 1 Corinthians 13:12. 'With
physical good' it says 'there exists also *physical evil* as long as
creation has not reached perfection',[8] reasserting the significance of the *eschaton*, 'that definitive sabbath rest' in
connection with creation.

Having said that, the CCC does provide one interpretation,
in its discussion of sin and the Fall, the story of which it relates
in a rather literal way. It states that, because of the original sin
of Adam and Eve, 'harmony with creation is broken ...
Because of man, creation is now subject "to its bondage of
decay"'.[9] Although it does not pursue this line with reference
to creation, but rather with the human race, it does seem to
be a rejection of alternative Christian views, such as Augustine's. Aquinas, following him, held that the Fall affected only
human beings and that predation and the death of nonhuman
creatures is all part of God's created order.[10] Aquinas' view
leaves the responsibility for the way nature is, in all its
savagery and rawness, to God alone, while it implies that
human beings and animals are of completely different natures
– the one fallen (and so subject to death and decay) because
of the consequences of sin; the other, subject to death and
decay from all time, by the Creator's plan.

One danger of this view is that, by separating man's Fall
from the state of nature, the latter becomes just a backdrop
against which the *real* drama of salvation is played out. Yet

another problem with considering that nature is as the Creator intended it to be, is that it therefore cannot be improved in any 'new creation', the eschaton.

Yet the CCC is emphatic about the eschaton. It links creation with eschatology by means of the 'eighth day'[11] whereby the new creation is in continuity with the original creation which was completed with the sabbath of the seventh day. The new creation, as described in Isaiah 11 and Hosea 2:18, is the original creation transformed to that which it should be. This is the 'real' world, the world which is the 'end' to which nature as a whole was called. And, according to a quotation from *Lumen Gentium*, the universe itself 'which is so closely related to man' actually 'attains its destiny through him'.[12] The 'man' here can be read not as the *human race* but as the perfect man, the second Adam, Christ.

The early Church expects the parousia imminently, and Church Fathers, such as Irenaeus, teach of the ultimate glorification of the whole universe. However, from the Enlightenment until the Second Vatican Council, church teaching on eschatology is concerned almost exclusively with the fate of the individual human soul. Now the CCC has no fewer than nine paragraphs, nn.1042–1050, devoted to the 'Hope of the New Heaven and the New Earth'. However, what has not yet received great attention in official Catholic theology is a more realized eschatology, such as called for by Pope John Paul II:

> The truth which the gospel teaches about God requires a certain focus with regard to eschatology. First of all, eschatology is not what will take place in the future, something happening only after earthly life is finished. Eschatology has already begun with the coming of Christ. The ultimate eschatological event was His redemptive Death and His Resurrection. This is the beginning of 'a new heaven and a new earth'. (Cf. Rev 21:1)[13]

How this eschatology has been realized in the life of some of the saints has been discussed in chapter four. Were the present Church to emulate their example, and to teach the solidarity between people and animals, its influence would be significant on the treatment of billions of animals worldwide.

2416:2. He surrounds them with his providential care

The CCC acknowledges that God does not abandon his creatures once they have been created. Paragraph n. 301 explains how God not only 'gives them being and existence, but also, and at every moment, upholds and sustains them in being, enables them to act and brings them to their final end. Recognising this utter dependence with respect to the Creator is a source of wisdom and freedom, of joy and confidence'. The paragraph then gives this lengthy quotation from Wisdom 11:24–6:

> For you love all things that exist, and detest none of the things that you have made; for you would not have made anything if you had hated it. How would anything have endured, if you had not willed it? Or how would anything not called forth by you have been preserved? You spare all things, for they are yours, O Lord, you who love the living.

What this expresses is that, to God, all creatures are good and loved – not just those that are beneficial or aesthetically pleasing to mankind. The CCC passage echoes the writings of an early Dominican writer, for long thought to have been Thomas Aquinas himself:

> It is God's custom to care for all his creatures, both the greatest and the least. We should likewise care for creatures, whatsoever they are, in the sense that we use them in conformity with the divine purpose, in order that they may not bear witness against us in the day of judgement ...[14]

This passage introduces an unusual element of the possibility of 'lesser' creatures being in a position to bear witness to the actions of mankind in the 'day of judgement', implying some form of existence, even exalted existence, at the eschaton. In this it echoes a text of the apocryphal II Enoch: 'There is one place in the great age for all the souls of the cattle, and one fold and one pasture; for the soul of an animal which the Lord has made will not perish until the judgement, but all souls *will* accuse man.'[15] The Dominican passage goes on to show providential care for all matter, including, rather Franciscan-like, inanimate matter:

> It is another of the ways or perfections of God that he cares for all that he has created the very smallest as well as the greatest, be they animals, fishes or birds. Two sparrows are sold for a farthing, yet not one is forgotten (Matthew 10:29). He cares even for the worms, great and small. He keeps all things in being and continually provides them with all they need for life. He cares for the four elements, for inert matter, for plants and trees and the whole animal world.[16]

2416:3. By their mere existence they bless him and give him glory [Cf. Matt 6:26; Dan 3:79–81]

This clause echoes the words of the seventeenth-century English poet Henry Vaughan:

> Birds, beasts, all things
> Adore Him in their kinds ... [17]

It also echoes a previous paragraph, n. 293,

> Scripture and Tradition never cease to teach and celebrate this fundamental truth: 'The world was made for the glory of God' [*Dei Filius*, can. § 5: DS 3025]. St Bonaventure explains that God created all things 'not to increase his glory, but to show it forth and to communicate it', [St Bonaventure, In II Sent. I, 2, 2, 1] for God has no other reason for creating than his love and goodness: 'Creatures came into existence when the key of love opened his hand' [St Thomas Aquinas, Sent. II, prol]. The First Vatican Council explains: [337, 344, 1361] 'This one, true God, of his own goodness and 'almighty power', not for increasing

his own beatitude, nor for attaining his perfection, but in order
to manifest this perfection through the benefits which he
bestows on creatures, with absolute freedom of counsel "and
from the beginning of time, made out of nothing both orders
of creatures, the spiritual and the corporeal ..."' [Dei Filius I:
DS 3002; cf Lateran Council IV (1215): DS 800] [759].

Similar to that paragraph, n. 2416:3 explains that, as animals
were loved into being by God, they in turn 'bless' and 'give
glory to' their Creator. It is a reminder of the Covenants
forged by God between himself and his creatures – no less
than those between God and mankind. The reference to
Daniel 3 is familiar to all Catholics who say the Canticle of the
Three Young Men, with its repeated refrain 'O bless the Lord',
in the Divine Office for Sunday mornings. As Hauerwas and
Berkman argue, animals will not manifest God's glory in so far
as their lives are measured in terms of human interests, but
only in so far as their lives serve God's good pleasure.[18]
Animals have their own *telos*, their own function distinct from
their use to us. They were not created simply to serve
mankind. Indeed humans themselves need to be truly what
God intended – redeemed, worshipping beings – before being
able to serve creation as *imago Dei*. The New Testament
commentator Charles Cranfield gives a description of nature's
praise and the place of fallen humanity's need for redemption
in order to 'complete the picture':

> The Jungfrau and the Matterhorn and the planet Venus and all
> living things too, man excepted, do indeed glorify God in their
> own ways; but since their praise is destined to be not a collec-
> tion of independent offerings, but part of a magnificent whole,
> the united praise of the whole creation, they are prevented
> from being fully what they were created to be, so long as man's
> part is missing.[19]

2416:4. Thus men owe them kindness

This 'thus' is significant, indicating that God gives us the key
to how animals should be used. The authority for a humane

and compassionate treatment of animals is in no way the benevolence of human beings, but that of God alone, in whose estimation they have value. This is of crucial significance in developing a Catholic ethic of the treatment of animals, just as the previous clause is significant in emphasizing what could be a truly God-centred Catholic theology of animals.[20]

Pope John Paul II's 1996 encyclical 'Gospel of Life', cites Ecclesiasticus 18:11: 'Human beings may be merciful to their neighbours, but the compassion of the Lord extends to every living creature', and follows it immediately with the line from CCC n. 2418: 'It is contrary to human dignity to cause animals to suffer or die needlessly.'[21] This encyclical, as a partial distillation of the CCC, calls for a 'culture of life' and it could be inferred, in this instance, that such a culture extends to *all* life, human and animal.

We 'owe' animals kindness. For one being to be 'owed' is to imply that someone else has 'duties' to him or her. This is not quite the same as concluding that animals necessarily therefore have rights in the legal sense (although the whole subject of rights will be discussed in chapter thirteen). Aidan Nichols, OP suggests that, 'While not ascribing rights to animals, the CCC speaks of what is their *due* – above all, kindness which, if we are to take seriously the etymology of the English word, means our sense of *kinship* with them.'[22] This view breaks down the separation, even alienation, between human and animal so redolent of much of Catholic teaching to date.

In avoiding 'rights' discourse, while emphasizing a strong element of 'duty', we can find allies among the avowed non-religious: 'Even Austin[23] admitted the existence of so-called "absolute duties", which include, for example, the duty "not to commit suicide, to do military service, to abstain from cruelty to animals". Such a duty, he said, neither implies, nor is implied by, a right.'[24]

While animals' *legal* rights are not at issue here, there remains the question of their *moral* rights. Cardinal Heenan's comment is appropriate: '[Animals] have very positive rights because they are God's creatures . . . God has the right to have all his creatures treated with proper respect.'[25]

In medieval jurisprudence, the concept of animal rights was taken quite seriously, if bizarre to modern thinking, as explored in chapter five. Those creatures which were thought to have been admitted to Noah's ark were considered to be responsible for their actions and brought to 'justice' if they had transgressed. Those who were not thought to have been included, were beyond the protection of the legal community.[26]

2416:5. We should recall the gentleness with which saints like St Francis of Assisi or St Philip Neri treated animals

The word here used to describe the ideal way to treat animals is the same as that used in Colossians 3:19 for the way husbands are to treat their wives –'with gentleness'. It is a strong indication of the CCC's approval – in this section – of a high degree of kindness towards animals. The appeal to the example of saints corrects the imbalance on the reliance of purely scholastic theology. Saints represent a significant Christian authority – the authority of holiness.

The importance of referring to saints in this context is two-fold: one is in their use as exemplars, as models of behaviour and right attitude. The saints serve as exemplars of the way that closeness to God affects men and women, enabling them to relate to God's creatures as God himself does. The other is in what their behaviour represents, a form of living realized eschatology – as is seen in chapter four in the lives of the Desert Fathers and Celtic saints. Dr Marie Hendrickx, a member of the Vatican's Congregation for the Doctrine of the Faith, ties these two together. She likens the way that holiness (in the legends of the saints) attracts wild creatures 'in a movement of overall reconciliation', to the Isaian vision of the Messianic times when 'the earth shall be full of the knowledge of the Lord as the waters cover the sea', and explains that the Hebrew word for the 'knowledge of the Lord' suggests something carnal, like a communion of life. 'Knowing the Lord' thus means becoming in some way consubstantial with him and, at the same time, being perfectly reconciled with creation. She describes the time of our [Christians'] definitive encounter with the Beloved [Christ], when 'our hearts will be like his, that all our past affections, however humble they may be, will find their place, having been purified, made right and ordered to him. For God,' she affirms, 'nothing human can be lost, not even the simple ties we have formed with the animal creatures, which filled, for example, our moments of loneliness.'[27]

St Francis of Assisi and St Philip Neri, the only two saints mentioned in the CCC – although many dozens more could have been[28] – are discussed in chapter four.

Notes

1 S. R. L. Clark, 'Is Nature God's Will?' *Animals on the Agenda*, edited by Andrew Linzey and Dorothy Yamamoto (London: SCM Press, 1998), p. 125.

2 Ambrose Agius, *Cruelty to Animals* (London: Catholic Truth Society, 1960), p. 15.

3 United States Catholic Conference, A Pastoral statement: *Renewing the earth: an invitation to reflection and action on the environment in light of Catholic social teaching* (Washington DC: USCC, 1992), p. 7.

4 Walter de la Mare, From *The Complete Works*, anthologized in *The Oxford Book of Short Poems*, edited by P. J. Kavanagh and James Michie (Oxford University Press, 1985), p. 182.

5 Stanley Hauerwas and John Berkman, 'The Chief End of All Flesh', *Theology Today*, 49.2 (1992), p. 204.

6 Ibid.

7 Alistair S. Gunn, 'Traditional Ethics and the Moral Status of Animals', *Environmental Ethics*, 5.2 (Summer 1983), p. 152.

8 Cf. CCC n. 310; CCC's emphasis.

9 Cf. CCC n. 400, citing Romans 8:21.

10 Margaret Atkins, 'Is God kind to animals?' in *Priests & People*, 13, 4 (April 1999), p. 157.

11 Cf. CCC n. 349, '... The seventh day completes the first creation. The eighth day begins the new creation ...'

12 *Lumen Gentium* 48, cited in CCC n. 1042.

13 John Paul II, *Crossing the Threshold of Hope* (New York: Alfred Kopf, 1994), pp. 184–5.

14 Aquinas, 'De cura Dei de creaturis', in 'De divinis moribus' (from Opusculum LXII), *Omnia Opera*, Vol. 28. There is also a translation by Bernard Delany, *On the Ways of God* (London: Burns and Oates, 1926), p. 24ff.

15 II Enoch, or 'Slavonic Enoch', XV, *The Apocryphal Old Testament*, edited by H. F. D. Sparks (Oxford: Clarendon Press, 1985), p. 350.

16 Aquinas, 'De cura Dei de creaturis'.

17 From 'The Morning Watch', by Henry Vaughan (which continues in part: Thus all is hurl'd/In sacred hymns and order; the great chime/ And symphony of Nature. Prayer is/ The world in tune …'.) From website < www.poetry-chaikhana.com/V/VaughanHenry/MorningWatch.htm >

18 Stanley Hauerwas amd John Berkman, 'The Chief End of All Flesh', *Theology Today*, 49.2 (1992), pp. 196–208.

19 C. E. B. Cranfield, 'Some observations on Romans 8:19–21', *Reconciliation and Hope*, edited by R. Banks (Grand Rapids, MI: Eerdmans, 1974), p. 227.

20 It is a key element of 'theos-rights', which will be discussed fully in chapter four.

21 *Evangelium Vitae*, 27.

22 Aidan Nichols, *The Service of Glory* (Edinburgh: T&T Clark, 1997), p. 216. 'Kind' from Old English *(ge)cynde*, from *cynn*, kin (*Chambers Dictionary*).

23 John Austin (1790–1859), British legal philosopher, friend of Bentham and Stuart Mill. In his 1832 work *The Province of Jurisprudence Determined* he attempted to provide an easily understandable ethical framework that could establish the rule of law as distinct from the rule of God and Christian morality. Cf. < http://www.bookrags.com/biography-john-austin/ >

24 Alan R. Wright, *Rights* (Oxford: Clarendon Press, 1984), p. 63.

25 Cardinal John Carmel Heenan, 'Foreword', to *God's Animals*, by Dom Ambrose Agius, OSB, (London: Catholic Study Circle for Animal Welfare, 1970), p. 3.

26 Mark Elvins, 'Animal Rights', *The Ark*, 189 (winter 2001), p. 11.

27 Marie Hendrickx, 'For a More Just Relationship with Animals', *L'Osservatore Romano* (December 2000, also 24 January 2001).

28 See, inter alia, *The Book of Saints and Friendly Beasts* by A.B. Brown (London: Longmans, Green and Co, 1901); and *Beasts and Saints*, by Helen Waddell (London: Darton, Longman and Todd, 1934, 1995).

Chapter Ten

Paragraph 2417: Stewardship of animals

2417. 1. God entrusted animals to the stewardship of those whom he created in his own image. [Cf. Gen 2:19–20; Gen 9:1–4.] 2. Hence it is legitimate to use animals for food and clothing. 3. They may be domesticated to help man in his work and leisure. 4. Medical and scientific experimentation on animals is a morally acceptable practice if it remains within reasonable limits and contributes to caring for or saving human lives.

2417:1. God entrusted animals to the stewardship of those whom he created in his own image [Cf. Gen. 2:19–20; 9:1–4]

The Genesis texts offered in support of this sentence are not the ones which might immediately suggest themselves in this context. The first describes the naming of the animals by Adam; the second, the blessing of Noah after the flood, with his rule over the beasts to be one of 'terror and dread'. This latter begins with a repetition of the blessing given to Adam in Genesis 1:28 – 'be fruitful'. However, the difference between the dominion given to Adam and that allowed to Noah is separated by both the Fall and the Flood, with God's new 'willingness to bear with sinfully violent humanity'.[1] The peace and harmony of Eden will not return before the eschaton so, as God has just covenanted to keep humanity from

destruction and as the *new* humanity – with Jesus Christ as its
'firstborn' – has not yet arrived, this is a description (not
prescription) of the way things were. It is likely that Genesis
9:1 was chosen in preference to Genesis 1:28, as that verse
follows the offer of dominion, not with 'fear and dread' for
animals, but with the provision of purely *vegetation* for food.
That could have presented the 'hence' of the following
sentence as even more of a non sequitur.

The relationship usually expressed as 'dominion' (from
Genesis 1:26, 28) is here given as 'stewardship' – for long the
preferred choice by many environmentalists and supporters
of animal welfare as it sounds less exploitative than 'dominion'. (However, this will be explored more thoroughly in
chapter twelve). Stewardship suggests looking after something in the absence of the landlord – which could arguably
imply a somewhat deist notion that God is no longer involved
in his creation. However, 'dominion' could still be more
appropriate – and at the same time not justify exploitation of
creation – by linking it with the preceding phrase, in Genesis
1:26, 'let us make man in our own image'.

The 'image of God' has long been used to differentiate
human from non-human animals, but as to what actually
constitutes that 'image' has not been consistently established.
Various theories have been suggested, Christopher Southgate
listing some of them as:

- The classical one that the image of God is in human rationality;
- The 'image' being grounded in other common characteristics – love, uprightness, dominion, creativity;
- The 'image' being understood in terms of capacity for
  authentic relationship (an understanding particularly
  attractive to certain Trinitarian theologians).[2]

Robert Murray, SJ,[3] Stanley Hauerwas and John Berkman[4] are
among those who do not consider that 'the image' means that
mankind has been exclusively created 'similar to' God by

possessing a godlike attribute, such as spirituality, intellect, or reason, but look rather to the origin of the biblical term. The 'God's image' language, they suggest, comes from a near-Eastern royal tradition whereby the kings represent their gods. By the time the priestly authors wrote their sections of Genesis, the kings in Israel had been replaced by the 'holy (priestly) people'. For Murray, the relationship here, in Genesis, of man with creation is essentially viceregal, with the people entrusted with the kind of rule of that which is proper to the ideals of kingship. As Hauerwas and Berkman put it, 'God simply chooses humans for the task of acting as God's deputies amidst God's good creation.'[5] In this they follow Millard Schumaker who describes the Genesis story as: 'Eden is to be considered as like a vassal state in the empire of the Great King, God: Adam is to be seen as ... a governor appointed by God to manage Eden.'[6] He suggests that popular suspicion of monarchy or hierarchy (although, perhaps much less so where benign monarchies rule, such as over the UK), is because of the inability to distinguish between the domination of a monarch and the domination of a tyrant, 'or more basically, the leadership of anyone who was not elected'. 'Christians too', he says, 'forget to make this distinction when they forget that what they long for is the Kingdom of God, a kingdom of love and peace, rather than one of tyranny and oppression.'[7]

Murray too stresses the *ideals* of kingship are what is assumed, 'not the abuses or failures: not tyranny or arbitrary manipulation and exploitation of subjects, but a rule governed by justice, mercy and true concern for the welfare of all'.[8] The model of kingly rule given throughout the Scriptures is that of God's, not Pharoah's; kenotic, not despotic. Christ's followers moreover are enjoined to be servants, not to 'lord it over' people like the pagans or to make their authority felt, but to serve (cf. Matthew 20:28).

Presenting the animals to Adam for naming, as we have seen under n. 2415, puts the animals both into relationship with Adam, and to some extent under his kingly control. The link

between naming and control is implied in the reluctance of
God himself to be named, and thus to fall under the control of
creatures, in Exodus 3:14 when Moses at the burning bush is
told only that God is the 'I am'. Here Adam displays the kingly
gift of wisdom, and by naming the animals, 'both defines their
natures and establishes authority over them'.[9]

2417:2. Hence it is legitimate to use animals for food and clothing

The 'hence' (*igitur*) here follows 'entrusted ... stewardship ...
[God's] own image'. Animals have been entrusted to
mankind: held in trust, to be cared for and given the conditions for flourishing. Stewards do not own that which they
control; they simply look after and manage their master's
goods to the best of their ability, ready to hand them back in
as good or better order, as the various Gospel stories show.[10]
Human beings are thus accountable to the Creator for the use
they make of his animal creation. This is a concept grasped
three hundred years ago by the Catholic poet, Alexander
Pope, who wrote: 'I cannot think it extravagant to imagine that
mankind are no less, in proportion, accountable for the ill-use
of their dominion over creatures of the lower rank of beings,
than for the exercise of tyranny over their own species.'[11]

The 'hence' in this sentence does not logically follow on
from the foregoing sentence (nor of the previous paragraph)
other than in the sense that the master's goods can be used
by the steward in the course of his stewardship. That would
not entail that any of these goods can be destroyed or harmed
in any way – on the contrary, it would be a poor steward who
would so treat his master's property.

'Legitimate' is a legal word indicating merely that which
does not infringe a law. It does not suggest any ideal or recom-
mend any exercise of virtue, or indicate compulsion. It simply
gives a 'bottom line' below which a member of the legal
community – that is, a human person – is not allowed to go
while remaining within the community.

It is difficult to get behind this CCC sentence to understand its intention. Do the writers mean that 'use' implies killing or harming animals? If it does, are there restrictions to be placed on the killing or harming of animals – particularly in the light of the previous paragraph? If not, does it mean that only animal-based food, such as milk, eggs and honey, which do not directly require the deaths of the animals, may be used? Even if the latter there are problems, as milk and eggs are produced by the females, whereas obviously male offspring are produced as well, and in far greater numbers than are needed for further reproduction. So newly-born young males of several species, from poultry to calves, are destroyed in large numbers. The science of genetics can now manipulate the procreative processes so that only further females are produced, apart from the occasional necessary male, but there are drawbacks to this technology, not least the potential ethical infringement of the 'integrity of creation'.

As few members of the Catholic hierarchy appear to be vegetarians or vegans, it is presumed that the right to kill animals for food is accepted in principle by the writers. They can look to St Augustine for authority who stated:

> When we hear it said, 'Thou shalt not kill', we do not take it as referring to trees, for they have no sense, nor to irrational animals, because they have no fellowship with us. Hence it follows that the words, 'Thou shalt not kill' refer to the killing of a man.[12]

The rationale here is summarized (but not approved) by Stephen Clark: 'Beasts have no share in reason; beasts are not persons; beasts cannot be members of our community.'[13] As noted in chapter two, the basis of fellowship, or belonging to the community, comes from the Stoic theory of *oikeiosis*, literally, belonging to the same household, whereby the treatment of one's own household *may* be extended to encompass other human beings. The later Stoics took the whole world – that is, the world of *rational* beings, gods and men – as forming a single city. Non-rational beings were excluded, so that the justice which applied to all citizens of this single global city did not apply to them.

If it were accepted that animals may, on occasion, be killed, are there conditions which could limit these occasions? Tardiff shows that St Thomas Aquinas provides a framework of principles in the context of violence and self-defence among human persons, but which could be applied further. This is from Aquinas's argument of proportionality:

> And yet, though proceeding from a good intention, an act may be rendered unlawful, if it be out of proportion to the end ... Wherefore, if a man, in self-defence, uses more than necessary violence, it will be unlawful: whereas if he repel force with moderation it will be lawful.
>
> *(Summa Theologiae.*, P.II-II, Q.64. Art.7)[14]

This argument means that the evil effect must not outweigh the good one. The choice a person makes must be the option 'which represents the least destruction of good possible under the circumstances'. Killing another person in self-defence is legitimate only as an unintended act of double effect (CCC, n. 2263), and public authorities who have the option of bloodless means of protection should use these (CCC, n. 2267). In the same way, the killing of an animal in self-defence could be seen as a legitimate, if regrettable, act if no other courses of action were available. Similarly, in order to sustain human life it may be that there are no other available sources of food (for example, among some Inuit of northern Canada, or at times of privation due to war or famine) and so the legitimacy of killing animals in this context is granted.

Another Thomistic principle can apply here in conjunction with proportionality: the hierarchy by which the lower serves the higher. As man is ontologically higher than animals, so are animals than plants – unlike plants, animals share with man such attributes as feeling, perception and memory. So, with the injunction that the least harm must be committed, the least violence suffered as possible, it is consistent to propose that where the lower, plants, can serve the needs of man –

which is virtually always and everywhere – then they should be destroyed for food, rather than should the higher category of animals.

But it would seem that shedding blood for any needs *other* than the absolute preservation of human life, that is, where no alternatives are possible, would be counter to the 'culture of life' and not in accordance with the actions of kindness towards them that we have been enjoined to perform in CCC n. 2416. The intrinsic goodness of the lives of animals, which Pope John Paul II calls a 'truth of nature',[15] entitles them to be treated with respect. While the ultimately highest value is placed on the preservation of human life, the lives of animals cannot be said to possess *no* value other than a monetary one. To be consistent in the promotion of a 'culture of life', there is a need to extent the scope of respect to include all sentient life. Human life from conception to natural death would be better safeguarded were the 'culture of life' to be encouraged towards all living creatures.

When it comes to choice, rather than the *necessity* of keeping alive, the refusal to kill and eat animals has a strong justification in the Christian tradition. The early monastic movement is influenced by rigorous asceticism, and embraces total abstinence from meat, the monks modelling their frugal lifestyle on Jesus' forty-day sojourn in the wilderness, which he spent peaceably in the company of 'the wild beasts'. As Athanasius says of Antony of Egypt: 'His food was bread and salt, and for drinking he took only water. There is no reason even to speak of meat and wine, when indeed such a thing was not found among the other zealous men.'[16] St Ambrose's homilies on Genesis includes the following exhortation: 'We ought to be content to live on simple herbs, on cheap vegetables and fruits such as nature has presented to us and the generosity of God has offered to us.'[17]

In the biblical world, the complex issue and praxis of religious sacrifice includes some eating of all, or part, of the animal victims. In the earliest, pastoral, times, possibly all animals killed for food were first offered as sacral sacrifices.

It is suggested that this is to deal with the taboo of killing, as:

> For the ancient Hebrew, as for the modern hunter-gatherer, the act of killing a living, breathing mammal, even for sustenance, was dangerous and threatening to the natural and social order. By sanctifying their butchers as priests, and by setting aside the precious life-blood of the animal to be eaten and sacrificed, the sanctity of life, and the safety of the community are both preserved.[18]

S. H. Webb argues that with Christ's death and the institution of the Eucharist – the perfect meal anticipating the eschatological banquet – has come the end of the need for animal sacrifices.[19] In John's Gospel, the death of Jesus coinciding with the Passover sacrifice allows the identification of his death as that of the ultimate lamb, the 'Lamb of God'. Earlier in the Gospel, Jesus identifies himself with the manna in the Exodus story, the true bread from heaven of John 6:32–5. The symbolic use of bread and wine – both of which have to become (bloodlessly) crushed and ground down in order to give life – is to give a new alternative to the killing associated with sacrifice. According to Webb, to treat the bloodless Eucharist as the ultimate meal in the Christian's life and then to kill and eat animals the rest of the time is inconsistent, and dishonours the Eucharist. In other words, Christians should safeguard the unique significance of the death of Christ on the Cross by refusing to shed the blood of any other 'sacrificial victim' – whether or not that victim is killed within a religious context.[20]

There is another argument which may find a readier ear within the Catholic justice and peace movement – and that is the one of the best use of the world's resources to feed people. It is demonstrably true that far more land is occupied by grazing animals, and far more grain consumed by them, than is required in producing for a vegetarian market. Protein is far more efficiently produced in the form of legumes and nuts than in raising livestock for slaughter. The over-consumption of meat, dairy and fatty products is one source of poor health in the prosperous West. Another is the ingestion and absorption of toxins, hormones, antibiotics and viruses in the modern meat diet, at great cost to the provision of health services. So individual choices should be limited by the requirements of the common good, and the use of animals for food seriously restricted to the preservation of life.

Under the principle of proportionality, as described above, the right to choose to eat animals simply for pleasure, for taste or by convention – it could be argued – should give way to the duty to preserve the life of animals; and the right to produce animals for meat should give way to the duty to provide sufficient healthy food for the world's entire human population. Even where the right to kill animals for food is granted, Dr Marie Hendrickx poses the following questions that seriously challenge today's agro-industrial treatment of animals:

> Does the right to use animals for food imply the right to raise chickens in tiny cages where they live in a space smaller than a notebook? Or calves in compartments where they can never move about or see the light? Or to keep sows pinned by iron rings in a feeding position to allow a series of piglets to suck milk constantly and thus grow faster?[21]

In similar vein, the present pope, Benedict XVI, draws attention to the modern manner in which food animals are raised, even if it is allowed that they can be used for food. In 1992 when still a cardinal, he is asked in an interview with a journalist if making use of animals 'even to eat them' is allowable, and gives the following reply:

> That is a very serious question. At any rate, we can see that they are given into our care, that we cannot just do whatever we want with them. Animals, too, are God's creatures, and even if they do not have the same direct relation to God that man has, they are creatures of his will, creatures we must respect as companions in creation and as important elements in the creation.[22]

In his consideration of whether killing animals for food is
permissible, he draws on the point made often by Christian
promoters of vegetarianism that, at first, the only food provision for human beings was plant-life: 'Only after the flood,
that is to say, after a new breach has been opened between
God and man, are we told that man eats flesh . . .' However, he
denies that this should lead to what he dismissively calls 'a
kind of sectarian cult of animals'. Killing for food is not forbidden although, at the same time, a person 'should always
maintain his respect for these creatures'. He then gives a
powerful denunciation of certain farming practices, namely
the method of producing *foie gras*, and intensive poultry
conditions:

> Certainly, a sort of industrial use of creatures, so that geese are
> fed in such a way as to produce as large a liver as possible, or
> hens live so packed together that they become just caricatures
> of birds, this degrading of living creatures to a commodity
> seems to me in fact to contradict the relationship of mutuality
> that comes across in the Bible.[23]

Such farming practices are protected by law, as if it were the
right of the 'producer' to treat animals in this way. However,
according to a Scottish bishop, Mario Conti, 'A right accorded
by law has to have an intrinsic relationship to what is in itself
right.'[24] What is 'right' in the context of using animals for food,
it is argued, can be found in the last sentence of this paragraph: the need to save human lives. Other than that, the logic
of this paragraph suggests, it is not legitimate. The consequences of that suggest the provision of an ethic towards
animals which favours a vegetarian or even vegan diet.

Similar ethical issues arise with clothing. The legitimacy of
using animal-based renewable sources of material, such as
wool and silk, is not at issue. What the CCC does not make
clear is whether such uses exhaust the limits of legitimacy, or
did the writers intend more than that? There is the use of
skins and hides as the by-products of the food industry, so
these really come under the heading of the ethics of using

animals for food. There is the further, and more problematic issue, of the use of furs and pelts which have been obtained by trapping, hunting or fur-farming. As with food, where alternatives exist, by the theory of proportionality, the intrinsic value of the life of an animal surely exceeds the value of mere pleasure or fashion, or worse, the seeking of status symbols. Where alternatives do not exist, or not sufficiently for human survival, then, so long as no animal would be involved in prolonged suffering, a case could be made for the use of animal fur.

A joint statement by the Catholic and Anglican bishops of Northern Canada in 1986 defends the fur trade and deplores the drop in income of four Inuit villages as a result of a ban on the local seal hunt. What they believe they are defending is an ancient tradition of indigenous people, as Inuit hunters have, for centuries, used every part of their quarry, including the fur for life-saving protection in Arctic winters. What they are overlooking is the fact that, since the arrival of European fur traders, 'native hunters were drawn into a larger economy, selling furs for cash to support a changing lifestyle'.[25] In other words, there is nothing traditional about engaging in a fur trade to supply the fashion markets of the affluent West, and Paul Hollingsworth, founder of the 'Native-American Brotherhood' and speaking as an Inuit, considers that his people 'were forced into a way of life that was not ours ... the problem isn't the fickle whims of fashion; the problem is our getting involved in it. Respect for Mother Earth and other creatures in it is central to native spiritualities'.[26] Subsistence trapping by Inuits using traditional methods no longer exists. In the fur-trapping 'boom year' of 1979, fewer than five per cent of them listed trapping as a main occupation. Even so, in the words of Dr Hendrickx again, 'Does the right to use animals for clothing mean letting those with valuable pelts slowly die of hunger, thirst, cold or haemorrhage in traps?'[27] Of the 40 million animals killed for their fur each year worldwide, some 30 million are killed on fur farms. These animals spend their entire lives in tiny wire cages, completely unable to exercise their instincts and natural patterns of behaviour. In Bishop Conti's terms, that does not seem 'right' treatment of wild animals.

2417:3. They may be domesticated to help man in his work and leisure

Part of this sentence makes sense in the light of the historic uses made by man in domesticating animals, from the time the first semi-tame dog helped with the hunt, and the first horse and donkey was enlisted in transporting people or goods. Oxen and horses still pull ploughs in parts of the world, and cats keep granaries free from mice and rats. Within the limits of good animal welfare, this relationship between man and animal is unobjectionable, although even the keeping of companion animals is not trouble-free. The RSPCA reports ever-increasing incidents of cruelty to pets, and millions of unwanted ones are destroyed each year world-wide.

Objections might be made in some of the uses of animals for 'leisure'. Again, the CCC writers are not specific. Where once the sport of horse racing, especially steeplechasing, was seen as a necessary training for cavalry troops, that reason no longer exists. Where amateur casual dog racing was once an occasion for local people to place a (reasonably innocent) wager, now the 'sport' is a highly organized and lucrative 'industry'. It is notoriously callous in its use of the dogs, destroying those not able to reach the desirable speeds, and discarding those whose racing days are over. Greyhound rescue centres, where they exist, are always full – although in some countries, such as Spain, the 'problem' is solved by hanging the dogs from trees. Innocent-seeming leisure pursuits, like pony riding and the keeping of pets, can be occasions for unintended cruelty, where gregarious animals are kept in isolation or in too-small pens or hutches. Inhibiting animals' natural patterns of behaviour can be an abuse of the 'integrity of creation' and the principle of proportionality might be brought into the account. Is the harm done to the animal so outweighed by the benefits to the human that it is positively *right* to do it, or does the principle articulated in n. 1756 of the CCC apply here, that 'one may not do evil so that good may result from it'?

What seems to be *excluded* in the context here of domesticating animals, is the 'right' of man to hunt wild animals as a leisure pursuit. This is despite Aquinas's acceptance of it, drawing on Aristotle, when he claims that 'It is in keeping with the order of nature that man should be master over animals, hence the Philosopher says[28] that the hunting of wild animals is just and natural, because man thereby exercises a natural right.'[29] Hunting animals for food when that is the only source of nutrition available is dealt with in the section above. Hunting for pleasure does not seem to be offered any justification in the CCC. Hunting practices evolved into stylized arena displays, such as bullfighting, seem to fit into this category of exclusion from legitimacy, as Pius V's 1567 Bull *De Salute Gregis* indicates (as mentioned in chapter five). Now these and similar practices are protected by European community law as 'traditional cultural pursuits'. Traditional and ethnic cultural identity is also used to support the continuation of practices involving the scapegoating and killing of animals in quasi-religious 'fiestas'. The cruelty and blood-lust encouraged by these, and similar, customs have hampered the work of animal protection agencies in these societies, and the late Pope John Paul II presented the unedifying sight of giving audiences to matadors. In relation to this clause in the CCC, as Dr Hendrickx again so eloquently expresses: 'Does the right to use animals for our leisure mean the right to stab bulls with *banderillas* after tormenting them at length? Does it mean letting horses be disembowelled? Does it mean throwing cats or goats from the top of bell towers?'[30]

2417:4. Medical and scientific experimentation on animals is a morally acceptable practice if it remains within reasonable limits and contributes to caring for or saving human lives[31]

In the original 1994 English edition of the CCC the last sentence of this paragraph read:

> Medical and scientific experimentation on animals, if it remains within reasonable limits, is a morally acceptable practice since it contributes to caring for or saving human lives.

The sentence, which 'provoked violent protests to the point that the Catholic position was accused of supporting vivisection'[32] was altered in the changes made for the revised translation of 1997. It now reads as above (in bold).

Is there an appreciable difference? The 'since' – meaning 'it is axiomatic that'– has been replaced by an 'if', that is, 'on condition that'. That does shift the ground considerably. It does not remove support for vivisection, but it does throw the emphasis onto the experimenters to prove that their actions are not only reasonable but also seriously useful. As Hendrickx explains, credit is now no longer allowed

> *a priori* to medical and scientific experimentation on animals 'to care for or to save human lives' and thus to be morally acceptable practices. Before experiments can be legitimately carried out, their usefulness must be shown. The admission that experimentation on animals is not morally licit except for its usefulness to man presupposes that an effort of discernment has been made to consider it as such. It can therefore be said with perfect logic that the Catechism has also clearly indicated the criteria for a sound and sensible reflection on how one should treat animals: 'It is contrary to human dignity to cause animals to suffer or die needlessly.' (n. 2418)[33]

'Within reasonable limits' is an unquantifiable term. What is reasonable to one may be beyond the pale to another. Can 'reasonable' include the deliberate infliction of suffering? At least the principle is established that there should be restrictions of some sort and that vivisectors are not being offered carte blanche. However restricted, many of the problems facing Catholic bioethicists today (embryonic cloning, genetic manipulation and 'designer babies', for example) would not have arisen if the experiments had not been practised at first on animals. There is also a long and documented catalogue of pharmaceutical products which have been tested on animals but which result in human beings suffering unanticipated negative reactions, many fatal.[34] Even if every experiment were successful and beneficial to humanity, the point is whether the human benefits exceed the costs to the animals involved, as John Berkman notes. Berkman is an eminent Catholic academic ethicist in the USA, who was converted to the cause of antivivisection by the books of Stephen R. L. Clark. He, Berkman, suggests that objectors to animal experimentation must never argue against it 'on the grounds that it has not been shown that there are sufficiently useful benefits. For once those who are concerned for animals argue in this way, they concede that vivisection is automatically acceptable if the benefits are shown to be great enough'.[35] Can the value of the lives of so-many monkeys or mice be weighed against the value of a cleaning product? There is also the quality of life for animals in laboratories to be considered, as they often exist in conditions which would be illegal for the keeping of pet animals.

The basic question is whether we have the moral right to inflict suffering on animals for our own ends. How can we apply here the principle of n. 1756 of the CCC, that 'one may not do evil so that good may result from it'? As mentioned in chapter five, the nineteenth-century Cardinal Manning was in no doubt:

> I do not believe [vivisection] to be the way that the All-wise and All-good Maker of us all has ordained for the discovery of the healing art which is one of His greatest gifts to man.[36]

Andrew Linzey gives three theological reasons why the use of animals in experiments is unethical:[37] one, that animals are not expendable for humans, they are God's creatures and hence have value in themselves, and we are responsible for them; two, that animals are not instrumental to humans, we are accountable to God for them; and three, that the Christ-like example of sacrifice is for the 'higher' to be sacrificed for the 'lower', which would exclude the sacrifice of animals for humans in experiments. Scientists and others who sometimes talk of 'sacrificing' animals for human good are misusing the term which, for Christians, involves a freely offered gift of self, and 'Animals, of course, cannot give their consent to scientific procedures performed upon them.'[38]

As for human choice, while there are demands for the right to choose to receive drugs or procedures which have been previously tested on animals, as Linzey points out,[39] there is no option for people using public health services who do *not* want to use drugs, et cetera, which have been so tested. They are, in fact, denied the right to choose and if they were, the adjustments necessary to providing alternative resources for experiments by the health services would quickly bring radical change. Alternative resources are constantly being discovered and provided by humane institutions (such as the Dr Hadwen Trust), but these are not nearly so well funded as those presently relying on animals.

Christian apologist C. S. Lewis is emphatic in his view of the effect of vivisection on desensitizing society: 'The victory of vivisection marks a great advance in the triumph of ruthless, non-moral utilitarianism over the old world of ethical law.'[40] As Berkman reminds us, 'If we are a people of peace, a people committed to trying to bring nearer the advent of the kingdom of God, then we will be a people not eager to shed the blood of our fellow creatures.'[41] Causing deliberate suffering, even if the ends are considered 'good', can never be justified, as cruelty is in itself a reprehensible act and, in the words of Lamartine, 'Cruelty is the same whether it is towards man or animal: only the victim is different.'[42] Aquinas is quoted in *Veritatis Splendor*

n. 80 as declaring 'No evil done with a good intention can be excused' and that encyclical explains that 'there are kinds of behaviour which can never, in any situation, be a proper response – a response which is in conformity with the dignity of the person' (CCC n. 52). The following paragraph in the CCC describes one act as contrary to the dignity of the person being 'to cause animals to suffer or to die needlessly'. There are certain acts which are 'incapable of being ordered' to God, termed 'intrinsically evil', always such, 'quite apart from the ulterior intentions of the one acting and the circumstances' (CCC n. 80). Mortal sin is described as existing when a choice is made which is 'gravely disordered', and such a choice 'already includes contempt for the divine law, a rejection of God's love for humanity and the whole of creation (CCC n. 70). Medical and scientific experimentation on animals, other than for their own good, can be considered gravely disordered acts, whatever the intention of the practitioners.

Notes

1 *The New Jerome Biblical Commentary*, edited by Raymond E. Brown et al (London: Geoffrey Chapman, 1989, 1991), p. 16.

2 Christopher Southgate, *God, Humanity and the Cosmos: a textbook in science and religion*, edited by C. Southgate et al., Book Two, 'Theology and the New Physics'. (Edinburgh: T&T Clark, 1999), p. 168. There is a useful history of the exegesis of the 'image of God' text in Claus Westmann's commentary, *Genesis 1–11*, Lodon: SPCK, 1974 (German), 1984 (English), pp. 147ff.

3 Robert Murray, *The Cosmic Covenant* (London: Sheed and Ward, 1992).

4 Stanley Hauerwas and John Berkman, 'The Chief End of All Flesh', *Theology Today* 49.2.

5 Ibid., p. 205. Claus Westmann also subscribes to the 'royal' interpretation, in his case particularly of the association of the term רדה (radah) being used of the dominion of a king in 1 Kings 5:4, see his *Genesis 1–11*, Lodon: SPCK, 1974 (German), 1984 (English), p. 159.

6 Millard Schumaker, *Appreciating our Good Earth: towards a pertinent theology of nature* (Kingston, Ont.: Queen's Theological College) 1980, p. 12, cited in Hauerwas and Berkman, 'The Chief End of All Flesh', p. 205.

7 Schumaker, cited in Hauerwas and Berkman, 'The Chief End of All Flesh', p. 205.

8   Robert Murray, *The Cosmic Covenant*, p. 98.

9   Ibid., p. 100.

10 For example, Matthew 24:45–51; Luke 12:42–6; 16:1–8.

11 Alexander Pope, 'Of Cruelty to Animals', *A Hundred English Essays*, edited by R. Vallance (London: Thos. Nelson & Sons, 1950), p. 159.

12 De Civ. Dei I, 20, cited in Aquinas *Summa Theologiae*, II-II, Q. 64, Art. 1 'On the Contrary'.

13 Stephen R. L. Clark, *The Moral Status of Animals* (Oxford: Clarendon Press, 1997), p. 15.

14 Andrew Tardiff, 'A Catholic Case for Vegetarianism', *Faith and Philosophy*, 15.2 (1998), pp. 210–22.

15 *Evangelii Nuntiandi*, 22.

16 *Athanasius: the Life of Antony*, translated by R. C. Gregg (New York: Paulist Press, 1980), p. 36.

17 *St Ambrose*, translated by J. J. Savage (New York: Fathers of the Church, Inc., 1961), p. 88.

18 Michael Northcott, 'Soil, Stewardship and Spirit in the Era of Chemical Agriculture', *Environmental Stewardship*, edited by R. J. Berry (T&T Clark International, 2006), p. 217. See also K. Eder, *The Social Construction of Nature* (London: Sage,1996), p. 58, n. 96, p. 99.

19 S. H. Webb, 'Whatever Happened to the Sin of Gluttony? Or, Why Christians do not serve meat with the Eucharist', *Encounter*, (Summer 1997), p. 243ff.

20 S. H. Webb, 'Whatever Happened to the Sin of Gluttony?, p. 243ff.

21 Marie Hendrickx, 'For a More Just Relationship with Animals', *L'Osservatore Romano* (December 2000, also 24 January 2001).

22 Joseph Ratzinger, *God and the World: a conversation with Peter Seewald*, translated by Henry Taylor (San Francisco: Ignatius Press, 2002), p. 78.

23 Ibid., p. 79.

24 Bishop Mario Conti, Speech to the Scottish Order of Christian Unity, 23 August 2001, *Briefing*, 31. 11 (16 November 2001), p. 17.

25 M. Arbogast, 'Fur, Conscience and Native Economies', *The Witness*, 76.10 (October 1993), p. 25.

26 Ibid., p.25.

27 Marie Hendrickx, 'For a More Just Relationship with Animals'.

28 Aristotle, *Politics* 1,5.

29 Aquinas, *Summa Theologiae*. P.I,Q.96, Art 1.

30 Marie Hendrickx, 'For a More Just Relationship with Animals'.

31 A previous paragraph in the CCC, n. 2293, considers that 'Basic scientific research, as well as applied research, is a significant expression of man's dominion over creation', which is 'placed at the service of man'. This is the perspective in which animals are to be fitted.

32 Marie Hendrickx, 'For a More Just Relationship with Animals', *L'Osser-*

vatore Romano (December 2000, also 24 January 2001).

33 Marie Hendrickx, 'For a More Just Relationship with Animals'.

34 For example, the British Anti-Vivisection Association film 'Bad Medicine: the human cost of animal experiments'; *Clinical Medical Discoveries*, by M. Beddow Bayly (London: National Anti-Vivisection Society, 1961*); Vivisection Unveiled: an expose of the medical futility of animal experimentation*, by Dr Tony Page (Charlbury, Oxon: Jon Carpenter, 1997), and many others.

35 John Berkman, 'Medicine, Animals and Theology', in *St Mark's Review* (Winter 1992), p. 32.

36 Cardinal Manning, 'Speeches against Vivisection', p. 48.

37 Andrew Linzey, *Animal Theology* (London: SCM Press, 1984), pp. 106–113.

38 Ibid., p. 111.

39 Andrew Linzey, 'Towards Ethical Science', Report of the International Animal Welfare Congress, Helsingborg (10 August 1996), p. 13.

40 C. S. Lewis, 'Vivisection' (1947), reprinted in *God in the Dock: essays on theology and ethics*, edited by Walter Hooper (Grand Rapids: Eerdmans, 1970), p. 228.

41 John Berkman, 'Medicine, Animals and Theology', in *St Mark's Review* (Winter 1992), p. 35.

42 Cited by Joanna Lumley, 'The Church Compassionate', in *Priests & People*, 16.7 (July 2002), p. 259.

Chapter Eleven

Paragraph 2418: Needless suffering

> n.2418. 1. It is contrary to human dignity to cause animals to suffer or die needlessly. 2. It is likewise unworthy to spend money on them that should as a priority go to the relief of human misery. 3. One can love animals; one should not direct to them the affection due only to persons.

This paragraph attempts to outline the practical applications of certain phrases in the first of these 'animal' paragraphs, n. 2415: how far 'man's dominion' and respect 'for the integrity of creation' and for 'moral imperatives' should go. It is summarized in the following quotation:

> In exercising his dominion, man must maintain concern for his neighbour's welfare, and respect for creation. He violates moral imperatives if he fails in either case. Spending money on animals when one's neighbours are suffering is a violation of the first. Causing animals to suffer or die needlessly is a violation of the second. Both are morally objectionable.[1]

2418:1. It is contrary to human dignity to cause animals to suffer or die needlessly

Depending on the meaning given, this sentence has radical implications. As with 'reasonable' in the previous paragraph, this hinges on the interpretation of 'needlessly'. If 'needless' simply means 'serves no purpose' then *any* purpose could be given to justify causing animals to suffer or die, for example, 'because I enjoy watching animals die, so my pleasure is a purpose for which it would be legitimate to kill them'. But this cannot be what the CCC means by 'needlessly'. In the principle of proportionality, as the Jesuit ethicist Thomas Higgins explains: 'There must be a proportionately grave reason for placing the act and permitting the evil effect. It would not be reasonable to allow a grave evil for a relatively insignificant good.'[2] To balance the taking of the life of one of God's creatures the resultant 'good' would have to be of significant gravity – mere taste, pleasure, financial gain, cultural conformity, and so on, are lightweight ends which could not suffice. If 'serving a purpose' was the meaning under which every deliberate animal death or cause of suffering was administered, then each act would have to be judged according to the quality of purpose, which would be of enormous complication and complexity. King Lear's exasperated cry: 'O! reason not the need'[3] comes to mind.

If, however, the meaning of 'needlessly' is 'that which cannot be avoided' then a different conclusion emerges. It would be legitimate to kill in self-defence if it could not be avoided (for example, when being attacked by a lion); to kill for food if no alternatives were available (for example, in conditions of extreme conflict or privation); to cause to suffer the pulling of ploughs or carts where tractors and motorized vehicles are unavailable or beyond the financial means, et cetera. This is the reading of 'needlessly' shared by Dr Hendrickx:

> ... we must repeat with the Catechism that man is not justified in 'causing animals to suffer needlessly'. He should therefore refrain from doing so *if he can avoid it*, or if there are no *serious* reasons for doing so. (My emphases)[4]

Thus would the conditions given in n. 2417 be limited in the spirit of n. 2416 where we must be actually *kind* to animals, and elsewhere. In n. 373, for example, the CCC talks of our stewardship of creation as 'not to be an arbitrary and destructive domination' but rather as images of the Creator 'who loves everything that exists ... to share in his providence towards other creatures'. Killing and causing animals to suffer needlessly *is* arbitrary and destructive and the 'image of God' language is a link to the first part of the sentence, referring to 'human dignity'.

The CCC does not say that causing needless suffering and death to animals is 'gravely wrong', or 'sinful', but 'contrary to human dignity'. The specific dignity of human persons is not in their possession of one quality or another, for ethologists today are finding that certain animals are far closer to humans in their abilities than they were ever thought to have been, and geneticists are finding that their DNA is surprisingly close and similar too. Human dignity consists in mankind having been made in the 'image' and 'likeness' of God, with a freedom of action and responsibility for creation given to no other creature (see also the discussion under n. 2415). 'If our dignity is to be like God, it follows that the more we behave like God, the more we are ourselves ...'[5] The reference to human dignity is echoed in the next sentence with 'likewise unworthy'. We are being offered the ideal, what it means to be a human person, with the worth and dignity accorded to the species both made in the image of God and having Jesus Christ as the 'first born' of the new humanity. All the choices made by human persons must bear this responsibility and high duty in mind – that we are to emulate the Son of the Most High, and not sanction unworthy choices which involve the destruction and suffering of the creatures given us in trust.

2418:2. It is likewise unworthy to spend money on them that should as a priority go to the relief of human misery

According to Aidan Nichols, OP, while kindness is owed to animals 'as their due' 'The relief of human misery always takes precedence over animal welfare: this is how the authors [of CCC] interpret, with the entire Judaeo-Christian tradition, the Genesis entrustment of animals to the stewardship of those, namely human beings, God created in his own image.' He goes on to qualify the limits of the precedence granted by quoting the previous phrase here: 'It is the *needless* [his emphasis] suffering or death of animals that the seventh commandment forbids as theft of the creation's riches.'[6]

As we have seen with the previous sentence, the priority of the relief of human misery is to be proportionate to the spending of money on animals. It cannot be the case that every single human being has to be declared thoroughly happy before even a penny is spent on the relief of suffering animals, or our duty of kindness would not be discharged. Arguably, the basic needs of people must take priority over the less essential needs of animals, but the basic needs of animals must take priority over the lesser needs of people, otherwise they would be suffering 'needlessly', without proportionate reason. For that we have seen that it is legitimate to kill for basic needs (the preservation of life), but not for lesser ones. On the other hand, if the logic of Christian 'lordship' is best expressed in *service*[7] then it follows that human service to other creatures requires that one must give sacrificially to preserve the interests of creatures other than ourselves in creation.

2418:3. One can love animals; one should not direct to them the affection due only to persons

The statement 'One can love animals' cannot be read in isolation from the next clause which largely vitiates it. However, it certainly improves on Aquinas's restrictions on the possibility of loving animals: he goes so far as accepting that we *can* love animals 'out of charity', but only if we regard them as 'good things' that we wish others to have, and we do so 'for God's honour and man's service'.[8] Aquinas's view of love is that it is expressed in friendship only among those with whom one shares fellowship. As it is not possible to share fellowship with irrational creatures, it is not possible to love them. In the *Summa Theologiae* 33 Q.25, we find a similar argument denying that animals can be our friends, because 'we will the good of our friend' and we cannot will good to irrational creatures. We cannot do this because they would not be competent to possess good things: possession depending on the ability of rational beings to exercise free will in using things and so being master of them. Another basic stop on our having the 'friendship of charity' towards an animal is grounded on the inability, in Aquinas's reckoning, of animals in sharing eternal life. The image of God, which is possessed fully by man, but only a trace of which is found in animals, confers this capacity. And this attribute is the basis of the 'fellowship of everlasting happiness' from which animals are obviously excluded, thereby excluding them from being the objects of either faith or charity.[9]

Of course, this Thomistic negation of the possibility of fellowship with animals is not shared by St Francis, whose sense of fellowship went even further, and acknowledged kinship. It is St Francis the CCC gives as the model (n. 2416) even if n. 2418 seems to give a limit to the relationship of man with fellow-creatures.

One Oxford Dominican scholar, the late Herbert McCabe, takes over the Thomistic view that lack of fellowship precludes the exercise of *justice* towards irrational animals, yet does apply another of Aquinas's favourite themes, the Virtues, to promote *kindness* to animals on the basis of their sentience. In the section of McCabe's own Catechism, under the cardinal virtue of temperance, he states that temperance is

> primarily exercised in respect of our attitude to our own pleasure in eating, and in sex. It is secondarily exercised in respect of our attitude to the suffering of others – thus it includes such dispositions as gentleness and compassion and we fail in it by callousness and by all delight in violence and cruelty.

The footnote after 'suffering of others' notes 'that this includes all God's creatures that are capable of suffering, not simply human beings'. Unfortunately, he goes on to state, following Aquinas: 'We cannot exercise the virtue of justice towards irrational animals for they are not, even potentially, fellow citizens either of secular society or of the Kingdom of God.' This denial of the virtue of justice to animals underpins the moral indifferentism of many Thomists towards animal creation. However, McCabe modifies it here by continuing: 'but we must exercise the virtues of gentleness and compassion towards them because they are fellow sentient beings'.[10] Temperance is the only one of the four cardinal virtues (the others being prudence, justice, and fortitude) 'whose practice is restricted to rational creatures that are simultaneously animals with bodily needs and appetites',[11] despite CCC dealing with all four of them under the heading 'The Human Virtues' (n. 1804ff).

The Latin of the CCC indicates that the love towards animals (*amare*) is to be expressed qualitatively differently from that directed (*affectio*) towards people. It may be taken to mean that *affection* should not be shown towards animals as it is behaviour appropriate only between people. It rather suggests that the writers of the CCC consider the human capacity to feel affection or love might 'run out' if directed towards animals, with none left for people. A theology is impoverished which can so limit love or fail to see the value of a loving relationship with animals. The fact is that most animal lovers are also active in causes which protect vulnerable human beings as well. Whereas, on the contrary, there is a wealth of evidence proving the link between abuse of animals and the abuse of children and domestic violence. In the materials for a conference on the relationship between animal abuse and human violence in Oxford, 2007, Professor Frank Ascione of Utah State University, USA, writes:

> Since the publication of the landmark case studies of animal abuse conducted by Fernando Tapia in 1971, a significant body of empirical research and conceptual analyses has emerged

linking animal abuse with various forms of interpersonal violence. The strongest links have been documented in cases where interpersonal violence takes the form of child maltreatment and intimate partner violence.

On the other hand, the CCC writers may be considering the distorted media image of animals in the West. A great amount of money is spent on exploiting a human emotion which can be detached from the reality of animals' lives and needs. This can lead to an extravagant misuse of money and resources. Sometimes the victims of over-sentimental attitudes can be the very animals their owners 'love'. These animals' natural instincts and physical needs may be thwarted by people in indulging their own needs. However, it is unlikely that the writers of the CCC had the welfare of animals in mind in this clause.

Some British Catholic clergy indicate a reluctance to tolerate demonstrations of affection towards animals. In a letter, reported in *The Ark*, the then Archbishop of Cardiff, Michael McGrath, congratulates the Catholic Church on 'reproving alike excessive fondness of and cruelty towards God's creatures, and pointing out that animals are neither to be fondled like little children nor abused as slaves were in former days'.[12] In the same issue of *The Ark* is a statement of a Monsignor Duchemin who, while declaring: 'so wonderful are the living creatures made by God for our use', suggests that people should be saved 'from the two excesses, thoughtless ill-treatment, and sentimental pampering of animals'. One of the founding members of the Catholic Study Circle for Animal Welfare, Dom Ambrose Agius, quoted, in a pamphlet on cruelty to animals, Cardinal Donnet,[13] who used words almost identical with those of this CCC passage: 'heaping excessive affection on animals and bestowing on them what has been denied to our fellow-men'. For Fr Agius, it was for the animals' own welfare that he was concerned, when animal lovers 'are sometimes cruel in their kindness, destroying the health and fine instincts of their animal companions by excessive pampering'.[14] (The attitudes of Catholic clergy towards animals will be examined in chapter twelve.)

Stephen Clark observes that 'there is a long tradition in the West which looks askance at animals, and zoophiles', considering the latter to be sentimentalists 'averse to proper human relationship'.[15] There is a tradition he points to which despises those concerned for animals and their environment 'because these represent our merely material natures, [and] we should not care much for our own material comforts'. A form of asceticism may be one element, the privileging of the spiritual over the material, and the elevation of the intellectual over the emotional.

This anti-material tradition was given impetus by the rise, in the Middle Ages (as we have seen in chapter three), of the academic theologians who increasingly dominated the intellectual life of the Church. Their form of analytic or deductive reasoning displaced other more intuitive or spiritual forms of reasoning and was defined by the possession of the faculty possessed exclusively by human beings.[16] Thus were animals – and the physical, emotional, bodily dimensions of life – distanced yet further from the concerns of influential Christians up to, and including, the present day. Certainly, anecdotal reports of the life and regimes of seminaries indicate that there has been a reluctance, to say the least, to give emotional development the same attention as the intellectual. Creation as a whole has been neglected in the theology of the last few centuries, partly because, according to Cardinal Ratzinger, 'it seemed a question devoid of concrete anthropological importance', or, 'At best it has been discussed as a detail of a current issue: the compatibility of creation and evolution.'[17] Maybe with the recovery of the sense of importance of creation and the material world in Catholic theology, there will be a more positive attitude developed towards it which will encompass the value of healthy emotional fellowship with all of God's creatures.

Compendium and Conclusion

The CCC gives testimony to the high dignity and calling of human beings to lead lives of holiness, and offers saints, such as Francis of Assisi and Philip Neri, as models (n. 2416). In their lives we see how holiness has helped to overcome the divisions not only between people and people, but also between people and nature, people and animals. In the words of Dr Hendrickx:

> For if holiness leads to reconciliation with nature, it is proba-
> ble that reconciliation with nature, properly understood,
> fosters in turn better relations with God. Or, if the right rela-
> tionship with God makes people just to others and kind to
> animals, kindness to animals could in turn reawaken senti-
> ments of admiration and praise in the human heart for the
> great work of the Creator of the universe.[18]

On 11 October 2002, on the tenth anniversary of its publica-
tion, John Paul II describes the CCC as a 'choice gift for all the faithful'. The Pope refers to the Catechism as,

> a complete and integral exposition of the Catholic truth, of the
> doctrine both of the faith as well as customs, valid always and
> for all, with its essential and fundamental contents, which
> enables one to know and study in-depth in a positive and
> peaceful manner what the Church believes, celebrates, lives
> and prays.[19]

In 2006, an official *Compendium* of the CCC was published,[20] having been drafted by a commission under the directorship of the then Prefect of the Congregation for the Doctrine of the Faith, Cardinal Ratzinger. Of the 598 paragraphs in it summa-
rizing key elements of CCC in traditional dialogical form, there is one paragraph relating to animals. This paragraph, n. 507, is presented in the appropriate seventh commandment section, under the question-heading: What attitude should people have towards animals? It answers it in one sentence:

> People must treat animals with kindness as creatures of God
> and avoid both excessive love for them and an indiscriminate
> use of them especially by scientific experiments that go
> beyond reasonable limits and entail needless suffering for the
> animals.

It is interesting that the commission and those whom they
consulted consider that the three main concerns of the CCC
paragraphs are

1. the treatment of animals with kindness;
2. the abuse of 'excessive love for them'; and
3. the inflammatory question of vivisection.

The first clause, 'People must treat animals with kindness as
creatures of God', is highly significant, suggestive of the
acceptance of a God-centred rather than anthropocentric,
theological approach. The second, about avoiding 'excessive
love for them', is questionable, as nowhere is the definition of
what constitutes 'excessive' love, and by whom, and it seems
to be a waste of the limited opportunity to develop the
Church's consideration of this issue. The third and lengthier
section, about avoiding 'an indiscriminate use of them especially by scientific experiments that go beyond reasonable
limits and entail needless suffering for the animals', brings in
a new third subjective term 'indiscriminate', to join 'reasonable' and 'needless'. However vague and imprecise it is, at
least this phrase takes further the thrust of the change in
wording between the two English editions of the CCC. The
impetus is now even more on the vivisectors to justify their
use of animals, and they have nothing here about 'caring for
or saving human lives' to fall back on. Perhaps at last the attention is turning towards consideration of animals in their own
right, and the Church is beginning to accept a humane animal
theology.

However, the authors of the *Compendium* are adamant that
it is not intended in any way to replace the CCC. It is the
reception of the CCC by large numbers of the 'faithful' that

ultimately matters. That reception has, naturally in the light of the presentation of the teachings in it, been mixed. Catholics who accept any publication from the Vatican unreservedly have welcomed it in every regard, while the views of others 'have ranged from serious caveats to shrill alarms'.[21] The 'animal' paragraphs have elicited strongly negative responses from animal rights advocates, some referring to them as the 'satanic verses'.[22] Some, indeed, have left the Church, including the 83–year-old Virginia Bourquardez, founder of the US-based International Network for Religion and Animals, 'after devoting a lifetime to bringing these two entities together ... because she could no longer support [the Church's] teachings about animals'.[23] However, how the general Catholic population in Britain understands them is the subject of the following chapter, so that the matter of reception will be dealt with there.

Notes

1 Andrew Tardiff, 'A Catholic Case for Vegetarianism', *Faith and Philosophy*, 15.2 (1998), p. 220.
2 Thomas J. Higgins, 'Man as Man: the science and art of ethics', (Milwaukee: The Bruce Publishing Co.), p. 76; cited in Andrew Tardiff, 'A Catholic Case for Vegetarianism', p. 212.
3 Shakespeare, *King Lear*, Act II, sc.iv, line 267.
4 Marie Hendrickx, 'For a More Just Relationship with Animals', *L'Osservatore Romano* (December 2000, also 24 January 2001).
5 Marie Hendrickx, 'For a More Just Relationship with Animals'.
6 Aidan Nichols, *The Service of Glory* (Edinburgh: T&T Clark, 1997), p. 216.
7 Luke 22:27.
8 Aquinas, *Summa Theologiae*. 1 Q.64:1.
9 Ibid.
10 Herbert McCabe, *The teaching of the Catholic Church: a new catechism of Christian doctrine* (London: Darton, Longman and Todd, 1985), p. 71.
11 Aidan Nichols, *The Service of Glory* (Edinburgh: T&T Clark, 1997), p. 231.
12 *The Ark*, 16 (July 1942), p. 28.
13 See this text, chapter one.

14 Ambrose Agius, *Cruelty to Animals* (London: Catholic Truth Society, 1960), p. 1.

15 Stephen R. L. Clark, *How to think about the Earth: philosophical and theological models for ecology* (London: Continuum International–Mowbray, 1993), p. 110.

16 Andrew Linzey, *Animal Rites: liturgies of animal care* (London: SCM, 1999), p. 8.

17 Joseph Cardinal Ratzinger, *'In the Beginning': a Catholic understanding of the story of creation and the fall* (Edinburgh: T& T Clark, 1990), p. 80.

18 Marie Hendrickx, 'For a More Just Relationship with Animals', *L'Osservatore Romano* (December 2000, also 24 January 2001).

19 Vatican internet news agency, < http://www.zenit.org/ >, 13 October 2002.

20 In the UK, by the Catholic Truth Society.

21 Stephen F. Brett, 'Reception and the Catechism', *The Homiletic and Pastoral Review* (October 1994), p. 4.

22 One Italian organization, the '4th Order of Franciscans' wrote a strongly worded letter of protest to the Pope saying that 'Catholics have been betrayed' and writing an article, translated with the title 'Satan has breached the Vatican'. *The Ark*, 167 (winter 1992), p. 9ff.

23 Evelyn Elkin Giefer, 'Religion and Animal Rights', *Mainstream* 27.1 (spring 1996), p. 15.

Part Three

Building The School Of Compassion

Chapter Twelve

Key issues and responses

As the previous two parts have demonstrated, any coherent Catholic theology of animals, or ethical consistency as to their treatment, is highly elusive. By limiting the community of 'persons' to rational human beings – and yet, as Pope John Paul II wrote in his pre-papal days, 'We would hesitate to call an animal ... a "thing",'[1] – the status of animals is left floating, as it were, with little to moor it. This leaves the question of their treatment equally undefined. Unlike so much else that is in the repertoire of the Church's moral laws, where the teaching is clear and unambiguous – such as in human reproductive and sexual ethics – this is one area in which no definition exists.

For example, the Church has not declared that a universal and unchanging moral norm governs any particular action in connection with the treatment of animals. Nor is there any official recommendation that moral virtue attends those who adopt or eschew particular practices. Yet there are Christians, and Catholics among them, who feel passionately that certain acts concerning animals, such as eating them, or using them for experimentation, are either highly sinful or, contrarily, entirely virtuous. Neither proponents are helped by the ambiguities in the CCC, whereby the CCC proposes the duty of kindness to animals (n.2416), but gives no suggestions as to the limits of the nature of the food and clothing for which it is legitimate to use them (n.2417). Medical and scientific experimentation on animals is 'morally acceptable' providing it 'remains within reasonable limits' (n. 2417), but it does not suggest what is 'reasonable'. Also the causing of animals 'to suffer or die needlessly' is condemned as 'contrary to human dignity' (n. 2418) but no definition is given of what could be construed as 'needless'.

Even if teaching were clear, reception by the Faithful, the body of the Church, cannot be speedily or easily guaranteed. Such was the case of the Nicene creed, which took fifty-six years from the time of its promulgation before it could be said to have been 'received' by the universal Church. With any new teaching, if it were to have any impact at all, and were it to begin

> to affect the practice of the faith, a new synthesis of under-
> standing and practice of the faith is initiated. Since this
> threatens the equilibrium of the community's self-understand-
> ing, it may cause a serious negative reaction in some quarters.
> Elsewhere, the good may be immunized by a superficial adap-
> tation.[2]

There can be no doubt that an official church teaching requir-ing kindness to animals – one that goes beyond the platitudinous, is clearly defined, and well-grounded theologic-ally – would seriously 'threaten the equilibrium of the community's self-understanding' and cause 'serious negative reaction' in many quarters – not least among those who earn their living in the meat and fur trades and in much of the leisure industry, not to mention the consumers of meat and fur and the many participants in those leisure pursuits which can be shown to be harmful to the interests of animals.

Yet reception of a teaching is as vital a part of the process of transmission of Catholic teaching as is the pronouncement of it.[3] Technically, the term is taken to mean, as Congar describes, 'the process by means of which a church (body) truly takes over as its own a resolution that it did not originate in regard to its self [sic], and acknowledges the measure it promulgates as a rule applicable to its own life'.[4] Examples include the acceptance by the pope of measures or resolutions put forward by the bishops, particularly in Council; also of the local churches (that is, national or diocesan) to the teaching of a Council; or the degree of ecumenical consensus arrived at by dialogue between Churches.[5]

Reception is therefore part of the process which originates elsewhere than with the receiver, or 'bearer of reception',[6] so that reception itself does not legitimize any teachings or conciliar decrees: 'they obtain their legitimisation and their obligatory value from the authorities who have supported them'.[7] This causes particular difficulty when there are various authorities each supporting differing views and where the teaching obliges the receiver to exercise personal judgement with no clear guidance, as in the case under discussion.

Within this heterogeneity, what is the 'ordinary' Catholic to think? How, in other words, has the 'ordinary' Catholic received the various messages from the teaching tradition about the status and treatment of animals?

Research in the UK[8] produced some interesting evidence of deep confusion by practising Catholics on the matter, reflecting the ambiguity of the teaching in the *Catechism of the Catholic Church* itself. Apart from numerous correspondents, a dozen people were interviewed in depth. None of the interviewees displayed knowledge of any church teaching about animals and their welfare. None had ever heard a homily on the subject, or given one, although most had heard of animal-blessing services. From the interviewees, two general groups emerged. One group of four could be labelled the 'positives' (those more sympathetic to animals), composed, as it happens, all of women and all of whom were converts from Anglicanism to Catholicism. Another group was those called the 'negatives' (those less sympathetic to animals), with some others falling into a 'grey' area. A subgroup within the 'negatives' comprised the three priests interviewed.

Issues raised by participants in the research will be dealt with shortly, but one particular question intrigued many of the 'positive' group. That is, how any Christian, caring person is able to hunt and kill animals, experiment on them and eat

them, use their fur, and so on, without a qualm. It seems as if
people are able to switch off a compassionate, caring impulse
when it comes to animals. The 'switch' is, it appears, a neuro-
physical reality situated in the hypothalamus of the brain of all
social animals, including humans. According to the Norwegian
biologist Bergjlot Børresen[9] there are only two positions of
the switch, 'on' and 'off'. In the 'on' position the whole spectrum of social emotions is at the disposal of the individual. In
the 'off' position, those emotions are not available. There are
times, for example, when hunting food-prey, when the 'off'
position is most effective – enabling calm attention, concentration and an analytical approach, and disabling any potential
pity or concern for the prey itself. When mutual co-operation
is needed or, conversely, fierce aggression, the switch is
turned 'on' and emotions come into play, for friendship or
fighting. After several hundred thousand years of hunting,
taming and herding animals, people have developed the
ability to turn the switch on and off appropriately for their
needs. As with all other social animals, we are able to see an
individual animal as either 'one of us' (switch 'on' for our own
pets) or 'one of them' (switch off to kill, or simply buy and
cook, an animal not our own). In this post-Enlightenment
period, emotional detachment has become a scientific virtue,
which enables vivisectors to do what they do. Whereas in
previous ages, small family farms induced a certain relationship to exist between humans and their animals, now
production animals in factory farms are treated with the 'off'
position switch at all times. The animals too have minimal or
no contact with humans, so keeping their own switches
turned 'off'. As Børresen says, the 'species barrier becomes
impenetrable'.

The research indicates that there is little consensus among
'ordinary' British Catholics about what constitutes Roman
Catholic teaching on animals. So in Part Three some of the
themes and principles which arose in the previous chapters
will be revisited and a theology which is both Catholic and
respectful of animal creation, a 'school of compassion', will be

outlined. To be Catholic requires that there is no radical discontinuity between this theology and elements of traditional theology – so there is nothing absolutely 'new' in content, only in new approaches and new emphases.

Three themes to be explored in this chapter are stewardship, anthropocentricity and gender. In chapter thirteen a range of ethical theories, both Christian and secular, will be analysed, including the Virtues and animal rights. There will also be a brief mention of how a pro-animal theology could lead to the practical treatment of animals in different situations. In the last chapter there will be the outline of an animal theology which is both theocentric and which pays attention to 'theos-rights' of animals. The 'image of God', that has run like a motif through so much of Part Two, will then be seen in conjunction with the human role as priest of creation, particularly in the context of the Eucharist. This leads on to discuss the nature of charity, the Christ-like kenotic service towards other living beings in order to build up the Kingdom of God and direct all things to their proper end in the eternal Sabbath at the eschaton.

The core principle underlying CCC nn. 2415 to 2418, is that of anthropocentricity modified by a stewardship concept of care. The anthropocentricity will be looked at presently, but meanwhile, is the phrase 'God entrusted animals to the stewardship of those whom he created in his own image' (n. 2417) adequate to form a basis for a theology of animals? I suggest that it could be *part* of such a basis, but only if certain views of Aquinas are given weight. Stewardship as a concept has many inherent problems, but can point to a valuable source for a theology for animals.

Stewardship

The words of one of the optional prefaces for Sunday Eucharistic prayers (V) gives the purpose of the stewardship of creation as continuously to give praise for it: 'You made man the steward of creation, / to praise you day by day for the marvels of your wisdom and power / through Jesus Christ our Lord.'[10] Not a hint here of the instrumentalization of nature.

In the research, mentioned on page 203, of British Catholics in response to the paragraphs, there is an acceptance by them of stewardship as human care for the created world. Yet, despite its implication of minding the property belonging to another, the link between it and the theme of the Seventh Commandment, of which the four paragraphs under discussion are explanatory, was understood only tenuously. The Seventh Commandment prohibits theft, whereby abuse of God's creation must be a form of theft of what, in stewardship language, belongs to God. That would provide the groundwork for a sound theology of creation. However, the Catechism itself confuses the issue by stressing the theft element as relating to the common good of the human race, past, present and future. Only in n. 2416 where animals are designated as God's creatures, is the idea expressed of God being the true owner of creation.[11] Another source of confusion were the words 'religious respect' in n. 2415, indicative, perhaps, of the anthropocentric culture in which those researched live.

Anthropocentrism is, by definition, inimical to the theocentric premiss on which stewardship is based. A theocentric stewardship points to a concept of theos-rights (to be discussed later) wherein, as Alistair S. Gunn points out, the duty not to mistreat animals is actually owed to the absent ruler, God, and not to the animals themselves. Gunn notes that this is a specifically Christian concept, as 'the secularist does not have the appeal to divine authority which justifies the stewards's role'.[12] Gunn himself prefers the term 'trustees' to that of stewards, as trustees act self-sacrificially, 'in order to benefit future generations'. He tends to see trustee-type obligations to whole ecosystems as the best way of preserving and valuing all within nature, rather than supporting any 'liberal-independent' notion of rights for individual animals. This tension between ideas that support a holistic, ecosystem-based conservationism and those that support the value of the welfare and rights of individual members of sentient species is highly problematic and one that will re-emerge throughout this study.[13]

a) Objections to stewardship

There are several objections to the stewardship model as an adequate basis for a theology of creation or, specifically, of animals. There is the implicit yet untenable separation of human beings from nature, as stewards are 'other' than – and superior to – that over which they have care. This dualism gives the impression of the human being not only as something set apart from creation, but even as having an equivalence with the whole of the rest of creation. As it was this very sense of distance and difference, or hierarchy and dualism, that 'made manipulation, indeed exploitation, possible in the first place', the model has to be treated with care.[14] Rosemary Radford Ruether opposes stewardship's vertical-linear hierarchical view of creation as the same which 'has afforded ruling-class men unbridled license to exercise their "dominion" over all human and nonhuman forms of life', and 'is replicated in human relations, men over women, rich over poor, white over black, able-bodied over disabled, heterosexual over homosexual, and so on'.[15] Environmentalist Edward P. Echlin also acknowledges that stewardship 'lends itself to a detached and manipulative view of creation', while his main objection to it is practical, in that it 'has not moved hearts'; especially, he notes with regret, it has not moved the hearts of young people.[16] One reason for its motivational weakness in Christian discourse could be, as Clare Palmer observes, that 'the associations frequently made between the idea of "stewardship of nature" and the Bible are misplaced'. Not only is the term 'steward' never used in Scripture in association with nature, but the different understandings of the term render it unhelpful in that it allows existing attitudes of domination and triumphalism towards the rest of creation.[17]

One of the understandings of the term 'stewardship' for many years has been that of 'stewarding' the financial and

personnel resources of parishes and churches, with 'stewardship schemes' being concerned exclusively with personal
giving of money or time to the local church. In more recent
years the churches have begun to respond to the image of
stewardship in creation or environmental terms, but too late,
and too feebly, to create a major impact with the image.
Despite efforts to reinvigorate the term,[18] it has been too
weakly presented to be effective.

One reason for this is the inevitable implication, as Gunn
describes, of God as an 'absentee landlord'. This leads easily
to the negative view that 'absence' is only a short step away
from 'uncaring'. This in turn allows a 'carte-blanche' attitude
to prevail, which is, sadly, all too obviously one that has been
taken up enthusiastically by many people, both Christian and
atheist. There is however a more positive way of understanding God's non-interference, seeing it not as 'absence' so much
as a 'standing aside', as expressed by Moltmann, whereby God
'rests' from the work of his creation. This enables creation to
pursue its own ways while God is being fully receptive to it
and fully present in it.[19] However, this more positive approach
needs considerable development before it can overcome the
prevailing 'absent parent' or 'absent landlord' view.

b) Positive aspects of stewardship
On the other hand, and bearing in mind the difficulties with
the term, the stewardship metaphor can be supported, to a
point, by the reality that real stewards do not ruinously exploit
the materials for which they are responsible. One contemporary equivalent to a biblical 'steward' is John F. D. Hoy, Chief
Executive Officer for one of England's foremost stately
homes.[20] He comments that: 'Given my own circumstances
here at Blenheim, it is unrealistic to assume that my role as
CEO provides me with the ability to "take" Blenheim Palace
for my own use.'[21] Following that, another 'steward', or estate
manager,[22] states that, while the estate manager has responsibility for the goods and persons within his care, he does have
the right to a fair remuneration for his work. That would be

drawn from the estate, but would not ruinously deplete the resources of the estate – or else he would be soon out of a job![23] With God as owner of the estate – the planet itself – *God*'s purposes for creation, not the steward's, should prevail, even though the steward would be remunerated from the resources of the estate. This would arguably preclude many modern practices, from widespread destruction of habitats to factory farming, as depleting the gene-pool of resources and as damaging God's property. Were it truly understood that God alone owns animals, the concept in n. 2416 of their 'giving glory to God', so difficult for many people to comprehend, would find a more ready acceptance.

c) Aquinas revisited: stewardship as justice

Helpfully, there is a strand of Thomist teaching that supports the description of the Christian stewardship of creation. Willis Jenkins describes that, for Aquinas, 'stewardship is rooted in justice, which is itself an act of God's providential love, bringing creation to its perfection in God'.[24] Nature is not an end in itself, but leads and is led towards the divine goodness as the end of all things. In Aquinas' own words:

> So, therefore, in the parts of the universe also every creature exists for its own proper act and perfection ... whilst each and every creature exists for the sake of the universe. Furthermore, the entire universe, with all its parts, is ordained towards God as its end, inasmuch as it imitates, as it were, and shows forth the Divine goodness, to the glory of God ... Thus it is plain that Divine goodness is the end of all corporeal beings.[25]

The *telos* of each creature and the inter-relationality of all for the good of the whole exists for the glory of God, not, as n. 2415 insists, only as resources for human beings. Creation in its enormous diversity is 'Because His goodness could not be adequately represented by any one creature alone, [so] He produced many and diverse creatures, that what was wanting to one in the representation of the divine goodness could be supplied by another.'[26] Each creature is a representation of

God, an 'icon', Jenkins calls it, 'into the divine life'.[27] As it reflects the likeness of God, so it is the recipient of the love of God – expressing what is meant in the Catechism by n. 2416: 'Animals are God's creatures. He surrounds them with his providential care.' As expressed in the preface to Eucharistic Prayer IV: 'Source of life and goodness, you have created all things, / to fill your creatures with every blessing.'[28] Jenkins deduces from that, that 'to say, therefore, that creation is an instrument of grace is to refute the very idea of nature's instrumentality'. So as creatures enable us to appreciate God through their representation of God, and because none can do so adequately alone, it follows that the more creatures and the more species there are of everything, the better the representation of God, and the more the praise of God rises to heaven. As Eucharistic Prayer III notes, 'all creation rightly gives you praise'.[29] As Jenkins puts it:

> The more kinds of created things we see, the more modes of God's availability [there are] for us. Ecological diversity is a sort of adumbration of God ... Ecodiversity is the fertile ground of a multi-chorused praise of God. With the extinction of species and despoiling of places we lose the ability to name and praise God, and find ourselves with only the names derived from things made in our own image, the artifices of our own technology.

Stewardship therefore is not only in the practical responsibility for sustaining species and seeing to the flourishing of individuals, but it also has a liturgical aspect. As we

> demonstrate the love of God for every creature, so too is it our liturgical work to hold up and bless the natural love every creature has for God. Noting that every thing loves God in its own way, Thomas remembers that Dionysius said, 'God leads everything to love of Himself', and comments in response, 'Hence, in the state of perfect nature man referred the love of himself *and of all other things* to the love of God as to its end.[30]

This could be the ground upon which another aspect of the

current Eucharistic Prayer IV in the 1975 Roman Missal is built, where the worshipper is 'United with [the countless hosts of angels], And *in the name of every creature under heaven*, We too praise your glory ...'.[31]

(This liturgical aspect will be examined more thoroughly in chapter fourteen.)

Eco-thomistic stewardship, then, calls for a radical environmentalism, concerned with whole ecosystems and, to Jenkins, it :

> avoids the determination of anthropocentric, ecocentric or even theocentric, by showing the harmony of several centrisms: It is in our own best interests to be able to perfect our nature (anthropocentric) by seeking the knowledge of God through worship (theocentric), which we are best able to do by understanding the many different perfections of the cosmos and our particular place amongst them (ecocentric).

This widening of concern to embrace all living beings, all ecosystems, and the suggestion of a inclusiveness of centricities could well help towards creating a real paradigm shift in the attitude of the Church towards animals while at the same time being consistent with Catholic tradition.

d) Summary
Stewardship in its present understanding has proved to be a weak and inadequate model, with problematic elements suggestive of dualism and the 'absent landlord'. However it does establish certain positive principles:

1. that the Catholic Church is committed to care for creation;
2. that all creation is the property of God, not of the human race, as supported by paragraph 2416;
3. that, established in justice, stewardship shows that all creation has been designed for the glory of God and to fulfil the *telos* of each creature;
4. that the very diversity of creation enables the praise of God to be fuller and richer, and that the damaging or

destruction of any part of that diversity is to diminish the praises of God, and be a form of blasphemy.

Anthropocentrism

a) Current anthropocentrism

However, the key stumbling block to the development of any theology which pays real attention to the environment or to nonhuman creatures is the overarching anthropocentrism apparent in all of the relevant paragraphs in the CCC. It is an insistence upon the ontological otherness, the unbridgeable difference, between animals and human beings. From the Enlightenment's stress on rationalism in the eighteenth century to the horrified reaction to Darwinism in the nineteenth century, Christianity has erected a barrier between human beings and animals which can seem insuperable.

This is what is referred to by Albert Schweitzer in his 1918 sermon 'Reverence for Life':

> Christianity, from the first centuries up until deep in the Middle Ages, did not ennoble people in their behaviour towards animals. Throughout the centuries one finds the greatest thoughtlessness and crudeness bound together with the most earnest piety ... One thinks less about what we ought to be toward the poor creatures than again and again about how one can make the most *of the difference between man and them*: 'You have an immortal soul. The animal does not. An unbridgeable chasm lies between us', as if we really knew about it.[32]

Schweitzer's agnosticism about the immortality or otherwise of animals' souls is refreshing. If it is the case, and it is ultimately unknowable, that animals have no immortal soul, it is surely even more incumbent upon those creatures who do to ensure that the animals' brief life on earth is the most comfortable possible. As Humphry Primatt asks in 1834:

> [W]hat hope is there to support and comfort the brutes under

their affliction? . . . The present moment is an eternity to them.
All their happiness is in this life only . . . therefore, when they
are miserable, their misery is the more insupportable.[33]

However, while discussion of the immortality of individual
animal souls as if they were identical to human ones poses
problems,[34] it may be possible to borrow again from the
Eastern Church Fathers in developing the Thomist line of
approach whereby a divine *telos* for all creatures (animals, of
course, included) is granted. For the early sixth-century
Dionysius the Areopagite, 'all creatures are called to perfect
union with God'[35] as the initial state of creation was simply an
'unstable perfection' in which the fullness of union is not yet
achieved. For St Maximus,[36] who followed Dionysius' thought,
the *telos* of all creatures is outside themselves and something
towards which they all tend, to which they are all in a state of
'becoming'. Of course, that to which they are all tending is the
uncreated Godhead. Vladimir Lossky describes the Maximian
belief in the wholeness of creation as contained within the
Logos, the Second Person of the Holy Trinity, who is the first
principle and last end of *all* created things.[37] For the Eastern
Tradition, grace is not an 'add-on' to nature, but is implied in
the act of creation itself, as integral to creation. So it is grace
which impels creation towards its final goal, its deification.
Philaret of Moscow, Lossky relates, considers that nothing
proceeding from the word of God can pass away; nothing ultimately ceases. This expands the Pauline teaching in Romans
8:18–22, whereby the whole of creation is groaning in a stage
of becoming renewed. There is nothing in this of the annihi-
lation of non-human living creatures after death.

However, the 'difference' teaching continues to finds cham-
pions. This is demonstrated in a paper presented by the
President of the Pontifical Pro Vita Academy, Professor Juan de
Dios Vial Correa. In it, while revisiting the evolution debate,
he condemns 'materialistic evolutionism' for eroding the
'qualitative difference' between human and non-human
primates[38] and, in a clumsy attempt to discredit this 'erosion',
evokes a monist (and profoundly racist) nineteenth-century

German biologist, Ernst Haeckel. His *General Morphology*, a book of extreme Darwinianism published in 1866, caused a furore by denying any intellectual or physical difference between humankind and nonhuman animals.[39] Haeckel declares that the consciousness of the highest apes, dogs, elephants, etc. differs from human consciousness in degree only, not in kind, stating that:

> the graduated interval between the consciousness of these 'rational' placentals [mammals] and that of the lowest races of men (the Veddahs etc.), is less than the corresponding interval between these uncivilized races and the highest specimens of thoughtful humanity (Spinoza, Goethe, Lamarck, Darwin etc.) ...[40]

De Dios Vial Correa then dismisses Peter Singer's dictum, 'All animals are equal' for placing humans within that category, and Tom Regan's animal rights position similarly, for equating the status of animals with that of 'man'. He equally condemns 'the ethics of the earth of [Aldo] Leopold' and the 'deep ecology of [Arne] Naess' for 'an outlook which in principle deprives man from any special consideration', although he concedes that this environmentalism does mean 'that objectively good values are being rediscovered'. Against the godless 'natural religion' just criticized, De Dios Vial Correa asserts the biblical view that provides man with 'the mandate received from the Creator to subdue, to dominate the earth' – a responsibility he modifies by acknowledging that man is accountable to God. That he can call for a 'renewed anthropocentric perspective' – albeit one that can 'range from the compassion for animals and the repugnance toward inflicting unnecessary suffering' – indicates how far from current discourse on animal welfare and the environment this Vatican body really is. Can anything be claimed for a *non*-anthropocentric case that would not alarm the official Church? Or can anything be said on behalf of a higher status for animals without it being seen as diminishing unacceptably the status of humankind? It seems a high hurdle to jump, but one that must be attempted.

The Church's adoption of the principle of anthropocentrism, however modified, is supported by the assumption that animals lack reason, and therefore, if reason is necessary for the possession of 'soul', then soul, and if possession of a soul is what defines a person, then personhood. The assumption needs to be challenged by both science and tradition, for it has not necessarily been held throughout church history. If, rather than Darwin, Thomas Aquinas could be called as a witness for the opposition, the Church might, possibly, begin to reconsider.

b) Aquinas re-visited: challenging anthropocentrism

In the picture of the eschaton shared by his contemporaries, Aquinas foresees only human bodies and the mineral world (for the bodies to stand upon, presumably). Plants and animals, serving only pre-resurrected bodies, are simply no longer needed and so cease to exist. Von Balthasar condemns this as a 'cruel verdict' and considers, rightly, that it,

> contradicts the Old Testament sense of the solidarity between the living, subhuman cosmos and the world of men, the prophetic and Jewish ideas of divine salvation in images of peace among the animals, and it also goes against a deep Christian sense ... and finally one can refer ... to the role of animals in the biblical heaven – the lamb, the dove, the living creatures with animal faces before the throne of God – and to their indispensable employment in Christian art.[41]

The book of Revelation, particularly, von Balthasar considers, draws God's creation, in all its multiplicity, into one.

But is Aquinas himself consistent in this discontinuity between human and animal life? Eco-thomist scholar Judith Barad provides a convincing case for a Thomistic theory of the continuity between humans and animals – a theory which also reconciles beliefs in creation and in evolution.[42] She shows that Aquinas, far from consigning all animals to the realm of the purely material, held that the souls of higher animals have some share in immateriality, and thus possess to some extent, an immaterial nature in the same manner as do humans. John Haldane, too, regards it as implausible that a human soul could be created directly by God and not as the result of any natural process, saying: 'It is odd to claim that my body's properties are created directly by God, whereas those of Felix the cat are not: where both sets of properties seem in principle empirically traceable to natural causal origins.'[43]

Barad shows that, unlike Aristotle, who thought that species were fixed and unchangeable, Aquinas maintains that new species pre-exist in the active power of the original species. His embryology is similar. He teaches that the human embryo goes through a biologically continuous process, developing in stages from the lower orders of life, the vegetative and the sensitive, before turning into the higher human one before birth.[44] This process is gradual, so much so that at certain times, the levels are almost indistinguishable from each other. In a similar way, in the whole structure of being, creatures overlap in such a way that there are no unaccounted-for spaces. As Aquinas puts it:

> And among individuals of these types [one] will find a diversity based on the fact that some are more perfect than others, inasmuch as the highest members of a lower genus seem quite close to the next higher genus; and the converse is also true; thus, immovable animals are like plants.[45]

In other words, the highest form of plants is similar to animals, and the highest form of animals is contiguous with the lowest form of human beings (that is, those with impaired intellectual capabilities). (We shall shortly see the implications of this for the various theories of 'rights'.) There is more.

Aquinas observes that the ascent from lower to higher life is dependent on the need for motion: the lower the form of life, the less movement it displays; plants and some molluscs moving least. Increased mobility is related to increased consciousness. In the *Commentary of the Metaphysics* Aquinas distinguishes three levels of animal life, ranging from the immobile, lacking a capacity for memory, to those whose capacities are broadened by learning. The first level, 'is had by animals having neither hearing nor memory, and which are therefore neither capable of being taught nor of being prudent'. The second level, however, is 'that of animals that have memory but are unable to hear, and which are therefore prudent but incapable of being taught'. The third level however is 'that of animals which have both of these faculties, which are both prudent and capable of being taught'.[46]

Barad notes that Aquinas' attribution of prudence to animals is found in several texts, notably where he shows that Aristotle 'allows wise judgment to a few animals, and not exclusively to man, because even animals have a sort of prudence or wisdom'.[47] Memory is necessary in allowing an animal to have a cognitive capacity beyond sense. Aquinas even states that,

> Animals, in which a trace of such an impression [of sensible objects] remains, are capable of having some knowledge in the mind beyond sense, and those are the animals that have memory.[48]

Only the animals on the lowest level are those whose instinct operates in a purely mechanistic way, while those on the higher levels are capable of intelligence. Their complex behaviour, adapting to new situations, results from both the exterior and interior senses, common to both humans and animals. The interior senses are 'the central sense, the imagination, the memory and the estimative sense'.[49] On the one hand while Aquinas *does* deny animals any share in immaterial existence, for they have 'no being whatever which is independent of the body',[50] yet on the other hand he accords the 'sensitive soul' (i.e. the animals') 'some measure of participation in reason, coming into contact at its highest level of activity with reason at its lowest'.[51] As Barad explains, he describes what that 'something' is, in *Commentary Posterior*, Lect. 20, as reasoning about *particulars*, whereas human intelligence is able to deduce from the particulars to the universals, or abstracts.

The fact that both animals and humans are able to reason,

albeit to a different degree, is evidence of the continuum, not the disparity, between them. They can both be classed as 'intelligent beings' as they are both adapted to 'have also the form of some other thing',[52] to apprehend material things in a cognitive and spiritual way. In order to do this there has to exist an element of immateriality in the receiver, or 'knower'. Thus 'an animal receives forms in a partly material and partly immaterial way'.[53] It is further proved, in ethological studies unknown to Aquinas, that some species of animals are able to abstract from particulars to form universal concepts which they can then apply to particular situations as, for example, dolphins (in a particular environment) learning that only new tricks provide rewards, not established routines.[54]

It has also been found that instinct itself, inborn behaviour, is measurable on a 'continuum', is not restricted to animals, and relies on judgement:

> An instinct is the innate ability of the central nervous system to turn on exactly the right emotions at the instant certain signals are picked up by the senses. It is necessary to add that: the behaviour triggered by these emotions is always shaped and modified by the individual's judgment, based on the actual scenario as well as accumulated experience.[55]

For Aquinas, the cognitive powers originate in the soul, enabling the creature to receive a form without matter, construct particular concepts, be able to know all sensible things, and manifest immaterial activity. Human intellectual activity, of course, is *more* abstract, implying greater immateriality and indicating more of an underlying spiritual existence, than that of animals. But still, animals' souls are not completely material, and so there is continuity between the animal and the human, a proof consistent with Aquinas' theory of embryology and hierarchy of being. This fact should not make humans feel diminished or their specific intelligence less valued. As Margaret Atkins points out:

> If God, in his goodness, has chosen to bestow his gifts widely, we have no more cause than the labourers in the vineyard to

be fearful or resentful.[56] ... The only area of traditional theology that might need a radical overhaul on account of our new understanding of animals concerns the treatment of animals themselves.[57]

c) Summary

Anthropocentrism has been largely asserted on the grounds of the ontological difference between human and nonhuman animals, particularly the human capacity for rationality. However, Aquinas supports the principles of the biological continuity between animal and human, and of animals' 'participation in reason'. Human beings cannot be identified *purely* on grounds of rationality, and the diversity of creatures within this continuum of creation is a cause of joyful gratitude.

With the ontological continuity and not disparity between animal and human life, the ethical implications can be developed into an inclusive theology of life, but first, another aspect of the results from chapter three needs to be explored, also involving differences and similarities, but this time between the two genders of the human species.

Gender issues

a) Women's responses

In the research of attitudes held by British Catholics towards the paragraphs, evidence was shown of gender differences in approach to the issue of animals – the women being generally more sympathetic towards animals, and the men, particularly the celibate clergy, being less so, even – in some cases – hostile. This would have little significance were it not for the fact that, to date, the formulation of theology and church teaching has been an exclusively male preserve, and a celibate male preserve at that. This is borne out in the fact that the CCC itself is the result of the work of a commission comprising twelve cardinals and bishops and an editorial committee of seven diocesan bishops – all celibate men.

A report in the *Wall Street Journal* assumes it to be uncontroversial to assert that white, Western, suburban women are generally more sympathetic to animals and to their welfare than are men.[58] The eighteenth-century moral philosopher Adam Smith believed that women were more disposed to humanitarianism,[59] but one based, in their case, more on moral sentiment than on reason. This 'sentimental' aspect was used to disqualify women from moral debate and to keep their sphere of moral influence confined to the private home.[60] Frans de Waal, a professor of psychology at Emory University, and a leading primatologist, gives an evolutionary basis for the theory:

> During the 180 million years of mammalian evolution, females who responded to their offspring's needs out-reproduced those who were cold and distant. Having descended from a long line of mothers who nursed, fed, cleaned, carried, comforted, and defended their young, we should not be surprised by gender differences in human empathy.[61]

He goes on to describe that the first sign of empathy – crying when another baby cries – is already more typical in girl babies than in boy babies. However, this observation, supporting an essentialist view of gender, is denied by others who fail to find that gender really can be discerned in infants.[62]

Even to put the question whether such a disposition in women is of genetic (essentialist) origin or of societal conditioning is deplored by psychologist Carol Gilligan as a restriction on the 'possibility for resistance, for creativity, or for a change whose wellsprings are psychological'.[63] Gilligan, continuing the methodology of Lawrence Kohlberg (1927–1987) and his 'stages of moral development' theory,[64] suggests that while female infants begin with the same selfish attitude as do male children, they are then conditioned to care for others, even to the stage of considering that to value their own interests before those of other people is selfish and wrong. Eventually, she concludes, women may graduate to the point of considering their own interests as members of an equal relationship with another, but even that is usually in order to preserve the quality of the relationship. In other words relating and caring are the key features in women's psychology, whereas men tend to approach situations more from a legalistic point of view, respecting the rights of others and restricting action. Men's morality, so Gilligan postulates, has a 'justice orientation' whereas women's has a 'responsibility orientation':

> The conception of morality as concerned with the activity of care [i.e. women's] centers moral development around the understanding of responsibility and relationships, just as the conception of morality as fairness [i.e. men's] ties moral development to the understanding of rights and rules.[65]

The picture of the male – autonomous, hierarchical and fearful of commitment – and the self-critical, caring, empathetic female is stereotypical, yet is strongly suggested by the interviews Gilligan also had with both (American) men and women. As Selma Sevenhuijsen points out, this dichotomous system needs to be treated with caution[66] – and it is not helpful to suggest that 'women's morality' is superior, or that men's is wrong – but it is necessary as an antidote and alternative to the dominant and traditional perspectives which have done little to improve the status of animals.

While Gilligan's research, which was much cited in the late 1980s and early 1990s, has been fiercely attacked,[67] in connection with animals, at least, it is borne out by other surveys. In the late 1980s, two wildlife experts conducted a survey of a broad spectrum of American society and discovered that 'male versus female differences in attitude towards animals were dramatic'. Men, it was found, tended, by a large majority, to endorse 'dominionistic' and 'utilitarian' attitudes towards animals – being keener to exploit them in various ways, with twenty-nine per cent of all men polled reported having been hunting during the previous two years. Women in the study valued animals differently, being more concerned about the infliction of pain and suffering on animals.[68]

When concern for animals and their welfare is translated into dietary choices, an obvious indicator is vegetarianism or carnivorism. Matt Ridley, an evolutionary anthropologist, suggests that the sexual division of labour between hunting (male) and gathering (female) from our primitive ancestors may have left their marks, as men 'are on average more carnivorous; women are roughly twice as likely to be vegetarians as men of the same age group, a discrepancy that is, if anything, increasing'.[69] Several recent surveys have borne this out.[70] Membership of animal charities is another indicator, with women far outnumbering men in, for example, the organization Catholic Concern for Animals, both as ordinary members and as committee members.[71]

This sympathetic disposition of women towards animals has served neither women nor animals well historically, as it has reinforced traditional patriarchal views associating rationality and spiritual matters with maleness, and bodily nature and material matters with femaleness.[72] Heather Eaton asks 'whether nature is devalued by virtue of a perceived association with women, or the reverse'.[73] She explains how in early cultures, the earth itself was perceived as female, as Mother Earth or as nurturing the Mother Goddess.[74] To some feminists, this is associated with an early, possibly mythical, benign matriarchal society, a Golden Age in which people lived more natural, agricultural, lives and respected the rhythms of the seasons and the diversity of species. This wondrous period was superseded by the patriarchal, hierarchical, militaristic, rationalist and carnivorous age persisting to the present and from which we need to emerge in order to save humanity, if not the planet.[75] The age of matriarchal innocence corresponds with the biblical prelapsarian universal vegan condition first willed for creation, described at the end of the first chapter of Genesis and much used by Christian vegetarians to support their cause. However, the Mother Goddess culture which forms the basis for much earth-based feminist spiritualities, such as Matthew Fox's creation spirituality,[76] is inimical to Catholic Tradition. In an attempt to influence Vatican thinking it would be would be counter-productive to base a Roman Catholic animal theology on it.

b) Ecofeminist responses

A Christian ecofeminism,[77] one which avoids Mother Goddess references and does not pursue a 'women's ordination' agenda, needs not attract the usual opposition as do militant forms of feminism.[78] It basically seeks to reconnect the 'complex web of interrelationships between all living organisms and their environment'.[79] Joan D. Chittister suggests that 'We need a new relationship with animals. We need to immerse ourselves in creation with new respect. We need to come to see ourselves as one more creature dependent on all the others more than they are dependent on us.'[80]

To a point, this is expressed in the CCC, in n. 340: 'Gods wills the interdependence of creatures'. The examples it then gives are all of the non-human world, commenting that: 'The spectacle of their countless diversities and inequalities tells us that no creature is self-sufficient. Creatures exist only in dependence on each other, to complete each other, in the service of each other.' Another paragraph shortly following this reinforces it, 'There is a solidarity among all creatures arising from the fact that all have the same Creator and are all ordered to his glory' (n. 344). These give support to a holistic eco-community view of nature, but leave the impression that somehow human beings are not involved in this diversity, and are not 'in the service' of these other species. Between the two paragraphs, this impression is reinforced by one headed: 'Man is the summit of the Creator's work' (n. 343), which continues: 'as the inspired account expresses by clearly distinguishing the creation of man from that of the other creatures'. It cites here Genesis 1:26 – which can be used instead to show that 'man' was created on exactly the same day as all the other mammals, and thus is not so different from them! Ecofeminism can point to this separation of 'man' from nature as one of the causes of the ecological problems to which we are finally awaking. As if commentating on these very CCC paragraphs, Elizabeth A. Johnson, CSJ, writes: 'Our human lives are interwoven with millions of other species in a great community of life. How we pray and live responsibly in this community will determine whether life on this planet has a glorious or miserable future. The very glory of God is at stake.'[81]

Some ecofeminists, particularly Carol J. Adams,[82] support the theory of animal rights.[83] Others, for example, Rosemary Radford Ruether, are critical of Tom Regan's view on rights for individual animals, favouring a more holistic, covenantal environmentalism. However, although most ecofeminists include animals within an overall concern for nature, and a few, like Adams, have made them their central concerns, Janet Biehl notes that, in three contemporary anthologies, 'ecofeminism has failed to locate animals as central to any discussion of ethics involving women and nature'.[84]

More disconcerting, however, are the criticisms of ecofeminism itself – not from the usual suspects – but from Lisa Sideris, who bases her arguments on a neo-Darwinian evolutionary theory, coupled with chaos theory. These, she maintains, undermine the 'ecosystem community model' espoused particularly by Rosemary Radford Ruether and Sally McFague. Far from being a benign Gaia – a self-healing, balanced network of biosystems and ecosytems – the planet, according to Sideris, is organized on a random, unpredictable basis, and is indifferent to predation, violence and the extinction of species on a massive scale. To base an ethic on 'the biological science of natural environmental communities' is, to her, unscientific, outdated, and unrealistic.[85] It deliberately ignores the reality of suffering in nature, and Ruether's articulation in *Gaia & God* of the Peaceable Kingdom as the final fulfilment of the covenant of creation is, to Sideris, the ultimate denial of the enmity and conflict within nature. Human beings, she opines, need to take a 'more modest role ... than that of arbiters of justice and purveyors of peace and health in nature'.[86]

However, I make three responses to the Sideris 'demolition-job'. One is that the eco-system community model may be outmoded in some academic spheres, but is still true on a basic observable level. The second is that while human humil-

ity and modesty in relation to nature is exactly the response
the ecofeminists espouse, a denial of all human responsibility
and care for nature runs counter to the very nature of compassionate women and men. To do nothing is a poor response in
the face both of the destruction of the natural world and of
the innumerable cruelties faced by animals. The third is
similar, in that Christian faith heeds the imagery of Scripture
and from that, certain consequences ensue. One is that the
eschatological goal described by Ruether provides more hope
and challenges behaviour more positively than does the
nihilism of chaos and random 'natural selection'. Another is
that the role of the human person in nature is privileged, not
by an arrogant anthropocentrism, but by virtue of the incarnated Second Person of the Trinity. In a Christian view of
nature, there is nothing impersonal and valueless, nothing
outside the interest of God. In poetic language, as described
in the legend in *The Protoevangelium of James*, mentioned in
chapter four, the whole of nature pauses, frozen in time, at the
moment of the nativity, the point of special contact between
heaven and earth. In the same way, the whole of nature is
caught up in the violence of the crucifixion: 'creation is caught
up in grieving over Christ's death'.[87] Nature witnesses to and
celebrates the resurrection too, and both the agony and the
ecstasy of nature is given expression in the Christian Tradition.
When recovered, this provides a more rounded and complete
basis for an ethic than does a purely scientific post-Darwinian
understanding of an impersonal, chaotic, random, nature.

c) Clerical responses

In the research of British Catholics' attitudes to the paragraphs, previously mentioned, the clergy's responses are less
sympathetic towards animals than are most of the women's
and even of the other men's. Having undergone many years of
training in all-male seminaries, and being formed for a lifetime
of emotional suppression in order to cope successfully with
celibacy,[88] as well as receiving a totally anthropocentric
academic education, it is not surprising, perhaps, that they

should be. Their training in a spiritualizing theological tradition would predispose them to give a lower estimation of the physical, the body, than would be found in the general population. Until relatively recently, physical sexual relations between married couples were understood, in clerical teaching, to be exclusively procreative acts; and the cultivation of bodily asceticism, such as fasting, abstinence and plain clothing, were highly valued as aids to sanctification.[89]

Another notable feature of the clergy used in the research sample is that, unlike nearly half of the population of the United Kingdom,[90] they had not and do not have responsibility for pet animals. As Rosemary Radford Ruether observes: 'This relationship to pets should not be trivialized, for it is the main arena where urban humans experience interspecies love and communication and come to recognise the personhood of animals.'[91] Pet ownership, properly conducted, is especially important in early life for developing a child's respect for animals and gentleness in the treatment of them. With regular contact and interaction with animals, it is more possible for a growing child to avoid developing the cognitive and affective developmental disorder recently identified as animal-insensitivity syndrome.[92]

With lives totally ordered to ministry towards people, and with a theological formation that excludes the natural world from its concerns, there would be only wonder why a priest in today's Church should be sympathetic to animals. It is greatly to the credit of the few who are that they should 'buck the trend'.

d) Summary

In order for a true *sensus fidelium*, the Church needs to attend to the insights of the half of its membership – women – which has not to date been influential in formulating the teaching of the Magisterium. The Church also needs to contribute to correcting the prevailing dualism which privileges maleness, reason, and culture over femaleness, emotion and body. Many of women's insights and approaches in relation to nonhuman animals are demonstrably different from those of men, particularly clerical men. They can be generally expressed as certain ecofeminist principles, particularly that of relationality and inter-connectedness (which includes a respect for diversity) between species and within humanity. It is modelled on the relational community of ecosystems, which despite current scientific theories, provides a useful basis for an eschatological theology which works for a future of peaceful justice for the whole of creation.

Notes

1 Karol Wojtila, *Love and responsibility*, translated by H. T. Willetts (First published in Polish, *Milosc I Odpowiedzialnosc*, Krakow: Wydawnicto, Zualosc, 1960; Revised edition, first published in English, London: William Collins Sons and Co., 1981; this edition, London: Fount Paperbacks, 1982), p. 25.

2 Edward J. Kilmartin, 'Reception in History: an ecclesiological phenomenon and its significance', *Journal of Ecumencial Studies* 21 (1984), p. 37.

3 As cited in chapter seven, 'In articles recently published by the bishops most involved with its development ... there is a clear recognition of the importance of the process of reception by the faithful.'
   David McLoughlin, 'The treasure-house of faith', *The Tablet* (28 May 1994), pp. 656–7).

4 Yves Congar, 'Reception as an Ecclesiastical Reality', in *Election and Consensus in the Church*, edited by Guiseppi Alberigo and Anton Weiler (Concilium 77, New York: Herder and Herder, 1972), p. 45; cited in Stephen F. Brett, 'Reception and the Catechism', *The Homiletic and Pastoral Review* (October, 1994), p. 5.

5 Thomas P. Rausch, SJ, 'Reception Past and Present', *Theological Studies* 47 (1986), pp. 497–508.

6 Edward J. Kilmartin, 'Reception in History: an ecclesiological phenomenon and its significance', *Journal of Ecumencial Studies* 21 (1984), p. 37.

7 Yves Congar, 'Reception as an Ecclesiastical Reality', p. 64; cited in Stephen F. Brett, 'Reception and the Catechism', *The Homiletic and Pastoral Review* (October, 1994), p. 5.

8 A project conducted by this author for a Ph.D. at the University of Wales Lampeter, in 2008, using qualitative research methods, enquired into the reception of the Catechism paragraphs 2415–2418 by a selection of practising Roman Catholics. The full report can be found in

the thesis 'Can there be a Roman Catholic Theology of Animals?' held in that university's library and at the National Library of Wales, Aberystwyth.

9 See Bergjlot Børresen, 'Friend, Foe or Food? Social vs Predatory Emotions in Dealings across the Species Barrier'; paper given at a workshop for Human Animal Relations, Oslo University (November 1999).

10 From the section of optional Prefaces to the Eucharistic Prayer, *The Sunday Missal*, edited by Harold Winstone (London: Collins, 1975, 1977), p. 67.

11 The concept of the universal (human) destination of goods is itself not a widely understood teaching of the Church, evidenced by the inability of some of the subjects of the research to apprehend the concept of ownership of property beyond that of the individual ownership of private property.

12 Alistair S. Gunn, 'Traditional Ethics and the Moral Status of Animals', *Environmental Ethics*, 5.2 (Summer 1983), p. 152.

13 It is addressed illuminatingly by Andrew Linzey in chapter four: 'The Conflict between Ecotheology and Animal Theology' in his book, *Creatures of the Same God* (Winchester University Press, 2007), p. 49ff.

14 Ruth Page, 'The Fellowship of all Creation', *Environmental Stewardship*, edited by R. J. Berry (T&T Clark International, 2006), p. 97.

15 Rosemary Radford Ruether, *Women Healing Earth* (London: SCM Press, 1996), p. 124.

16 E. P. Echlin, *The Cosmic Circle: Jesus and Ecology* (Blackrock, Co. Dublin: Columba Press, 2004), p. 16.

17 Stewardship: a case study in environmental ethics', in *Environmental Stewardship*, edited by R. J. Berry (London: T&T Clark International, 2006), p. 64.

18 For example, by Douglas John Hall, *The Steward: a biblical symbol come of age* (New York: Friendship Press for the Commission on Stewardship, National Council of Churches (USA), 1982). In it he suggests that the symbol of stewardship, relating to creation, redemption and accountability (in contradiction of Palmer) 'so powerfully expressed in the New Testament' was lost sight of in succeeding generations with the influence of Greek notions of sin as failing to reach one's potential, compared with the Hebrew concept of sin as a breaking of relationship with God. Thus the Hebrew faith's earth-rootedness was replaced by a personalist spiritualizing that diminished stewardship's material nature.

19 Jürgen Moltmann, *God in Creation* (London: SCM Press, 1985), p. 279.

20 Blenheim Palace, Woodstock, Oxfordshire, owned by the Dukes of Marlborough.

21 Private email correspondence, 10 October 2006.

22 T. R.W. Moore, the General Manager and Land Agent for the Marquis of Bath's Longleat Estate.

23 Private email correspondence, 12 October 2006.

24 Willis Jenkins, conference paper, entitled: 'Biodiversity and Salvation: notes for an Eco-Thomism', delivered at the conference 'Ecology, Theology and Judeo-Christian Environmental Ethics' at the University of Notre Dame, Indiana, 21–24 February 2002, and to be found on the website: <www.nd.edu/~ecoltheo/text_Jenkins>. All citations of Jenkins are from this paper. See also See Jill LeBlanc, 'Eco-Thomism', *Environmental Ethics* 21.3 (Fall 1999), p. 293 ff for an endorsement of this 'holistic ecophilosophy' of Aquinas.

25 *Summa Theologica*, I.65.2 (Jenkins uses the 1948 English Dominican Fathers Translation)

26 Ibid., I.47.1

27 See note 16. All Jenkins' references are taken from his conference paper: 'Biodiversity and salvation'.

28 From the Preface to Eucharistic Prayer IV, *The Sunday Missal*, edited by Harold Winstone (London: Collins, 1975, 1977), p. 45

29 The beginning of Eucharistic Prayer III, *The Sunday Missal*, p. 41.

30 *Summa Theologica*, I-II.109.3 (Jenkins' emphasis).

31 From the Preface of Eucharistic Prayer IV, *The Sunday Missal*; my emphasis. Following it in the same prayer, the 'Praise to the Father' notes that 'man' was 'set over the whole world' with the object of serving 'you, his creator and to rule over all creatures' and acknowledges that this rule was granted before the disobedience of the Fall. Unfortunately, the connection between serving God and ruling over the creatures has never been emphasized. However, in the 'Memorial prayer', the 'acceptable sacrifice' of Christ 'brings salvation to the *whole world*' and then, just before the final doxology, the kingdom is anticipated, when 'we shall sing your glory *with every creature* through Christ our Lord'. The liturgical theme is referred to later in chapter fourteen.

32 Albert Schweitzer, *A place for revelation: sermons on reverence for life*, edited by Martin Strege and Lothar Stiehm (New York: Macmillan, 1988), p. 24.

33 H. Primatt, *A Dissertation on the Duty of Mercy and the Sin of Cruelty to Brute Animals* (London: T. Constable, 1834), p. 65; cited in Andrew Linzey, *Christianity and the Rights of Animals* (London: SPCK, 1987), p. 57.

34 There has been previous discussion on this point in chapter two.

35 Dionysius the Areopagite, *De Coel. Hier.*, III, 3; P.G.,111,168; cited in Vladimir Lossky, *The Mystical Theology of the Eastern Church* (Cambridge and London: James Clarke and Co, 1944, 1957), p. 97.

36 St Maximus the Confessor, *c*.580–662.

37 Vladimir Lossky, *The Mystical Theology of the Eastern Church*, p. 98.

38 J. de D. Vial Correa, 'Ethics of Animal Experimentation', IX General Assembly, Pontificia Academia Pro Vita (24–26 February 2003), see

website: www.academiavita.org/template.jsp?sez=Pubblicazione&pag=testo
/et_ricbiorn/vial.co

39 See the responses of Christian contemporaries, and particularly those of
    the Catholic Mivart, to the monism of Haeckel, in Jacob W. Gruber, *A
    Conscience in Conflict: the life of St George Jackson Mivart* (New York:
    Temple University Publications, 1960), p. 40.

40 Ernst Haeckel, *Die Welträthsel* (1899), translated in 1899 as *The Riddle
    of the Universe*, by Joseph McCabe (Prometheus Books, 1992), p. 182,
    cited in de D. Vial Correa, 'Ethics of Animal Experimentation'.

41 H. U. von Balthasar, *Theo-Drama: theological dramatic theory: last Act.*
    Vol.5, translated by G. Harrison. (Fort Collins, CO: Ignatius Press, 1998),
    p. 421.

42 Judith Barad, *Aquinas on the nature and treatment of animals* (San
    Francisco: International Scholars Publications, 1995), and, more briefly,
    as Judith Barad-Andrade, 'Aquinas and Evolution: a compatible duo',
    Medievalia 13 (Instituto de Investigaciones Filológicas, Universidad
    Nacional Autónoma de México) (abril 1993), p. 1ff. The following ideas
    on this subject are, unless otherwise attributed, taken from these
    sources.

43 Cited by Ricard Cross, 'Aquinas and the Mind-Body Problem', *Mind,
    Metaphysics and Value in Thomistic and Analytic Traditions*, edited by
    John Haldane (Indiana: Notre Dame University Press, 2002), p. 46.

44 *Summa Theologica*, I, 76, 3 ad 3. Also 118, 2 ad 2; *Commentary on the
    Second Book of the Sentences*, Dist 18, q.2, art. 1 and 3; *Summa Contra
    Gentiles* 86–9; *Quaestiones Disputatae de Potentia*, q.3, art. 9 to art. 12.

45 *Summa Contra Gentiles*, III, 97.

46 *Commentary Metaphysics*, I, Lect.1, n. 13.

47 *Commentary on De Anime*, III, 3, n. 629.

48 *Commentary Posterior*, II, Lect. 20.

49 Barad-Andrade, 'Aquinas and Evolution: a compatible duo', p. 6. Cf.
    Summa Theologica I, 78, 4.

50 *Summa Contra* II, 82.

51 *Disputed* 25, 2.

52 *Summa Theologica*, I, 14, 1. This is disputed by Igidius Doolan, in
    Philosophy for the Layman (Dublin: Dominican Publications, 1944,
    1954), who accepts the four 'internal senses' (common sense, imagina-
    tion, and the estimative and memorative powers) are possessed by
    'higher' animals, but denies them the 'intellectual powers'. However he
    accepts that Aquinas allows animals to possess judgement, even though
    they cannot reason about their judgement metaphysically.

53 Barad-Andrade, 'Aquinas and Evolution: a compatible duo', p. 9. See
    Paul Hoffman, 'St Thomas Aquinas on the halfway State of Sensible
    Being', *The Philosophical Review*, 99 (1 Jan 1990), pp. 73–92.

54 For examples, see Bernd Wursig, 'Dolphins', *Animal Societies and*

Evolution: readings from Scientific American, by Howard Topoff (San Francisco: W. H. Freeman , 1981), p. 86.

55 Børresen, Bergjlot, 'Friend, Foe or Food? Social vs Predatory Emotions in Dealings across the Species Barrier', paper given at a workshop for Human Animal Relations, Oslo University (November 1999), p. 4.

56 'Have I no right to do what I like with my own? Why be envious because I am generous?', Matthew 20:16.

57 Margaret Atkins, 'I think therefore I love', *The Way*, 41.3 (July 2001), p. 197.

58 A report in the *Wall Street Journal* (Tuesday, 7 November 2006), p. 1, by Brody Mullins of the Humane Society of America (HSA), mentions that, after a series of mergers with other animal-welfare groups, HSA now counts 10 million Americans as members, and that the HSA's motivating issue – the promotion of animal welfare – 'resonates with the white suburban women who could be the key block of voters who decide this election' [the 2006 Mid-term elections for Senate and the House of Representatives].

59 Adam Smith, 'The Theory of Moral Sentiments', *The Glasgow Edition of the Works and Correspondence of Adam Smith* (New York: Oxford University Press, 1976), pp. 190–1.

60 Joan C. Tronto, *Moral Boundaries* (New York & London: Routledge, 1993), p. 56.

61 From *Our Inner Ape*, by Frans de Waal (New York: Riverhead/Penguin, 1995), p. 6.

62 Jacques Lacan, for example, posits that it is only with speech that gender identity is formed, and that it is wholly conditioned by the culture, see Elaine Graham, *Making the Difference: gender, personhood and theology* (London: Mowbray, 1995), p. 173ff.

63 Carol Gilligan, *In a different voice: psychological theory and women's development* (Cambridge, Mass.: Harvard University Press, 1982), page xix.

64 See the series *Essays in Moral Development*, by Lawrence Kohlberg (New York and London: Harper and Row, 1981, 1984).

65 Carol Gilligan, *In a different voice*, p. 19.

66 Selma Sevenhuijsen, *Citizenship and the Ethics of Care* (London: Routledge, 1998), p. 51.

67 As being anecdotal, unrepeatable, unhelpful to women and anti-male, by Christina Hoff Sommers, *The war against boys: how misguided feminism is harming our young men* (New York: Simon and Schuster, 2001). Also by Carol Stack in 'Different Voices, Different Visions: gender, culture, and moral reasoning' *Uncertain Terms: negotiating gender in American culture*, edited by Faye Ginsburg and Anna L. Tsing (Boston: Beacon Press, 1990), pp. 19–27, who found, while testing Gilligan's hypotheses, no gender differences. See also 'Gender Differences in

moral reasoning', *Sex Roles* 15 (1986), pp. 645–53 by M. K. Rothbart, T. Hanley and M. Albert; cited in Joan C. Tronto, *Moral Boundaries* (New York & London: Routledge, 1993), pp. 81–2, n. 56. Tronto herself finds Gilligan's conclusions too supportive of an essentialism (p.85) – thereby reinforcing women's traditional role – and reports the criticism of Kohlberg and Jürgen Habermas of Gilligan's work as suggesting a too narrow, non-universal type of moral thinking, more suited to the private sphere than the public (pp.87–8). For a further range of negative critiques, see Barbara Houston, 'Gilligan and the Politics of a Distinctive Women's Morality', *Feminist Perspectives: philosophical essays on method and morals*, edited by L. Code (Toronto University Press, 1988).

68   Reported in Stephen Kellert and Joyce Berry, 'Attitudes, knowledge and behaviours towards wildlife as affected by gender', *Wildlife Society Bulletin*, 15.3 (Fall 1987), p. 365 ff; cited also in Joni Seager, *Earth Follies: feminism, politics and the environment* (London: Earthscan, 1993) p. 219 ff.

69   Matt Ridley, *The Origins of Virtue* (London: Viking, 1996), p. 95.

70   Gallup poll for 1999: male vegetarians 3.2 per cent (of population), female vegetarians 6.7 per cent; JMA Student Omnibus, January 2000 (survey of 1141 students, 17–24 years), male vegetarians four per cent, female 11 per cent; Food Standards Agency National Diet and Nutrition Survey (young people 4–18 years), 2000, boys 1 per cent and girls 10 per cent claimed to be vegetarian or vegan; ICM Poll for the Daily Telegraph 2001, 7 per cent men, 10 per cent women (do not eat meat); National Diet and Nutrition Survey 2001, (2251 adults 19–64), 2 per cent men, 7 per cent women claimed to be vegetarian; JMA Marketing and Research Survey for Scolarest Eating on Campus Report 2005, (1051 university students), 11 per cent women, 4 per cent men claimed to be vegetarian. Statistics provided by The Vegetarian Society, who also noted that in their society the ratio of women to men is about 2:1. Thanks to Chris Olivant, their Information and Customer Services Manager.

71   See also Joni Seager, *Earth Follies: feminism, politics and the environment* (London: Earthscan, 1993), p. 207, where figures are given of 70–80 per cent of animal activists in the USA being women.

72   Beth Dixon, in 'The Feminist Connection between Women and Animals', *Environmental Ethics*, 18, 2 (summer 1996), is particularly scathing about this: 'Feminists have little to gain by concentrating exclusively on how the concepts of woman and animal overlap' (p.193). She maintains that feminists have obligations to liberate any oppressed population, but not because of theoretical, practical or symbolic connections between animals and women, which can only lock both women and animals into essentialist characteristics. For Dixon, while animals may be naturally subordinate to rational human beings, that does not of itself imply oppression and exploitation, any more than children are subordi-

nate to adults (p.186).

73 Heather Eaton, *Introducing Ecofeminist Theologies* (London: T&T Clark, 2005), p. 68.

74 Ibid., p. 75.

75 For an account of this theory and its influences on a variety of ideologies, see Rosemary Radford Ruether, *Gaia & God* (London: SCM Press, 1992), p. 144 ff.

76 A celebratory, cosmic-oriented, neo-pagan alternative to traditional Christian theology and praxis; see Matthew Fox, *Original Blessing: a primer in creation spirituality* (New York: Jeremy P. Tarcher/ Putnam, 1983, 2000); and, *Bringing Life to Ethics: global bioethics for a humane society* (Albany, NY: State of New York University Press, 2001).

77 A term coined in 1974 by the French writer Françoise d'Eaubonne in *Le Féminisme ou la mort.*

78 Although the pursuance of justice is an integral element in all feminism, so that 'the concern for animal rights is ... seen as a logical extension of the more general feminist concern for nature or for less privileged human groups, all of whom are seen to share some features of oppression within patriarchal society', Lynda Birke, 'The Feminist Challenge', in *Animal Rights: a historical anthology*, edited by Andrew Linzey and Paul Barry Clarke (New York: Columbia University Press, 2005), p. 175.

79 Anne Primavesi, 'Ecofeminism', *An A to Z of Feminist Theology*, edited by Lisa Isherwood and Dorothea McEwan (Sheffield Academic Press, 1996), p. 45.

80 Joan D. Chittister, *Heart of Flesh* (Grand Rapids and Cambridge, Eerdmans, 1998), p. 167.

81 Elizabeth A Johnson, 'Passion for God, Passion for the Earth', *Spiritual Questions for the 21st Century*, edited by Mary Hemrow Snyder (Maryknoll, New York: Orbis Books, 2001), p. 121.

82 See Carol J. Adams, *The Sexual Politics of Meat* (New York: Continuum, 1990, 2000), pp. 180–6.

83 See the website < www.farinc.org/ > of the network 'Feminists for Animal Rights: an ecofeminist alliance'. This proposes that 'Animal advocacy is a feminist issue'.

84 Janet Biehl, *Finding Our Way: rethinking ecofeminist politics* (Montreal: Black Rose Books, 1991), p. 110.

85 Rosemary Radford Ruether, *Gaia & God* (London: SCM Press, 1992), p. 1.

86 Lisa Sideris, *Environmental Ethics, Ecological Theory and Natural Selection* (New York: Columbia UP, 2003), pp. 59–60.

87 Mary C. Grey, *Sacred Longings* (London: SCM Press, 2003), p. 139 ff.

88 It is interesting that the young priest interviewee considered 'love' purely in contractual terms.

89 There are very many pamphlets, particularly those published by the Catholic Truth Society, which describe enthusiastically the life of saints

in terms of their 'bodily mortifications' and ascetic practices.

90 The report 'The state of animal welfare in the UK 2005', by the RSPCA, p. 59, notes that nearly half of the UK households include pet animals.

91 Rosemary Radford Ruether, *Gaia & God* (London: SCM Press, 1992), p. 219.

92 See Michael W. Fox (2001) *Bringing Life to Ethics: global bioethics for a humane society* (Albany, NY: State University of New York Press); also 'Animal-Insensitivity Syndrome', *The Ark*, 205 (spring 2007), p. 11ff.

Chapter Thirteen

Ethical theories and practical treatment

So far, certain principles have been outlined which can contribute to the development of a Roman Catholic theology of animals, but there already exist relevant ethical theories that need to be explored in order to find elements to incorporate into a theological framework. Theological considerations with no grounds for ethical praxis would be simply high-minded vacuity.

Of the six specific ethical theories identified by Andrew Linzey: humanocentric, contractualist, humanitarian, welfare, rights, and generosity;[1] all are problematic in some way, and some can be dismissed at once. The first to go is the humano- or anthropo-centric, which, as we have seen, accords animals no moral status and imposes no duties on human beings towards animals. This tendency is behind most of the Church's teaching, but goes even further by imposing *no* duties on humans, whereas, as we have seen, both the model of stewardship and CCC n. 2416, as well as modifying clauses in nn. 2415, 24167 and 2418, do limit the human treatment of animals to some extent. The contractualist or deontological, is a variant of this, using the language of rights and duties, and stressing that rights pertain only to those who can make contracts or engage in mutual obligations. The humanitarian wishes to prevent cruelty to animals and promote kindness, not for the animals' sake, but for the moral benefit of human beings. The welfare supporter considers that sentience, and therefore the capacity to suffer, deserves moral consideration and that all sentient beings have – although not invariably – equal consideration. Linzey does not give specific categorization to utilitarian liberation theory, which could come at this point. This is one that weighs up consequences, privileging the higher number of beneficiaries over the lower number of sufferers. Animal rights supporters reject the instrumentalism of animals, considering each to be the subject of a life with inherent value and therefore rights. All animals, human and otherwise, are to be considered as equals, whatever the consequences. Generosity – a major basis for the theology proposed in this thesis – proposes more than rights, aspiring to the generous, self-sacrificial work by human beings to promote the well-being of other species. It draws on the kenotic and service principles of Christianity, applying them, radically, to relations between species. Theos-rights comes under this heading, with the value of each creature being assigned by God whose rights are to be recognized, as mentioned in the section on stewardship.

Some of these theories are based on the interests of the moral agent, the acting human being, rather than of the moral patient, just as the Charity Commission of Great Britain does not recognize the welfare of animals as a suitable cause for recognition, but only inasmuch as the welfare can contribute to the good of human society. Some Catholic teaching, particularly that in n. 2415, is totally 'moral agent' oriented, such as declaring that the purpose of all nonhuman beings and objects is the service of human beings. The earliest Christian ethical system, virtue ethics, is concerned only with the moral agent, but lends itself to an 'animal-friendly' orientation.

a) Virtues

Virtue ethics, originating with Aristotle and developed by Aquinas, are described in the CCC as based on cultivating 'an habitual and firm disposition to do the good ... The virtuous person tends towards to the good ... [and] chooses it in concrete actions' (n.1803). It includes considering what a good person would do in a given situation, and modelling oneself and one's actions on such a person. It is in practising virtue so diligently and consistently throughout life that good actions are the inevitable consequence and one's behaviour becomes naturally conformed to the four cardinal and three theological virtues.[2] These can today all be related to the treatment of animals so that there could, to some extent (limited as it is to attention to the moral agent) be a 'virtuous' ethic towards animals. The virtuous exemplars would be, of course, St Francis of Assisi and St Philip Neri, as mentioned in n. 2416. To them could be added the Celtic saints and Desert Fathers discussed in chapter four, as well as the more contemporary Cardinals Newman and Manning, and the very many secular proponents of a virtuous ethic towards animals. The best exemplar, of course, is Christ – and how the Christian can model his or her behaviour on Christ's is to be discussed further in this chapter.

Of the traditional virtues *Prudence* helps the moral agent to apply ethical principles to particular cases in order to bring about the good and avoid evil. As we have seen, even animals, according to Aquinas, can possess this virtue. Achieving the good for all living creatures and avoiding the evil of cruelty is a simple goal, but prudence is especially necessary in helping to decide between the competing claims of moral patients. To Richard Wade, in order to exercise prudence, it is necessary to identify the *telos* of human life, both in terms of the natural world (where natural law operates) and of the human person's relationship with God. When both are in harmony, the right moral choices will, presumably, become 'natural'.[3] The *dis*harmony of human relations with animals which we see around us is, in traditional Catholic teaching, a result of the Fall, since when animals have become 'enslaved and accommodated to the uses of others'.[4] *Justice* is the virtue of giving to God and neighbour what is owed them. CCC n. 2416 states that animals are owed kindness, so the principle is established that justice is to be extended to them, either as a form of neighbour or, as the n. 2416 seems to intend, as part of the justice owed to God. Raymond Gaita appeals to the

Christian virtues, preferring the virtue of 'justice' over the notion of 'rights', in relation to animals and nature. He specifically admires 'renunciation', as exemplified in the writing of Simone Weil, and cites approvingly her comment that 'The supernatural virtue of justice consists of behaving exactly as though there were equality when one is stronger in an unequal relationship.'[5] *Fortitude* enables the agent to be firm and constant in one's struggle to achieve the good, which must include the justice owed to animals; while *Temperance* ensures that a proper balance is struck and extremes not indulged in. This can ensure that in matters such as diet, clothing and leisure, nonhuman animals are not sacrificed for the indulgence of appetite, fashion, taste-preference or entertainment. It can also provide a correction to an over-sentimental attitude towards animals where inappropriate anthropomorphizing can diminish or even destroy the dignity and integrity of an animal.

While *Faith* and *Hope* include a belief in the ultimate transformation of all creation, *Charity*, the primary virtue, would extend to encompass all sentient beings as worthy recipients. To limit charity to those who can reciprocate, such as fellow human beings, or even to companion animals alone, is to diminish the concept of disinterested and generous love to the point of its being one unworthy of a fully virtuous person. *Mercy* is relegated to one of the fruits of charity, along with joy and peace (n. 1829), but the *works of mercy* are included in the same section, under the Seventh Commandment, as are the four 'animal' paragraphs. These are explained as 'charitable actions by which we come to the aid of our neighbour ...' (n.2446). Who is my neighbour for whom I should be merciful? In the following passage by Pope John Paul II the impression is given that the answer is wider than a purely anthropocentric one:

> The present-day mentality, more perhaps that that of people in the past, seems opposed to a God of mercy, and in fact tends to exclude from life and to remove from the human heart the very idea of mercy. The world and the concept of 'mercy'

seems to cause uneasiness in man, who, thanks to the enormous development of science and technology, never before
known in history, has become master of the earth and has
subdued and dominated it. This dominion over the earth,
sometimes understood in a one-sided and superficial way,
seems to leave no room for mercy.[6]

Jay B. McDaniel suggests three more 'moral virtues': the first
is 'reverence for life'; the second is 'ahimsa' [borrowed from
Hinduism, especially Jainism] or noninjury [which could be
borrowed from the Jewish injunction, *tsa'ar be'alei chayim*,
'not to cause pain to any living creature', as mentioned in
chapter two]; the third is the exercise of active goodwill
[which Cardinal Manning endorses, as will be seen below].[7]

Summary
The virtues represent a helpful adjunct to the ethical dimension
of an animal theology, but they need a sound hermeneutical
basis by which to interpret behaviour in relation to animals. The
plight of animals worldwide requires more than reliance upon
the disposition and circumstances of individuals, however well
motivated. However, they, especially McDaniel's, offer useful
basic guidance for Christians to inform their responses to a
range of issues.

With the eighteenth-century Enlightenment, however,
virtue ethicists were replaced by the deontologists, using the
language of 'duties' and 'rights' – translated today by both
contractualists and animal rights supporters. These tend to
draw attention to the animal-object, rather than to the person-
agent. Then the nineteenth-century Utilitarians stressed the
importance of the consequences of actions, with the maximizing of happiness or pleasure and the minimizing of its
reverse, whether of agents *or* objects. Today, Peter Singer
leads that school in connection with animals. Richard Ryder,
one of the small group of Oxford writers in the 1970s who
revived interest in the ethical treatment of animals,[8] and the
first to use the term 'speciesism', posits a fourth approach,
that of 'painism'.[9]

b) Animal liberation

For Peter Singer, a liberation movement is 'a demand for an end to prejudice and discrimination based on an arbitrary characteristic like race or sex'.[10] Species is for Singer the 'arbitrary characteristic', with 'speciesist' the term of opprobrium for those who discriminate on grounds of species. To liberate is to demand 'an expansion of our moral horizons'.[11] For many, to associate species as merely an 'arbitrary characteristic' is to expand their moral horizon over one boundary too far.

The supposedly unique characteristic of 'rationality' is the one Singer highlights as being the one most used by people to maintain their powers and privileges. He would support the recognition by Aquinas and modern science that reason or intelligence can be rated on a continuum. His mentor is Jeremy Bentham (1748–1832), whose utilitarian philosophy Singer adopts, and who dismisses the human 'faculty of reason or the faculty of discourse' as having significant absolute value, for 'a full-grown horse or dog is beyond comparison a more rational, as well as a more conversable animal, than an infant of a day or a week, or even a month old'.[12] One end of animal life comprises mature, healthy human beings, followed – and in some instances overlapped by – many 'higher mammals', dogs, elephants, pigs, primates, dolphins. At the other end, there are molluscs and single-celled creatures. They are different, but should, according to Singer's 'principle of equality' between species, be treated with equal consideration. However, his ethics operate largely on behalf of 'higher mammals', and he admits that 'consideration for different beings may lead to different treatment and different rights'.[13]

His principle of equality is based on that between human beings. This, to him, is not a *de*scription of alleged actual equality, but a *pre*scription of how people should treat other people.[14] Human beings are patently unequal in many ways, in intelligence, talents, emotional maturity, and so on, yet those differences do not matter as the basis for treating them with equal consideration. When applied to other species as well, the main interest shared by all is the avoidance of suffering and maximizing of pleasure. The answer to the famous question Bentham asked about animals 'Can they suffer?' is obviously, yes – despite the denial by Descartes and all those of his followers to the present day, who disregard the infliction of pain on animals *as if* they could not suffer. Can animals experience pleasure and happiness? Anyone with a pet dog or cat knows exactly the triggers and responses of pleasure – the flourishing of the 'walkies' lead, the fireside, the food treats, and so on, all elicit expressions of pleasure by their pets. Some of the most horrific clinical experiments are to test precisely the limits of pain endured before unconsciousness or death intervenes, while ethologists have discovered the evolutionary benefits of feelings, emotions and pleasures in species' survival.[15] Therefore, as both people and animals have the capacity to experience pleasure and suffering, and therefore possess interests in increasing the one and minimizing the other, Singer argues that both people and animals have the moral right to equal consideration of these interests. To experiment on animals and to eat their flesh constitute, for him, the two major forms of speciesism in our society. Although, as a Utilitarian, Singer can justify the use of some animals in experimentation where the positive results of experiments benefit a greater number of another species, such as humans.[16]

There are certain grave problems in Singer's approach for it to be used for a Catholic theology. To categorize, as he does, some non-human primates as 'persons' does nothing to enhance their welfare or that of the other – 'non-person' – animals, and only provides ammunition to those who claim that the dignity of the human person is being undermined. It is reasonable of him to ask why all humans – and here he lists infants, the mentally defective, psychopaths, Hitler, Stalin, and the rest – have some kind of dignity or worth that *no* elephant, pig or chimpanzee can ever achieve. However, his argument that there is no moral reason why mentally handicapped or immature human beings (such as fetuses or new-born infants) should not be selected for scientific experiments rather than mature, healthy animals, would find no place in any Catholic theology.[17] As an avowed atheist, he would regard this as of no concern,[18] and any Christian defence of the unique status of human beings as only empty rhetoric or 'fine phrases'.[19] The Christian response would have to run the risk of this attack. It could not ignore the biblical phrase of human beings being made 'in the image of God' – although the interpretation of that phrase needs to be clearly defined as being endowed with responsibilities for the planet. To touch on a further Christian argument, it was through human persons that sin came into the world and through a human person that the world has been redeemed – taking responsibility for the entirety of creation to its sublimely highest point. This does not mean that other creatures are no less deserving of consideration: in fact, as carers, or servants, of creation – and creation of course includes the most vulnerable human beings, those unborn, disabled or dying, this should make human beings *more* considerate of the interests of other creatures.

Utilitarianism can be helpful – to a point – in determining between competing interests. However, there are inherent problems with it, for which a system of rights is often invoked as a necessary corrective. One problem Singer admits to, despite it tending to undermine his own argument. It is the natural instinct for people to give special consideration to their family and relatives. The human species is no different from any other in this respect. It is 'hard-wired' into all animals as part of their natural genetic make-up for the survival of their genes, as well as of their species. The utilitarian theory breaks down when it involves conflicting claims between what is of universal utility and what motivates us on this personal and intuitive basis. For if one were to agree that it was better that a new-born child should be killed in preference to an unknown mature healthy dog, it would be unlikely that one's *own* newborn child would be offered.[20] An example of the unnatural nature of utilitarianism is in the behaviour of the father of Jung Chang, author of *Wild Swans*. In his efforts to be the perfect Communist, he suppresses all feelings and behaviours which could have been interpreted, by a strictly totalitarian regime, as showing favour to his own family.[21] Thus he is described as an abominable human being precisely because his treatment of his family deviated from the norm, based on the natural human instinct of preferential care and protection for one's partner, parents and offspring. Because there will always be a *degree* of humanocentricity in our dealings with nonhuman animals and nature as a whole, it is necessary to stress vigilance in these dealings so that this prejudice is checked by justice to the moral patient.

There is a final, if minor, problem: that is the difference between an animal liberation movement and that of its human models (for race, sex, age, etc). For, as David Lamb notes,[22] whereas reform movements, on the Gandhi model, depend on the appeal to the consciences of the oppressor group, liberation movements have to arise from the oppressed groups themselves. Animals cannot liberate themselves, but depend on people doing it for them. Ultimately, it relies on the degree of awareness, sympathy and conscience of people and appeals to their sense of equality beyond the species barrier. The appeal to equality beyond the species barrier is one which Mary Midgley considers inadequate. Equality can be a tool for rectifying injustices within a given group, she maintains, but is not appropriate for widening that group or for deciding how the group ought to treat those outside it.[23]

Summary
Animal liberation is helpful in challenging the species barrier, with its human arbitrary characteristic of rationality, and in broadening the moral community. However, its utilitarian base is too rigid and crude to be wholly co-opted for a Catholic theology of animals, and some elements, such as advocating the (theoretical) use of human infants and mentally impaired people in experiments, are unimaginable in such a theology.

c) Animal Rights

i) rights and duties

Animal rights is another approach, one for which Singer has little time.[24] For pioneering humanitarian Henry Salt (1851–1939), whose work *Animals' Rights*[25] had considerable influence on Gandhi and G. Bernard Shaw, animals have rights which consist of 'restricted freedom' to live a natural life which permits individual development. The rights approach is derived from the concept of human rights, a legacy of the natural rights tradition in Anglo-American and French political thought.[26] Because it was a product of the secular Enlightenment, the Christian Churches' reaction to it was negative at the beginning. Gradually the Churches have come to espouse human rights, although Christian history shows that charitable and educational institutions have long been serving sick and poor people *as their right*.[27] Slavery and social deprivation were (albeit eventually) seen as needing, respectively, abolition and reform, and it was Christians (admittedly, mostly Anglicans and Methodists rather than Catholics) who largely spearheaded the movements for both. Of course, the just treatment of significant numbers of people, as of animals, is still to be won in the Church.

However, it is not plain sailing. With the word 'rights', the whole deontological world is opened up. Nicholas Boyle, for example, dismisses 'rights', whether of humans or animals, because they are treated as if they were property or possessions, symptomatic of a 'property-obsessed age' and thus 'one of the most potent temptations to idolatry'.[28] He prefers the discourse of 'duties' – imposed as the law of God – as the foundations of social, political and legal life, and which avoids the absurdity of attributing property (rights) to non-human owners. (Here again, theos-rights is implicated, an idea treated more fully later.) An influential Dominican, Benedict M. Ashley,[29] while deploring cruelty to animals, excludes 'moral rights' from all but human beings on the grounds that only human beings are 'persons', which he defines as beings 'with spiritual intelligence and free will'. He does not explain why rights should be confined to 'persons', so defined, apart from resorting to the 'image of God' and 'dominion' references of Genesis 1:26.[30]

Boyle is far from alone in considering duties as a necessity correlative to 'rights' discourse. A typical contractualist view is that of Richard A. Watson, who considers that only a 'moral agent' can possess rights as only a person of self-consciousness, free-will – and other uniquely human characteristics – can have duties. He derives his reciprocity of rights and duties largely from a (mis)interpretation of the Golden Rule; 'to do unto others as you would have them do unto you', whereby he sees that as implying a contract between two equal and rational agents.[31] This, of course, leaves infants and the mentally impaired unqualified, logically, to be recipients of rights. Watson's views are soundly rebutted by Anthony J. Povilitus,[32] who rejects Watson's Cartesian privileging of reason, replacing it as a value with the higher one on life itself, the life of nature as a whole, citing H. H. Iltis: 'Not until man accepts his dependency upon nature and puts himself in place as part of it, not until then does man put man first!'[33] Animals and ecosystems are deserving of primary rights, as a means of restraining human beings from exploiting them.

The logical, or reverse, deontological argument deserves consideration, although not everyone would agree with it. If an agent has the duty not to do something, such as inflict pain on a patient, so, it can be inferred, the patient (person or animal) has the right *not* to have the pain inflicted upon him or her.[34] Raymond Gaita suggests that rights are promoted when: 'Good-hearted people find it intolerable that just treatment of the powerless should depend on the generosity – on the charity in the old-fashioned sense – of the powerful.'[35] However, he declares the appeal to rights to be illusory: 'Unless an appeal to rights has force to back it, an appreciation of the wrong being protested depends entirely on a spirit of justice in those to whom the appeal is made.'[36] Rights do need laws to enforce them, but first the spirit of justice has to be kindled in order for pressure to be put on the authorities to pass appropriate laws.

ii) Regan on animal rights

Animal rights are defined as 'the recognition that animals are sentient beings possessing inherent value, having interests of their own, and belonging to themselves, that is, they are not mere things, not objects to be used in any way we want, and not our property'.[37] Tom Regan, one of the earliest propo- nents of the term, challenges the moral community to widen its circle to include the whole of creation. He argues from biology and other branches of science that animals have their own 'biographies', being subjects of their lives, with the same degree of self-awareness as is possessed by human infants of more than one year old.[38]

Rights are invoked particularly when conflicts of interests are encountered, such as when the interests of individuals are in danger of being submerged by the collective interests of a larger number; in other words, when utilitarianism threatens personal subjects. In Regan's view, all killing of animals for food, clothing and so on, is morally wrong, and people in advanced societies, with plenty of alternatives, have no excuse for killing animals. He does make allowances for people living in the harsher conditions of the developing world who hunt and kill animals for food and clothing. The act itself is always wrong, but the degrees of culpability depend on circumstances. It is wrong because thousands of species of animal are subjects of a life – they have experi- ences, particularly those of pain and suffering, which must be taken into account. Just as the infliction of pain and suffering would be taken into account when applied to one species, how, Regan reasonably asks, can it not be wrong when applied to another when no relevant difference separates them? Humans have the right not to have non-trivial pain inflicted, for one reason, because it prevents us from pursu- ing our own good, our *telos*. Animals too have their own good, the pursuance of which they demonstrate by appro-

priate behaviour. They too have desires, wants, needs and so
on which should be met.

iii) Ryder and 'painism'

For Richard Ryder, pain and suffering is the one criterion that
overrides all others, and the theory this generates he calls
'painism'. Regardless of species, pain, 'broadly defined to
include all forms of suffering, is the only moral evil. All other
moral objectives are means to reducing pain'.[39] Like Regan, he
rejects the trade-offs allowed in Singer's Utilitarianism,
whereby harm to one can be justified by the greater benefits
accrued to another or to a greater number of others. (In
Ryder's theory, would one interfere in an attack by a fox on a
rabbit? While one suffers deeply for an instant, the other could
slowly starve and thereby also suffer pain.) For both Regan
and Ryder there is no 'collective' pain, as pain is only suffered
by individuals. Ryder refines Regan's solution when faced with
a conflict of rights. Instead of deciding which party has more
interests, and therefore is more deserving of rights, for Ryder,
precedence is given to whichever party suffers more or
deeper pain.

However, there are two significant objections to Ryder's
cause. In an attack on Singer, but relevant here, Lisa Sideris'
quotes J. Baird Callicott over the importance of the biological
function of pain: 'If nature as a whole is good, then pain and
death are also good.'[40] And she adds, sarcastically, that if the
problem of sentient suffering is to be solved, maybe all the
animals should be removed from the wild and placed in zoos
where they could be fed and protected.[41] Certainly, pain has an
evolutionary value by enhancing a species' prospects for
survival, and warns sufferers of the existence of bodily
damage. Better life with pain than nonexistence without.
However, although nature is good in many respects, the Christian view of it is that it is also fallen, and pain and suffering are
a consequence of that: the true 'goodness' of nature is the
prelapsarian vision before sin, predation, death and suffering
were introduced by human beings. But by allowing suffering

does not mean that God is indifferent to it. It may be difficult for some Christians to consider that God is concerned with the pain of animals; the philosopher Peter Geach, for example, considers that 'The Creator's Mind ... seems to be characterized by mere indifference to the pain that the elaborate teleologies of life involve' and that God 'does not share with his creatures ... the virtue of sympathy with physical suffering'.[42] That Deistic view is not shared by others:

> Christian believers may ... find themselves driven to affirm, with the medieval theologian Peter Abelard, that the cross of Christ reveals the suffering in the heart of God which all creation entails for the creator. There we see him taking on himself not only the wickedness and suffering of humans, but also the pains of all his creatures. The cross, it might be argued, manifests in time the suffering of God throughout the creative process until it is complete.[43]

This is, in my view, consistent with the view of a loving God, and one who redeems the full consequences of the Fall, which include the suffering of all.[44]

The other objection is of a different nature. It is that the prevention of the infliction of pain and suffering is not the *only* right which should be claimed for animals. Indeed, as Lamb argues, there is more to life than avoidance of suffering, and avoidance of suffering itself could even be in conflict with other interests, such as liberty. For example, songbirds live shorter lives in the wild than they do in cages, and sheep on wintry hillsides succumb to death by natural causes more than do their sheltered counterparts.[45] The wild rabbits in *Watership Down* try to persuade a captive rabbit to join them in their great adventure, but fail, as the captive prefers a coddled and safe life to a free one full of risks.[46]

iv) Wild animals and rights
How can rights apply to conflicts of interests between animals in the wild? The rights of one animal to exist could threaten the right of another. As the writer Brigid Brophy asks:

Are we humans justified in intervening to save, for example, tigers from the extinction that now threatens them as a species, given that the preservation of one individual tiger necessarily means the premature extinction of a large number of harmless, vegetarian, ruminant individuals whom the tiger will inevitably prey on?[47]

To answer this we take as a given that, whereas we have duties towards animals, and they have rights in regard to our treatment of them, they have none towards each other. It is only in the relationship that humans have with them that the language of rights is relevant, particularly with those over which we have direct responsibility, such as domestic and household animals. Rights theory is weakest in relation to a more holistic view of nature, as it applies only to individual holders. As it would preserve only a community of subjects, and not the biotic community as a whole, it is criticized on environmental and evolutionary grounds. In rights theory, species as such have no value, as only individuals can be endangered, but evolutionary forces and natural selection do not respect individual rights and interests.[48] In a conflict of interest between non-domestic animals when humans can influence the outcome in any way, our duty is to the environment as a whole, which depends upon the balance of nature. To deprive nature of predators could cause an exponential growth in the number of ruminants to the detriment of the latter species' gene pool (by weaker individuals not being culled) and the possible destruction of the habitat by overgrazing. The tiger's right to exist, in this case, supersedes the right to life of the prey species, and our duty is to see to it that the tiger's right is upheld. Similarly, if a person could stop a fox attacking a rabbit, non-intervention should be the rule, however emotionally painful to the person that might be. The case is different in relation to domestic cats preying on wild birds and small mammals, as human interference is already involved in the keeping and feeding of cats, so that intervention is justified. (See later for a general account of the appropriate treatment of wild animals.)

v) Christianity and animal rights

Unlike Peter Singer's, Regan's analysis of the Christian Scriptures and tradition is positive, drawing out those elements which should, in his view, inspire Christians to accept his premisses.[49] For example, he stresses how the creation, before Adam, was declared 'good' by God, and that with mankind being created on the same day as animals a sense of kinship between them was intended. Also, he declares that animals were created as 'independently good expressions of the divine love', and that, as a vegan diet was instituted in the perfect state of creation, that demonstrates that animals were created not to be utilized by humans, but for humans to protect. Two further arguments he makes are: that throughout Judaism and Christianity every form of life is seen as an expression of God's love and that, while vegetative life has been provided as food, God makes binding covenants with both humans and animals.

These are strong arguments which should appeal to all Christian traditions. That they have not been effective demonstrates the strength of innate opposition to the cause of animals within these traditions. A typical comment by the reactionary element in the Catholic Church is given by Joseph Sobran in the ultra-traditionalist magazine *Christian Order*. In concluding an article about the unlovability of dolphins, he says, 'Broadly speaking, animals are violent, predatory ... and lacking in compassion. We owe them no apologies. Besides, many of them taste good.'[50]

vi) Aquinas revisited: rights

Is it possible to reconcile Catholic theology with any theory whereby animals can be rights' holders? Here again, Aquinas can be called as a *non*-hostile witness. In another closely argued article,[51] Judith Barad demonstrates that Aquinas, despite the licence he gives human beings to use animals, clearly affirms that animals have natural rights, defended by justice. Rather than Aristotle's civic community, the polis, as the locus for claims of justice, for Aquinas it is the larger community, the community ruled by God. All beings, animate and inanimate, obey eternal law, defined as God's 'wisdom directing all actions and movements'.[52]

> Conserving the existence of all beings, God orders them to the common good of creation. All the manifestations of law concern the common good, and God's eternal law concerns the common good of the universe ... Aquinas's emphasis upon all creatures' membership in the community of the universe suggests a panorama of all creatures as related to one another and to God.[53]

This eternal law, objectively discoverable, this *jus* in Latin, is the object of justice, or doing what is right. Justice serves as a defence of natural rights. Unlike the other cardinal virtues,[54] which concern the moral agent only, this one, justice, is 'set up by its relation to others'.[55] It supersedes mere man-made laws, as Aquinas contends that slaves, for example, are not bound to obey their master with regard to marriage[56] – the right to marriage belonging to this natural or eternal law. The physical laws of the universe, the movement of planets and molecules, are subject to God's eternal laws, or the natural law, as is the behaviour of living creatures. Each creature, human or non-human, is to realize its specific nature and end, to achieve fullness of its being, through correctly ordered behaviour. 'Thus Aquinas's discussion of eternal law underlies his principle that every creature moves towards its end by the development of its potentialities.'[57] The end or *telos* of an animal is to be fully itself – a dog, for example, is to be truly a dog, doing all the doggy things that is natural for it to do, for God's sake. It is in this way that CCC n. 2416 means that by animals' '*mere existence* they bless God and give him glory'. However, there is an inconsistency in Aquinas' teleology, as it is in conflict with his instrumentalist view of animals. As Barad notes, his concept of teleology implies the concept of duty:

> A thing is a matter of precept, in so far as it is something due. Now a thing is due in two ways, for its own sake, and for the sake of something else ... now in every genus that which is for

its own sake takes precedence of that which is for the sake of another.[58]

She applies this principle to animals whereby, 'If an animal has a capacity that is for its own sake yet can be used by human beings, then the end that "takes precedence" should be the end that is for the animal's own sake.'[59] On the basis that it is wrong to frustrate the natural end of an animal's activity, such as growing to maturity, producing offspring, and the like, it is logical therefore to conclude that animals are not given their 'due' by treating them as mere instruments and things for human benefit. That would be to offend against natural law, God's law.

Of course, not all creatures are protected by this law to the same degree. Inanimate objects cannot know that they have interests, and the immanent life of plants is limited. But more complex creatures possess 'sensitive souls' involving memory and imagination, and are able to exercise immanent, self-realizing, or self-perfecting activity (*actio immanens*). Aquinas considers animals to be such[60] and so

> the common good cannot take priority over any innocent animal, human or non-human. On Aquinas's account, since animals are self-perfecting beings, the common good cannot have priority over the welfare of an innocent animal ... Aquinas does hold that the good of the individual must never be lost sight of ... In short, every self-perfecting individual within the community of creation has moral status and a claim to protection.[61]

Does this mean that Aquinas grants natural rights to animals? Yes, according to his *Commentary on the Nichomachean Ethics* where he describes human beings as possessing two natures, one in common with other animals, and one which is exclusively human, and that, 'Jurists call only that right natural which follows the inclinations of nature common to man and other animals, as the union of male and female, the education of offspring, and so forth.'[62] More than that, he states that 'Non-human animals have rights considered absolutely, distinguishing them from mere property: "Now it belongs not only to man but also to other animals to apprehend a thing absolutely; wherefore the right which we call natural is common to us and other animals".'[63]

Barad notes that Aquinas follows neither Justinian, who refers natural law only to humans, nor his teacher Albert the Great, whose idea is that natural law and the law of reason are the same, and exist only in humans. Instead, he makes use of the Roman jurist Domitus Ulpianus (Ulpian)[64] and his definition of natural law as 'what nature has taught to all animals'.[65] This is more than just instinct, as it involves the apprehension of things, but provides a biological contingency for what is good for the species, both human and non-human. All rights and duties proceed from its first principle of doing good and avoiding evil. What these rights and duties are, Aquinas suggests, can be learnt by observing natural behaviour, and discovering what the *telos* of each individual could be. Then our treatment of each being should be in accordance with what helps it to achieve its telos and not prevent it from fulfilling it. The ethical consequences of this are expanded by another Catholic theologian, Richard Wade,[66] who suggests that violation of the natural inclinations of animals;

> for example, [by] the infliction of pain and abuse, deprivation of water, food, space to run free, and so forth, is against the interests they require to have their natures fulfilled ... Failure to respect the prima facie interests of animals based upon their nature is to deny them natural justice.

Because animals, unlike inanimate things, have the capacity to enjoy living, it matters to them how their lives fare; they are 'morally considerable'. As Aquinas avers, animals are ontologically superior to vegetables, which are superior to inanimate objects. As the treatment of human beings is to accord to their ontological status – the treatment of animals should be different from that of mere things.[67] They thus have claims upon people to treat them appropriately. Human beings will inevitably have *more* rights than animals as it is appropriate for people to have those which pertain to their condition, such as the right to order their society as they wish, to worship as they wish and claim other freedoms as they wish. These would not be appropriate for animals. But the 'Five Freedoms', a code of the Farm Animal Welfare Council, would be entirely appropriate as an absolute basis for animals:

> freedom from hunger and thirst;
>> from discomfort;
>> from pain, injury and disease;
>> from fear and distress,
> and the freedom to express normal behaviour, which includes providing sufficient space, proper facilities and company of the animal's own kind.

These are ensured only by the sense of responsibility in humans. As Wade puts it, 'The claims of animals thus generate in us a duty to care for their welfare.'[68] This claim, however, according to Wade, may be overridden 'to preserve a proportionate good', such as in self-defence, or in the destruction of a mosquito. The key word is 'proportionate', and in determining right action when interests, human and animal, compete, the moral virtue of prudence is required. Jill LeBlanc describes that 'in the state of innocence, animals are the subjects and not the slaves of humans; after the Fall, however, they are slaves'.[69] According to St Thomas, the Fall affected not animals' nature, but human nature – and the loss of real leadership that we see restored only in the great saints, such as the Desert Fathers, as described in chapter four.

A benefit of natural law theory is in its universalism. It can be applied by everyone and anyone – it is not necessary even to posit the existence of God as creator of natural law in order to adhere to its principles – and it can apply to all living beings, a true biocentrism, rather than be limited simply to higher mammals or even sentient creatures. It should ensure a truly responsible and sustaining environmentalism. Everything, every species, has its God-given purpose in the general scheme, even if human science knows little of what it is. Natural law respects 'raw' nature and wildness, and can deduce ethical conclusions simply by an observation of nature. As biologist Robert A. Angros deduces:

> If there were no wisdom in nature, it would be pointless to use nature as a measure of human acts. If our ability to eat, or our sexual faculty, or our power of speech, do not have natural purposes, then it will be impossible to abuse them, since abuse means using a thing in a way contrary to its natural purpose [and we instinctively *do* recognise abuses in these faculties] ... if wisdom and goodness are found in nature, this can give us insight into the wisdom and goodness of God.[70]

However, natural law is itself a source of criticism from some theologians, especially Protestant ones, as being deficient in not being based on revelation, particularly that of Scripture. Natural law is also attacked by secular philosophers as being 'inexplicable intertwined' with theology and insufficiently rational.[71] It also invokes the accusation, identified by David Hume and named by G. E. Moore, of 'naturalistic fallacy', whereby what is natural is necessarily right or moral, or deriving an 'ought' from an 'is'.[72] However, 'although one cannot go directly from "is" to "ought", an "ought" can and often does imply an "is"'.[73] Catholic theology, though, holds firmly to the natural law principle, and assumes that it will be used intelligently. Pope John Paul II, in particular, made much of the application of rationality as a complement to revelation, as together they provide an ethic which is based on an objectively valid moral order perceived by the divine gift of reason.[74] The use of reason or, perhaps better, prudence, or discernment, upon natural justice can prevent regression to a Rousseau-like idealization of wild nature in human behaviour, and at the same time, can enable humans to transcend their own species barrier with sympathy and compassion, qualities which are rarely observed in the wild.[75]

A further Thomistic principle, already referred to in chapter ten, can be used in situations of competing interests – that of proportionality. Basically, an action is unlawful if the good effect could have been secured without the evil effect. This ties in with the statement in the CCC that: 'One may not do evil so that good may result from it' (n.1756). For example, animals can be used for food and clothing *only* if food and clothing cannot be obtained by plants and minerals, or by animals only when real need demands, rather than preference, taste, and so on – otherwise it would be unlawful to harm that which is higher in the chain of life, the animal. In most conflict of interest situations, an application of proportionality combined with consideration for the interests of all living, especially sentient, parties will help in determining action.

Summary

Regan's ethics of rights can contribute to a Catholic theology by acknowledging the interests of non-human creatures and allowing them moral consideration. However, the development in Thomistic teaching has more to offer by allowing the *telos* of each creature to be given the protection of natural justice, a justice grounded in God. It is not just in avoiding the evil of frustrating the *telos* of creatures, but Aquinas suggests that we have a duty to nurture the flourishing of such *telos*, the more that glory to God will exist in and through creation. This ensures protection of the diversity of species and respect for ecosystems, as well as high welfare standards. Individuals are also brought into consideration by the principle of proportionality as animals, having a higher ontological status than mere 'things', should be treated with greater consideration.

Examples of how the Church might approach the practical treatment of animals

Just how, in practice, different categories of animals should be treated is suggested here:

a) Domestic animals (pets) As they are required to live in homes as 'members of the family', the natural behaviours and instincts of 'pet' or 'companion' animals have been highly moderated. As a result, their welfare is entirely a human responsibility. The breeding of dogs, cats and others must be regulated to ensure that unwanted animals are not killed or abandoned as strays. It would be better for all rescued dogs and cats to be found homes, and rescue centres to be made redundant worldwide, than for any commercial breeding to take place – but that would require powerful institutions such as the Kennel Club to cease operation, which would be most unlikely. Animals which naturally would live in packs or herds should not be kept in solitary conditions, nor should birds be kept in cages, as their natural instinct to fly and congregate in flocks is seriously compromised. When animals can no longer be treated for their illnesses by veterinarians, and painful death would only be prolonged, then a fatal administration of painkillers to alleviate their sufferings, one where death is a foreseen and tolerated inevitability, is acceptable – as it is with people (see CCC n. 2279). As animals are not in a position to inform us of the degree of their suffering, this may be administered at an earlier stage than with human beings, and the ensuing death be seen more in terms of euthanasia. But, as with people, ordinary care should not be interrupted, nor should an animal's life be terminated earlier than is necessary, and not for lack of funds for veterinarian bills or for any other lower cause. Real human poverty would, of course, mitigate the culpability.

b) Food animals Ideally, human beings would not terminate animals' lives prematurely for the sake of meat. Human beings do not need meat, as protein is found in a rich variety of other sources. However, while the Church could promote the advantages of a vegan, or at least, vegetarian, diet (both for the sake of animals and for social justice)[76] and endeavour to practise it, it is only realistic to acknowledge that most people will continue to eat meat. Therefore, what must be paramount is the welfare and comfort of the animals used for food, both in their lives and in the manner of their deaths. This requires a radical reversal of current 'factory farming' policies and practices, and a full and generous implementation of the Five Freedoms listed earlier. The kind of 'hog farming facilities' as described so graphically in Matthew Scully's book *Dominion*[77] must be considered anathema in a welfare-oriented industry. For as long as meat has to be produced, let it be more expensive, good quality, and organic, from humanely raised animals on welfare-oriented family farms, with the minimum transport for the animals involved, and where the slaughtering is done humanely 'on the farm'. Let the criteria for selective breeding be on welfare grounds rather than for maximizing meat, milk, eggs, etc. At the very least, the Church could adopt the request of Brother Alex, of the vegan Hindu Skanda Vale Community of the Many Names of God, in Carmarthenshire, who asks that 'before consuming that piece of lamb or beef, people should take a few minutes to be aware that an animal has had to die'.[78]

c) Animal for clothing While leather remains a by-product of the meat industry, the same welfare criteria apply as for food farming. If wool is produced humanely, then there is little to comment upon there. But, as mentioned in chapter eleven, all fur farming and trapping must be seen as the inhumane and unnecessary relic of a past age which has no place in the modern world, where substitute furs both look and feel similar to the real thing.

d) Draught and traction animals Animals, such as donkeys, camels, oxen and llamas used for carrying loads and pulling ploughs, carts and so on, need to be given every support and consideration so that any suffering is minimized. These are normally used only in impoverished countries where culpability for poor welfare is mitigated by poor education about animals and intense poverty. It is hoped that higher standards of living will improve the situation, whilst, in the meantime, charities funded in wealthier countries may offer support.[79]

e) Wild animals (culling and hunting) The management of large numbers of wild animals can sometimes be devolved onto human beings, who have already destroyed the balance of nature by eliminating many of the natural predators. In which case, if the welfare of whole herds is threatened by either disease or over-population, it would be preferable to treat the sick animals and to remove excess numbers to other locations, but it is admitted that with some animals and in some conditions this is not possible. In which case, regrettably, on a purely utilitarian basis, culling may be required of the weakest and sickest. This should be undertaken only by trained and authorized marksmen, and no element of entertainment or pleasure-seeking involved – for God's creatures' lives are being taken. Game-shooting and 'recreational' hunting are activities no Christian or humane person should engage in;[80] although hunting for food – where other sources of protein are genuinely not available – would mitigate the culpability as it would come under the category of 'self-defence'; one life taken so that another may survive.

e) Experimentation on animals This is a highly complex subject which stirs strong emotions on both sides of the argument. On one side, much of it is seen as a regrettable necessity where a few 'lower' animals are 'sacrificed' for the good of many 'higher' beings, usually people. On the other, it is seen as an extreme form of instrumentalization, and one where the interests of the animals themselves are totally overlooked. The comments of Cardinals Newman and Manning (see chapters five and six) can be invoked to give weight to the degree of abhorrence induced by the practice. Whatever conditions they are kept in, however high the standard of comfort and care received, the fact remains that the animals' lives are shortened, abused and frequently subjected to pain and suffering. It is incumbent upon the Church to support those agencies and institutions which do not use animals and particularly those that seek viable alternatives to animals.[81] The Church could also call for an immediate cessation of all duplicated or unnecessarily repeated experiments and a complete end to the use of animals as quickly as possible. There is a wealth of literature supporting the claim that the use of animals is detrimental and counterproductive to the health of human beings,[82] but that is a different argument – and lends itself to the counter-argument: were it shown to be of use, would it then be considered all right? It is an abuse of the integrity of creation to genetically engineer, modify or clone any animal for scientific or medical uses. Changes to the genetic constitution of any creature, other than occur naturally or by natural processes, trespass against the divine law and intention for that creature. The last word on this is given to an eminent former professor of surgery in the Harvard Medical School, Dr Henry J. Bigelow, who declares: 'There will come a time when the world will look back to modern vivisection in the name of science as they now do to burning at the stake in the name of religion.'[83]

f) Animals for gaming and entertainment Horses and greyhounds in the racing industry are bred to unnatural standards, and if not selected or have finished their racing lives, are often discarded and abandoned, or worse. In their racing lives, horses are whipped mercilessly and frequently suffer stress and fatal injuries from over-taxing jumps.[84] The Church (and its members) should withdraw support from the racing industry, as it should from circuses or any entertainment which exploit animals or compromise their dignity. Zoos should ensure that welfare standards are of the highest quality, that space and conditions closely replicate those of the natural environment for the particular species, and that there are sound conservation reasons for keeping the animals. With high-quality visual records of animals in their natural habitat, the reason for the existence of zoos is no longer to educate the public, nor should they be simply to entertain it if the animal is to suffer in any way.

Notes

1 'Animal Rights', *Dictionary of Ethics, Theology and Society*, edited by Paul B. Clark and Andrew Linzey (London and New York, 1996), pp. 29–33.

2 The cardinal virtues are Prudence, Justice, Fortitude, and Temperance; and the theological virtues are Faith, Hope and Charity.

3 Richard Wade, 'Towards a Christian Ethic of Animals', *Pacifica* 13.2 (June 2000), p. 210.

4 *Summa theologica*, II-II, 64, 1 ad 2.

5 Simone Weil, from *Forms of the Implicit Love of God*, cited by Raimond Gaita, *The Philosopher's Dog* (London and New York: Routledge, 2002), p. 202.

6 Pope John Paul II, Encyclical letter; *The Mercy of God*, 1.2; cited in Matthew Scully, *Dominion: the power of man, the suffering of animals, and the call to mercy* (New York: St Martin's Press, 2002), p. 287.

7 Jay B. McDaniel, *Of God and Pelicans: a theology of reverence for life* (Louisville, Kentucky; Westminster/John Knox Press, 1989), p. 73.

8 Others included the philosophers Roslind and Stanley Godlovitch, John Harris and Peter Singer, and were supported by Brigid Brophy, Tom Regan and Andrew Linzey.

9 Richard D. Ryder, *Painism: a modern morality* (London: Centaur Press, 2001), p. 8.

10 Peter Singer, *Animal Liberation* (London: Jonathan Cape, 1976), p. x.

11 Ibid., p. xi.

12 Jeremy Bentham, *An Introduction to the Principles of Morals and Legislation*, 1781, quoted in Peter Singer, *Animal Liberation*, p. 8.

13 Peter Singer, 'All Animals are Equal', chapter eight of *Applied Ethics*, edited by Peter Singer (Oxford UP 1986), p. 217.

14 Ibid., p. 220.

15 See *Pleasurable Kingdom: animals and the nature of feeling good*, by Jonathan Balcombe (London and New York: Macmillan, 2006).

16 This Singer implied during a discussion in Oxford for the BBC2 programme 'Monkeys, Rats and Me: animal testing', broadcasted in the UK on Monday, 27 November 2006.

17 Other utilitarian theories of his are challenged on Christian grounds. See *Rethinking Peter Singer: a Christian critique*, edited by Gordon R. Preece (Downers Grove, IL: InterVarsity Press, 2002). This set of essays by Australian evangelical Anglicans provides some thoughtful criticisms of Singer's claims, but also tends to justify and be complacent of the status quo.

18 Indeed, in *Animal Liberation*, 1976, he makes some trenchant criticisms of Christianity's contribution to the culture of cruelty to non-humans in the West, see especially chapter five: 'Man's Dominion: a short history of speciesism'.

19 Singer, *Applied Ethics* (Oxford UP, 1986), p. 228.

20 See Mary Midgley, *Animals and Why They Matter* (London: Penguin, 1983), especially chapter nine.

21 Jung Chang, *Wild Swans: three daughters of China* (London: Harper-Collins, 1991).

22 David Lamb, 'Animal Rights and Liberation Movements', *Environmental Ethics*, 4.3 (Fall 1982), pp. 215–32.

23 Mary Midgley, *Animals and Why they Matter*, p. 190ff.

24 Singer says that 'all that needs to be said about our moral relationship to animals can be said without thinking of animals as having rights', in 'The Parable of the Fox and the Unliberated Animals', *Ethics*, 88 (January 1978).

25 Henry Salt, *Animals' Rights* (London: The Humanitarian League, 1912), p. 6.

26 Hiram Caton, 'Human Rights', *The Dictionary of Ethics, Theology and Society*, edited by Paul B. Clark and Andrew Linzey (London and New York: Routledge, 1996).

27 See Revd A. L. Lilley, 'The Church's view: the Christian spirit and ideal', in *The New Charter: a discussion of the rights of men and the rights of animals*, edited by Henry S. Salt (London: George Bell & Sons, 1896).

28 Nicholas Boyle, 'Human rights and our human God', *The Tablet* (18 March 2006), p. 13.

29 Influential in that he is a senior Fellow of the Pope John Center of Medical Ethics in Boston, Mass., and is a Consultant on Doctrine of the US Bishops Conference.

30 Benedict M. Ashley, OP, *Living the Truth in Love* (New York: Alba House, 1996), pp. 299–300.

31 Richard A. Watson, 'Self-consciousness and the rights of nonhuman animals and nature', *Environmental Ethics*, 1.2 (summer 1979), pp. 99–129.

32 Anthonly J. Povilitus, 'On Assigning Rights of Animals and Nature', *Environmental Ethics* 2.1 (spring 1980), pp. 67–71.

33 H.H. Iltis, 'Man first? Man last? The paradox of human ecology', *BioScience* 20 (1970), p. 820.

34 An objection has been made to this by W. D. Ross, who argues that the object of a duty can only be expected to have a right to it if it can claim that right for itself, W. D. Ross, *The Right and the Good* (Oxford: The Clarendon Press, 1930), p. 50. Yet rights are accorded to infants and mentally impaired people who cannot claim them for themselves.

35 Raimond Gaita, *The Philosopher's Dog* (London and New York: Routledge, 2002), p. 201.

36 Ibid., p. 201.

37 Professor Priscilla Cohn, 'Animal Rights, Animal Liberation and Animal Welfare', a paper delivered to the IV International Meeting for Animals, in Tossa del Mar, Spain (30 September–2 October), 1994.

38 See Tom Regan, *The Case for Animal Rights* (Berkeley, CA: University of California Press, 1983, revised edition, 2004), especially chapters 8 and 9.

39 Richard Ryder, *Painism: a modern morality* (London: Centaur Press, 2001), p. 65.

40 J. Baird Callicott, 'Animal Liberation: a triangular affair', *Environmental Ethics*, edited by R. Elliott (Oxford University Press, 1995), p. 54; cited in Lisa Sideris, *Environmental Ethics, Ecological Theory and Natural Selection* (New York: Columbia UP, 2003), p. 145.

41 Ibid., p. 146.

42 Peter Geach, 'Divine Indifference'; see Andrew Linzey, *Animals and Christianity: a book of readings* (New York: Crossroads, 1988), pp. 52–5.

43 Brian Hebblethwaite, *Evil, Suffering and Religion* London: SPCK, revised edition 2000), pp. 114–15. Only the Appendix deals specifically with animal suffering, but the book covers the resources offered by world faiths to the problem of suffering in the world.

44 Heresy-hunters who sniff out Patripassionism here are taking too androcentric a view of God. For a more female-imaged Creator, see Sally McFague, *Models of God: theology for an ecological, nuclear age* (Philadelphia: Fortress Press, 1987), especially pp. 97–123.

45 David Lamb, 'Animal Rights and Liberation Movements', *Environmental Ethics*, 4.3 (Fall 1982).

46 Richard Adams, *Watership Down* (London: Puffin Books, 1973).

47 Brigid Brophy, 'The Darwinist's Dilemma', *Animal Rights: a symposium*, edited by David Paterson and Richard Ryder (Fontwell, Sussex: Centaur Press, 1979), p. 83.

48 See Lisa Sideris, *Environmental Ethics, Ecological Theory and Natural Selection* (New York: Columbia UP, 2003), pp. 152–164.

49 See Tom Regan, 'Christianity and Animal Rights: The Challenge and Promise', chapter six, pp. 73–87, in *Liberating Life: contemporary approaches in ecological theology*, edited by Charles Birch, William Eaken and Jay B. McDaniel (Maryknoll, New York: Orbis Books, 1990).

50 Joseph Sobran, 'The Dark Side of Dolphins', *Christian Order*, 47.10 (October 2006), p. 75.

51 Judith Barad, 'The Ontology of Animal Rights', *The Future of the Middle Ages and the Renaissance*, edited by R. Dahood (Turnhout, Belgium:Brepols, 1999), pp. 30–42.

52 *Summa Theol*.2.1.93.1.

53 Judith Barad, 'The Ontology of Animal Rights', pp. 31–2.

54 Cf CCC n. 1805.

55 *Summa Theol.*, 2.1.57.1.

56 See A. S. McGrade, 'Aristotle's Place in the History of Natural Rights', *The Review of Metaphysics* 49 (1996), p. 814, cited in Judith Barad, 'The Ontology of Animal Rights', p. 30.

57 Judith Barad, 'The Ontology of Animal Rights', *The Future of the Middle Ages and the Renaissance*, edited by R. Dahood (Turnhout, Belgium: Brepols, 1999), p. 32.

58 *Summa Theol.*, 1–11, 44, 2. Cited in Judith Barad, 'Aquinas' Inconsistency on the Nature and the Treatment of Animals', *Between the Species*, 4.2 (spring 1988), p. 108.

59 Judith Barad, 'Aquinas' Inconsistency on the Nature and the Treatment of Animals', p. 108.

60 Judith Barad convincingly counters Dennehy's denial that animals' actions can be self-perfecting and so be part of the common good or have their interests considered. Cf. Raymond Dennehy, 'The Ontological Basis of Human Rights', *The Thomist* 42 (1978), 460, cited by Judith Barad, 'The Ontology of Animal Rights', *The Future of the Middle Ages and the Renaissance*, edited by R. Dahood (Turnhout, Belgium:Brepols, 1999), pp. 34–5.

61 Barad, 'The Ontology of Animal Rights', p. 35.

62 *Commentary on the Nichomachean Ethics*, translated by C. I. Litzinger (Notre Dame: IN, 1993), 5.12.1019, cited in Barad, 'The Ontology of Animal Rights', p. 35.

63 Barad, 'The Ontology of Animal Rights', p. 36; *Summa Theol.*, 2.1.57.3.

64 Ulpian, *c*. AD 170–228

65 *Institutes of Gaius and Rule of Ulpian*, translated by James Muirhead (Holmes Beach, Fl., 1994), Digest 1.1.1.3; cited in Barad, 'The Ontology of Animal Rights', p. 37.

66 Wade supports Barad's reading of Aquinas and Ulpian, in 'Towards a Christian Ethic of Animals', *Pacifica* 13.2 (June 2000), pp. 202–12.

67 Judith Barad, 'Aquinas' Inconsistency on the Nature and the Treatment of Animals', *Between the Species*, 4.2 (Spring 1988), p. 102.

68 Wade, 'Towards a Christian Ethic of Animals', *Pacifica* 13.2 (June 2000), p. 210.

69 Jill LeBlanc, 'Eco-Thomism', *Environmental Ethics* 21.3 (Fall 1999), p. 298.

70 Robert M. Angros, 'Nature acts for an end', *The Thomist* 66.3 (2002), p. 536.

71 Murray N. Rothbard, 'The Ethics of Liberty' on website of the Ludwig von Mises Institute: www.mises.org/rothbard/ethics/one.asp

72 A good description of the nineteenth-century debate between Herbert Spencer's value-laden evolutionary theory in his 1879 *Data of Ethics*, and G. E. Moore's 'Human separation of the natural sciences from ethics in his 1903 *Principia Ethica* is given by James Rachels, *Created from Animals: the moral implications of Darwinism* (Oxford UP, 1991), pp. 62–70.

73 Philip E. Johnson, 'Metaphysics matters' (book review of *In Defense of Natural Law* by Robert P. George, Oxford UP, 1999), *First Things*, 97 (November 1999), p. 74.

74 Charles M. Murphy, *At Home on Earth* (New York: Crossroad, 1989), p. 124.

75 See Laura Westra's article 'Ecology and Animals: is there a joint ethic of respect?' *Environmental Ethics*, 11.3 (Fall 1989), pp. 215–30, for a detailed attempt to reconcile animal ethics with a holistic environmental ethic.

76 It is well documented that the production of meat protein is far more costly in terms of land, crops and water, than is non-meat protein. The destruction of the tropical rainforests for meat production is another example of how unnecessary desire for meat is causing catastrophic extinction of millions of species.

77 Matthew Scully, *Dominion: the power of man, the suffering of animals, and the call to mercy* (New York: St Martin's Press, 2002). See especially chapter six: 'Deliver me from my necessities', pp. 247–86, about one such 'farm' in North Carolina.

78 From an interview by Jeremy Clark in the article 'Shambo looked like a finalist for "best in show", not a condemned invalid', *The Spectator* (2 June 2007).

79 For such charities that work with draught and traction animals, see the Brooke Hospital, <www.thebrooke.org/> and the Society for the Protection of Animals Abroad,

80 See Fr James Legge's defence of hunting as a 'natural, selective and humane way of managing the environment', in his article 'Animal Rights: a perspective on the hunting debate', *Faith* 36.1 (Jan–Feb 2004). This is answered in an article by Deborah Jones (me) in the following issue, 'Animal Rights: another perspective', *Faith* 36.2 (Mar–Apr 2004).

81 For arguments and resources on alternative or 'scientific' use of animals, see the website of Doctors and Lawyers for Responsible Medicine, www.dlrm.org/resources/alternative.htm; also the Dr Hadwen Trust, www.drhadwentrust.org.uk/.

82 As the previous entries, also see www.navs.org.uk/research/; www.buav.org

83 Cited by George R. Farnum, *Vivisection: a dark blot on civilization* (Boston, MA., New England Anti-Vivisection Society, 1947), p. 14.

84 As in the Cheltenham Gold Cup of 2006, when nine horses lost their lives – during a 'Festival' which is strongly supported by Catholic clergy over from Ireland.

Chapter Fourteen

The School of Compassion

We have seen how the theory of natural justice is grounded in God's providing each living being with a *telos* beyond mere instrumentality. This segues neatly into the next area of interest: the development of a theocentric view of animals. In the CCC are two expressions[1] that form the basis for 'theos-rights' of animals, a term coined by Andrew Linzey and developed by him.[2] Theos-rights melds the intrinsic rights of each and every animal with the right that their Creator has over his creation. Therefore humane treatment of them is not a matter of charity, but of justice.[3] The key sentence of CCC n. 338 reads: 'Nothing exists that does not owe its existence to God the Creator'; an obvious statement, but one not to be taken for granted. The next paragraph describes the variety of creatures as reflecting God's goodness and then draws the conclusion that 'Man must therefore respect the particular goodness of every creature, to avoid any disordered use of things *which would be in contempt of the Creator* ...' (my emphasis). Respecting the particular goodness of any creature implies the 'natural justice' principles – enabling the *telos* of all creatures to be achieved without inter-ference, and that *telos* being God-oriented. The reason for so doing is given here as acknowledging the right of God not to have his creation abused. This is not an entirely new concept: the nineteenth-century Cardinal Tommaso Zigliara includes the following in his work *Philosophia Moralis*, giving one side of the 'rights' question even if not accepting the full equation that animals therefore have derived rights:

When man, with no reasonable purpose, treats the brute
cruelly he does wrong, not because he violates the right of the
brute, but because his action conflicts with the order and
design of the Creator.[4]

Had this argument prevailed in the Church, a positive attitude
towards animals could have ensued, which in practice has not.
Several Catholic moral theologians accept the principle that
animals are God's creatures without that affecting their basic
assumptions. For example, the Jesuit Henry Davis in a much
reprinted text of moral and pastoral theology states first that,
'animals have no rights .. [and] we have no duties of justice or
charity towards them', then, because 'they are God's creatures', he concedes that 'we have duties concerning them and
the right use we make of them'. These go only so far as to avoiding wanton cruelty, for the usual reason that it encourages a
cruel tendency, but that 'reasonable sport is not cruelty for its
own sake, and the pain of animals may be permitted, as may
also their suffering in vivisection', again, for the usual
reasons.[5] Germain Grisez, another influential moral theologian, similarly denies rights to animals and draws the
inference that it can be appropriate deliberately to kill them
'not only to put them out of their misery, but to serve any
significant human interest'.[6] Then Grisez goes on to state that
'Nevertheless, animals do have their own special value. Like
everything else God created, they are good in themselves.'
The reason he gives is that they lead us to 'admire, praise and
thank their Creator'. Then, in a seeming adumbration of
theos-rights, he states that 'reverence towards God requires
us to respect their value'. That respect, however, goes only so
far as to avoid the usual 'wanton' cruelty – not the systematic
cruelty of, for example, intensive factory farming. A note to
this statement comments that it is not the animals' value that
should determine humans' actions, as the moral value of
those is determined purely by 'relevant human good'. Anthropocentrism is brought to bear even upon an apparent and
partial theos-rights position.

Cardinal Zigliara's point is amplified and made more humane by another nineteenth-century cardinal, the Englishman, Edward Manning, already mentioned. He affirms that people owe each other rights and obligations which are not owed to animals, but avers, in Thomistic language, that:

> we owe a seven-fold obligation to the Creator of those animals. Our obligation and moral duty is to Him who made them and if we wish to know the limit and the broad outline of our obligation, I say at once it is His nature and His perfections, and among these perfections one is, most profoundly, that of eternal mercy ... And in giving a dominion over His creatures to man, he made it subject to the condition that it should be used in conformity to His perfections which is His own law, and therefore our law. [7]

At least here we have the quality of mercy (mentioned above) stressed in relation to the treatment of animals, and an emphasis on God's own nature as a model.

One of Manning's successors as Cardinal Archbishop of Westminster, John Carmel Heenan, as President of the Catholic Study Circle for Animal Welfare (now Catholic Concern for Animals), writes a Foreword in 1970 in one of the charity's publications, replying to the proposition that animals have no rights. He suggests, in the traditional formula, that this is true in the sense that, not being human persons, they can have no rights 'in their own right'. But then he spells out the theos-rights principle:

> But they have very positive rights because they are God's creatures. If we have to speak with absolute accuracy we must say that God has the right to have all his creatures treated with proper respect.
>
> Nobody should therefore carelessly repeat the old saying that animals have no rights. This could easily lead to wanton cruelty ... This book [draws] attention to the many ways in which the rights of God can be transgressed through ignorance as well as malice.[8]

In this short piece of writing Heenan also develops an ethic of kindness as a Christian duty as ensuing from these rights. After discussing the nature of cruelty – that much of it is practised as 'a matter of business', rather than deliberately (except by 'the perverted') – he then remarks that:

> It was once pointed out to me that the catechism[9] had no question about cruelty to animals. This was true but in giving lessons on Christian doctrine teachers now include the subject of cruelty to animals.[10] The best and most experienced teachers do not, of course, talk of cruelty to animals. They talk of kindness to animals. Christians have a duty not only to refrain from doing harm but also to do positive good. This book will help Christians to do their duty. This is why I wish it a wide circulation.

The above authorities all deny that animals can be rights-holders 'in their own right', whereas the theos-rights as advocated by Andrew Linzey does not deny them rights, but proposes that their rights are precisely because God's own absolute rights can extend, and be applied, to them. To explain this, he offers a three-point definition of theos-rights, beginning with animals as rights-possessors:

> To affirm animals as possessors of rights means:
> i) that God as Creator has rights in his creation;
> ii) that Spirit-filled, breathing creatures, composed of flesh and blood, are subjects of inherent value to God; and
> iii) that these animals can make objective moral claims which is nothing less than God's claims upon us.[11]

The difference between this and Regan's theory of rights is that, while Regan considers individuals as 'subjects-of-a-life', with inherent value and therefore objective rights, Linzey's theory values 'Spirit-filled individuals because God especially values them'.[12] In this theory, while all creatures of 'spirit, flesh and blood' (rather than 'sentience')[13] are subjects of inherent value, human beings have no special value to God by virtue of their faculties or 'personhood', although they are uniquely placed in 'God's redeeming purpose precisely because of [their] unique ability to co-operate with the Spirit'.[14]

Imago Dei and the priesthood of creation in the Eucharist

In a theocentric theology, the term 'image of God' has particular relevance, for attention is focused on how the image-holder can reflect the image of the God who values all living beings. It is a term that begs many questions of meaning, yet is frequently invoked by proponents of the status quo of human beings in relation to animals. Various explanations of the term are presented in Part Two, chapter eight, under the heading of n. 2417, although it may be helpful now to turn again to Eastern Christianity for some further suggestions to supplement them.

As mentioned above, the only significant difference between the human and the non-human animal is that the human being has the potential for great sin and great goodness: the sin of the first human being in the Fall being mirrored in each generation by the callous and inhumane attitude to the suffering of other living creatures; the goodness of Jesus of Nazareth being mirrored, although weakly, in all authentic followers of his.[15] The human being has, as just mentioned, 'a unique ability to co-operate with the Spirit'. In Eastern thought this is seen as the human being uniquely uniting the forms both of uncreated spirit and created body.[16] Each human person therefore contains the whole in microcosm, wherein the whole is present in every part (as demonstrated in Quantum mechanics), or a hypostasis, expressing and embodying in one identity the totality of a nature.[17] While being the image *of all of creation* we can also be the dynamic image *of God* towards that creation. As the first human, Adam, according to St Maximus, united in himself the whole of created being; his function, his *telos*, was to reach perfect union with God and thus deify the whole creation. He could do this only by conquering the divisions and temptations within himself, and by abandoning himself to love. Only then could he return to God the whole created universe gathered together in his own being. Then would God give himself to man who would, by grace, possess all that, by nature, is possessed by God. Adam failed this task, and 'it is in the work of Christ, the second Adam, that we can see what it was meant to be'.[18] James B. Torrance describes Christ's work in this respect:

> The good news is that God comes to us in Jesus to stand in for us and bring to fulfilment his purposes of worship and communion. Jesus comes to be the priest of creation to do for us men and women what we failed to do, to offer to the Father the worship and praise we failed to offer, to glorify God by the life of perfect love and obedience, to be the one true servant of the Lord. In him and through him we are renewed by the Spirit in the image of God and in the worship of God in a life of shared communion.[19]

The human follower of Christ is at one with, and not set apart from, creation, and has the divine task of offering in love the whole of creation to God. This is what we offer at the Eucharist – ourselves in the fullness of our being: our 'bodies', our material lives and the material life of all creation; and our 'blood', all our failures, all that is death-oriented in us and in all creation. That is the priestly role of mankind – to present the fallen world ('disfigured', in Eastern parlance) to God who can then transform it.[20] As Hans Urs von Balthasar explains: 'as a result of its violated condition, the whole created world (at least) has been drawn into the destiny of redeemed man'.[21]

Adam's Fall had consisted in making mankind the 'ultimate point of reference in creation'[22] – and thereby not overcoming the limitation of creation's inherent mortality. Had Adam acted as the Priest of Creation, in the way that Christ was to do *par excellence*, mortality could have been transcended. It is Christ, as representative and perfect Man, who is truly the subject of George Herbert's verse in his 'Man is the world's

High Priest: he doth present / The sacrifice for all.'[23] Christ, the one true 'image of God', sums up all creation under his headship; he is the embodiment of the *anakephalaiosis* of all creation, and shows us how we can, symbolically and liturgically, offer to God elements of creation (bread and wine) in recognition of God's true ownership of *all* things. We receive them back and consume them,

> no longer as death but as life. In this way creation acquires for us a sacredness which is not inherent in its nature but 'acquired' in and through our free exercise of our imago Dei, that is, our personhood. This distinguishes our attitude from all forms of paganism, and attaches to the human being an awesome responsibility for the survival of God's creation.[24]

As Pope John Paul II expresses, celebrating Mass in different environments 'in chapels built along mountain paths, on lakeshores and seacoasts' gives him a sense of the 'universal and, so to speak, cosmic character' of the Eucharist – 'Yes, cosmic!' he emphasizes. On whatever altar it is celebrated, 'The Eucharist is always in some way celebrated *on the altar of the world*. It unites heaven and earth. It embraces and permeates all creation.' He goes on to explain that creation's redemption is achieved because the Son of God became man

> in order to restore all creation, in one supreme act of praise, to the One who made it from nothing. He, the Eternal High Priest who by the blood of his Cross entered the eternal sanctuary, thus gives back to the Creator and Father all creation redeemed. ... Truly this is the *mysterium fidei* which is accomplished in the Eucharist: the world which came forth from the hands of God the Creator now returns to him redeemed by Christ.[25]

The reception of the life and death of Christ into our very bodies at the same time as our own self-offering 'as a holy sacrifice, truly pleasing to God'[26] bonds us in the Eucharist into the one mystical body of Christ.[27] So when we turn to go back into the world, we do so as members of that body, as

limbs, feet, hands, and so on, to be as Christ in the world and
do as Christ would do. As Christ and the Father are one God,
and as God 'loved the world' (the *cosmon*) 'so much', the
vocation of the Christian is to love that world similarly, the
world of human beings and animals, eco-systems and habitats.

Catholic eucharistic theology and Orthodox-inspired sacra-
mentalism in relation to creation can combine to form this
theology of animals. It can provide a view, an attitude, that
informs one's whole life, and generates an increased attitude
of reverence towards creation. It is a reminder that sacraments, as well as celebrating the present reality, point forward
to the state when the reality that they symbolize is actualized
in the Kingdom of God. Lest such sacramentality be confused
with sentimentality, creation itself, still subject to predation
and the struggle for survival, reminds all that, while there is
beauty and awesomeness to be admired, the goal of the Peaceable Kingdom is still to be sought. Action must follow
celebration.

The elevation of the human being within creation as its
priest is not to deny the ability of nonhuman creatures to
praise and worship God in their own way.[28] Even the
seventeenth-century scientist Roger Boyle accepted that all
creatures 'glorify their Creator ... in a way and Language
unknown to us tho naturall to them'. He also considered that
in our mistreatment of animals we disturb 'their Gratitude &
Devotion to God'.[29] Richard Bauckham considers the 'priesthood of creation' theory to be too anthropocentric. He draws
from the Psalms (19:1–3; 97:6; 98:7–9; and especially 148) the
description of non-human creatures praising God in their own
right, without any need for people to voice their praise for
them, and considers that the idea of the mediating role of
humans as priests 'intrudes our inveterate sense of superiority exactly where the Bible will not allow it'.[30] But I consider
that there are responsibilities upon our species in several ways
and that the highest of these is to represent the whole of
creation in our praise and worship. Christopher Southgate
notes, in an article largely supportive of the concept, that 'talk

of priesthood does not tell us what or how much we may do, only how we should do it'.[31] Yet how indeed we 'should do it' does matter, and an excellent and haunting description of this is given by Wendell Berry in a passage cited by Southgate:

> To live we must daily break the body and shed the blood of creation. When we do this knowingly, lovingly, skilfully and reverently, it is a sacrament. When we do it ignorantly, greedily and destructively, it is a desecration. In such a desecration, we condemn ourselves to spiritual and moral loneliness and others to want.[32]

Charity and the eschaton

The Church, as the priestly people chosen on behalf of the whole creation to fulfil Christ's priestly function on earth as in heaven, needs the 'charitable heart' described by St Isaac the Syrian (or 'of Nineveh') in a passage which is worth repeating in full:

> What is a charitable heart? It is a heart which is burning with charity [love] for the whole of creation, for men, for the birds, for the beasts, for the demons – for all creatures. He who has such a heart cannot see or call to mind a creature without his eyes becoming filled with tears by reason of the immense compassion which seizes his heart; a heart which is softened and can no longer bear to see or learn from others of any suffering, even the smallest pain, being inflicted upon a creature. That is why such a man never ceases to pray also for the animals, for the enemies of truth, and for those who do him evil, that they may be preserved and purified. He will pray even for the reptiles, moved by the infinite pity which reigns in the hearts of those who are becoming united to God.[33]

A theological underpinning of this ethic of charity is developed in the work of the Orthodox theologian, Sergei Bulgakov, for whom sophiology is central.[34] He develops the idea of the dynamic creative outpouring of Divine Wisdom as inseparable from the kenotic, or divine self-giving, dispossession of God. Creation can come fully to share in the life and liberty of God as God lovingly withdraws and makes space for it. God's kenosis is continual and eternal, and the creation, just what God desires, becomes truly itself when it too lives *into* self-giving. The human calling is to share the love and liberty of God, and, in a similar way, to 'let be'; not imposing the human will, not in *self*-expression, but in expressing kenotic charity, through justice and reconciliation. The world is 'soaked through' with the Wisdom of God, imbued with his sophiatic life. And the incarnation affirms the goodness of creation and fills the created order with life. Human beings, and the Church as the community of Christians, are tasked with being carriers of Wisdom, to rejoice in being creatures, not aspiring to God and God's powers. The kenotic principle must underlie all that the Christian is and does, towards God and towards both human and nonhuman neighbour. The image of Christ as the mother pelican, feeding her chicks by the blood of her body, is a model for the Christian self-giving towards all vulnerable and dependant creatures.

Borrowing from this theology of Bulgakov,[35] and adopting our human priestly role in creation we can see how the ethic of kenotic charity, of love, has eschatological significance. The calling of each person to be charitable to all creatures is not simply for sentimental reasons, to feel better about it, but to fulfil a divine mandate on behalf of the cosmos. As the then Dean of Westminster Abbey, Edward Carpenter, expresses, man is 'to commit himself to the divine task of lifting up creation, redeeming those orders of which he forms part, and directing them towards their end'.[36] As we embrace that which we share with all other created beings, and take responsibility for the flourishing of all life, so we become more perfectly human and, through the redemption won by Christ, attain the 'glory of the sons of God' of Romans 8. The 'whole creation' is eagerly waiting for this (Romans 8:19) and the whole creation, with each individual animal being within it, will find that 'shalom', that completeness and fulfilment of *telos*, that wholeness not experienced in their earthly life.[37] This cannot mean the merging of all life into the Life of God, wherein each individual loses its different identity, for that would not be love. Love respects the 'other' while drawing it close, and the love of God 'which passeth all understanding', cannot be less than any love that creatures are able to feel and express.

Conclusion and the Catechism

The theology so far described is, I believe, to be in accordance with Catholic theology and Tradition, especially with the support for it given by Aquinas, read anew. Thus it should be of little matter to change or 'correct' the next edition of the Catechism of the Catholic Church. Would such change be countenanced? There have been changes made in the second edition of the CCC itself, particularly with regard to the teaching about capital punishment and a rewording of n. 2417 about the use of animals in experiments. Of course, teaching has changed over the centuries, for example, regarding the legitimacy of slavery. Papal Bulls have been subject to change, as mentioned in Part One chapter five, when Puis V's *De Salute Gregis* was largely revoked under pressure.

If changes in the passages about animals were to be made to a future edition of the CCC, of what might they consist? The following is my suggestion for how the paragraphs might read in a future edition of the CCC, involving as little change as possible while reflecting the theology expressed in this chapter:

> n. 2415. The seventh commandment enjoins religious respect for the integrity of God's creation. The mineral and vegetable resources of the universe are the common patrimony of the world's people: the use of these resources cannot be divorced from environmental considerations for present and future generations. Economic development must proceed only in consideration of the flourishing of eco-systems that support life. All living creatures have been created for their own purposes and with their own interests, which must be respected by human beings. People's stewardship over them,

granted by the Creator, must not be abused, for human dominion is a role of service, not tyranny. People's treatment,
therefore, of other creatures must be governed by moral
imperatives.

n. 2416. no changes – but perhaps the inclusion of further
examples of saints who have treated animals respectfully and
compassionately

n. 2417. God entrusted animals to the stewardship of those
whom he created in his own image [Cf. Gen 2:19–20 ; Gen 9:
1–4]. Hence human beings must remember that animals, both
domestic and wild, belong to God, not to them, and so treat
them with all kindness and consideration. When people use
animals to meet their legitimate basic needs, which cannot
otherwise be met, they must do their utmost to secure the
well-being of the animals to the highest possible degree, and
not give priority to the concerns of income and profit. People
will not make animals work beyond their strength, nor impose
living conditions contrary to their natures. They will not
engage in leisure pursuits which, directly or indirectly, cause
suffering to animals. The use of animals in experiments, other
than for the benefit of the individual animals concerned, (or, in
rare cases, for the sake of the animals' own species) is not an
appropriate exercise of human stewardship.

n. 2418: By adopting in love the roles of servant and priest of
creation, the human being goes beyond simply fulfilling duties
towards animals. People's love for them must be appropriate
to the needs of the species. It is contrary to God's rights
over his creation for animals to be caused any suffering, and
especially premature death, except under exceptional circumstances and where no alternative cause of action is available.
While the relief of human suffering must always be a duty of
the highest priority, that is not to disregard the legitimate use
of resources for the relief of animal suffering.

The pastoral consequences of such amendments to the principal teaching document of the Catholic Church would be
profound. Such new wording would also be a witness for the
world at large that Christianity truly supports and values life in

an inclusive way, and also abjures cruelty to the most weak and vulnerable. It would signal the Church's commitment to the 'integrity of creation' and to today's ecological challenges. Human beings would not lose anything of their unique role in creation, although the emphasis would be on responsibility and service rather than on the anthropocentrism which has defined the status quo. The Church would be seen to be helping to create a more humane society, one modelled on the true humanity of the loving Christ. (The epithet 'humane', used to identify animal welfare societies in the USA, is a telling one, signifying that cruelty to animals betrays the authentic humanity of the perpetrators.)

Were the school of compassion for all living creatures really to take root in the hearts of the over one billion individual Roman Catholics throughout the world, the treatment of animals would undergo root and branch reform. Meanwhile, in local parishes, small changes could be effected. There is no room here to detail all the changes to Catholic life resulting from this pro-animal theology, except to mention briefly the following. Liturgies could be amended and created to express thanksgiving for animal creation and contrition for the human acts and attitudes which have caused suffering to animals. At the simplest level, prayers for animals could be included in the Prayer of the Faithful (Bidding Prayers) of the Mass, and attention drawn to those parts of the Mass which refer to 'all creation' (as in the Prayer of Offering and the Prayer to the Father in Eucharistic Prayer III). Many liturgical prayers and practices are already in the Tradition, but have been long neglected. As Andrew Linzey wrote in the first-ever book of rites for animal services, 'It is still not too late for the Christian community to develop and expand its rites so that its latent sensitivity can be manifest and in such a way that those who care for animals can identify the Christian vision of peacefulness as their own.'[38] The practice of holding animal blessing services could be expanded and, on a regular basis, people encouraged to bring their (well-behaved) pets forward for a blessing at Communion. These pets are often considered to be 'members of the family' and attention given to them would be warmly welcomed by their owners, especially when some people have to forego attendance at services rather than leave their animals alone. People frequently feel the need for pastoral and liturgical support to cope with the death of pets, and suitable services and prayers could be devised to offer comfort at this time. Educational and homiletic materials which reflect the positive teaching of the Church towards animal creation could be developed, and the virtues which enhance a positive and merciful treatment of animals be included in the work of spiritual direction and formation. The works and spirituality of the many pro-animal saints could be revisited and encouraged to be widely disseminated. The many animal charities and charitable activities would welcome the support of the millions of Catholics. Special days could be set aside within the Church's calendar to focus attention, for example Animal Welfare Sunday, the one nearest to the 4 October feast of St Francis, could be officially adopted, as could the 'Feast of Creation' on 1 September, initiated by the Orthodox Church in 1989, when it asks God 'to protect nature from calamities of human origin', and asks Christians 'to become the voice of creation … by bearing its supplication before the throne of God'.[39] Church groups, parishes and leaders could become beacons of ethical consumption within society, eschewing all products tainted with cruelty, and withdrawing patronage from all leisure and sporting activities involving cruelty.

As a result of all this, a child's instinctive empathy for animals would not meet the harsh reaction of the clerically-trained theologian who today still regards nonhuman life as of little or no account. This poem by a Jesuit scholar, Robert Murray, sums up the transition from antipathy to empathy, the metanoia hoped for from the development of a Catholic theology of animals:

The School of Compassion[40]

Clare, do you remember the child who asked me
To bless the corner where you buried your mouse?
And I who had unlearned the logic of childhood
Gave you cold answer of book-theology:
'Mice have no need of grace or blessing,
but only humans who choose evil and good.'
But now I have learned in the school of compassion
I did not pass over the yearling squirrel
Lying cold and stiff in the Wealden lane,
But lifted him gently and reverently laid him
Cradled by roots of a wayside oak,
Briefly his playground and now his long home.
Over his body, torn head to still tail,
I traced the sign of the world's mending
And said 'Little brother, more innocent than I,
Remember me in the peaceable kingdom.'

Notes

1 CCC n. 2416: 'Animal are God's creatures', and the section 'The Visible
   World', paragraphs 337ff.

2 Especially in *Christianity and the rights of animals* (London: SPCK,
   1987), chapter five, pp. 68–99.

3 A brief clarifying summary of Linzey's ideas of theos-rights is given in the
   chapter 'Responding to the Debate about Animal Theology', *Creatures
   of the Same God: explorations in animal theology*, by Andrew Linzey
   (Winchester UP, 2007), especially pp. 87–8.

4 Tommaso Maria Cardinal Zigliara, *Philosophia Moralis* (9th edition,
   Rome), p. 136.

5 Henry Davis, SJ, *Moral and Pastoral Theology*, Vol. 2, 'Commandments
   of God/Precepts of the Church', Heythrop Series II (London: Sheed and
   Ward, 4th edition 1943), p. 258. He repeats Aquinas's view that the feelings of pity for pain in animals can induce similar feelings for people,
   and suggests that biblical anti-cruelty texts were 'to recall the Jewish
   people – naturally prone to cruelty – to a sense of pity', p. 259. I repeat
   this touch of anti-Semitism as an example of the distance traveled in
   moral theology since that time.

6 Germain Grisez, *Difficult Moral Questions* (The Way of the Lord Jesus,
   Vol. 3) (Quincy, IL: Franciscan Press, 1997), p. 289 – the note for this citation refers both to Genesis 9:1–3 and CCC n. 2417.

7 Edward Cardinal Manning, *The Zoophilist*, London (1 April 1887).

8 *God's Animals*, by Dom Ambrose Agius, OSB (June 1970), p.2.

9 That is, *The Penny Catechism*, or *A Catechism of Christian Doctrine*, approved by the Hierarchy of England and Wales in 1911, and intended for the teaching of children, particularly in preparation for their First Communion. Its questions and answers were learnt by rote.

10 This may be an example of wishful thinking on the part of the Cardinal as no evidence, either textual or even anecdotal, can be found to support it. This does not mean none was ever so taught.

11 Andrew Linzey, *Christianity and the Rights of Animals* (London: SPCK, 1987), p. 69.

12 Ibid., p. 83.

13 See Linzey's discussion of sentience as a basis for rights, in Ibid., p. 81 ff.

14 Ibid., p. 76.

15 Of course, such goodness is found not only in authentic Christians, but in all who, albeit unknowingly or unconsciously, follow his way to full humanity.

16 Not only Eastern, Aquinas too held that 'Man in a certain sense contains all things; and so according as he is master of what is within himself, in the same way he can have mastership over other things', *Summa Theologiae*, I, 96,2. But although this concept had been brought out in the allegorical tradition of both Eastern and Western Christianity, it did not lead to the concept of priesthood of creation as it did in the Eastern Church.

17 Of course, this has its critics. St Gregory of Nyssa denigrates this view as a 'grandiloquent title' which 'honoured man with the characteristics of the mosquito and the mouse', from 'De hominis opificio, XVI', P.G.,t.44,177D-180 A., cited in Vladimir Lossky, *The Mystical Theology of the Eastern Church* (Cambridge and London: James Clarke and Co, 1944, 1957), p. 114. See also Zizioulas, 'Priest of creation', in *Environmental Stewardship*, edited by R. J. Berry (T&T Clark International, 2006), p. 286ff.

18 Vladimir Lossky, *The Mystical Theology of the Eastern Church*, p.110.

19 J. B. Torrance, *Worship, Communion and the Triune God of Grace* (Downer's Grove, IL.: InterVarsity Press, 1996), p. 14.

20 Not only Orthodox Christianity, but also Hasidic Judaism holds this concept of the priesthood of creation, cf. Larry Rasmussen, 'Symbols to live by', *Environmental Stewardship*, 2006, edited by R. J. Berry (T&T Clark International, 2006), p. 181. Also the 'Evangelical Declaration on the Care of Creation' gives humanity's calling to 'offer creation and civilisation back in praise to the Creator', *The Care of Creation*, edited by R. J. Berry (Leicester: Intervarsity Press, 2000), pp. 17–22; cited in 'To Render Praise', by Murray Rae, *Environmental Stewardship* (2006), p. 301.

21 Hans Urs von Balthasar, *Theo-Drama: theological dramatic theory: last Act.* Vol.5, translated by G. Harrison (Fort Collins, CO: Ignatius Press, 1998), p. 420.

22 Zizioulas, 'Priest of creation', *Environmental Stewardship* (2006), p. 288.

23 George Herbert, 'Providence', *The Works of George Herbert*, edited by F. E. Hutchinson (Oxford: Clarendon Press, 1959), p. 117.

24 Zizioulas, 'Priest of creation', *Environmental Stewardship* (2006), p.289.

25 Pope John Paul II's 2003 Encyclical letter, *Ecclesia de Eucharistia*, From the Introduction, paragraph 8. It can be found on the website: <http://www.vatican.va/holy_father/special_features/encyclicals /documents/hf_jp-ii_enc_ 20030417 _ ecclesia_eucharistia_en.html>

26 Romans 12:1.

27 Romans 12:4.

28 This is, however, the implication given in the words of a Preface of a eucharistic prayer published in 1985 by the International Commission on English in the Liturgy: 'You gave us breath and speech, / that all the living might find a voice to sing your praise.' However, as a result of the US bishops rejection of the prayer, its use is confined to eucharistic celebration at creation-theology workshops. See Sean McDonagh, 'Communion and the cosmos', *The Tablet* (5 March 2005), pp. 14–15.

29 Cited by Alan Rudrum in 'Ethical Vegetarianism in Seventeenth-Century Britain: its roots in sixteenth-century European theological debate', *The Seventeenth Century*, 18.1 (spring 2003), p. 88; from a Royal Society MS transcript of a letter by Boyle by Professor J. J. Macintosh in the paper 'Roger Boyle on Animal Rights'.

30 Richard Bauckham, 'Modern Dominion of Nature', *Environmental Stewardship*, edited by R. J. Berry (London: T&T Clark International, 2006), pp. 48–9. See also Ruth Plant, 'The Fellowship of All Creation' in the same book: 'We may not be able to hear or understand the praise given by animals, insects or plants, but then, for all our abilities, we are limited humans and it is to God that the thankfulness for being is expressed', p. 98.

31 Christopher Southgate, 'Stewardship and its competitors', *Environmental Stewardship*, p. 187.

32 W. Berry, *The Gift of Good Land* (San Francisco: North Point Press, 1981), p. 281; cited in Christopher Southgate, 'Stewardship and its competitors', *Environmental Stewardship*, p. 187.

33 *Mystical Treatises by Isaac the Syrian*, translated from the Syriac text by Bedjan Koninklijke (Amsterdam: Akademie van Wetenschappen te Amsterdam, 1923); cited in Vladimir Lossky, *The Mystical Theology of the Eastern Church* (Cambridge and London: James Clarke and Co, 1944, 1957), p.111.

34 Unless otherwise attributed, these references to the work of Bulgakov
    are taken from notes at a lecture by Dr Rowan Williams, Archbishop of
    Canterbury, 'Creator, Creativity and Creatureliness: the wisdom of finite
    existence' at a study day on Holy Wisdom, at the Oxford Centre for
    Mission Studies (23 April 2005).

35 In one of his sermons, 'Pentecost and the descent of the Spirit', he
    describes the descent of the Spirit as 'the fulfilment of Christ's work and
    the realization of God's conception of man, since man was created to be
    the temple of the Holy Spirit *together with the world of nature* of which
    he is meant to be the head and the soul'. Sergei Bulgakov, *The Wisdom
    of God*, in *A Bulgakov Anthology* edited by James Pain and Nicolas
    Zernov (London: SPCK, 1976), p. 184. He explicitly reaffirms the univer-
    sality of Romans 8: 'not only man but nature as a whole is predestined
    for [the] glory [to come]' (p. 186), and declares that 'the Lord is already
    united to his creation. He has deified it and abides in it' (p. 187).
    Bulgakov describes the world as being both *in* God ... (Romans 11:36),
    and at the same time, *outside* God. Bulgakov adopts 'panentheism',
    which, unlike pantheism, does not consider that the world is identical
    with God, but belongs to God 'for it is in God that it finds the founda-
    tion of its reality' (p. 155).

36 Edward Carpenter, then Dean of Westminster Abbey, 'Christian Faith
    and the Moral Aspect of Hunting, *Against Hunting: a symposium*,
    edited by P. Moore (London: Gollanz, 1965), p.136; cited in Andrew
    Linzey, *Christianity and the Rights of Animals*, (London SPCK, 1987),
    p. 98.

37 For an account of a 'process theology' approach in which the resur-
    rected life of all living beings, even plant and micro-organism life, is
    absorbed into a 'remembering' of God, see Jay B. McDaniel, *Of God and
    Pelicans: a theology of reverence for life* (Louisville, Kentucky; West-
    minster/John Knox Press, 1989). Absorption, however, is an inadequate
    expression of the eschatological mystery of redemption.

38 Andrew Linzey, *Animal Rites: liturgies of animal care.* (London: SCM,
    1999), p. 19.

39 Oliver   Clement,   *Conversations   with   Ecumenical   Patriarch
    Bartholomew I* (1987), p. 99; cited in Paul McPartlan, 'Mastery or
    Mystery: the Orthodox view of nature', *Priests & People*, 14.2 (February
    2000), p. 63.

40 First published in *The Month* (July 1991), and *Theology in Green*, 5.2
    (June 1995), p. 44.

Bibliography

Articles and papers consulted

Addison, Joseph, *The Spectator*, 120 (18 July, 1711).

Agius, OSB, Ambrose, 'Building "The Ark"', *The Ark*, 75 (April 1962).

—— 'Obituary [for Pope John XXIII]', *The Ark* 79 (August 1963).

—— 'Pius XII loved animals', *The Ark* 69 (April 1960).

—— 'The Popes and Animal Welfare', *The Ark* 74 (December 1961).

Altmann, A., 'A Note on the Rabbinic Doctrine of Creation', *The Journal of Jewish Studies*, 7.3–4 (1956).

Anderson, B.W., 'From Analysis to Synthesis: the interpretation of Genesis 1–11', *Journal of Biblical Literature*, 97 (1978).

Angros, Robert M., 'Nature acts for an end', *The Thomist*, 66.3 (2002).

Arbogast, M., 'Fur, Conscience and Native Economies', *The Witness*, 76.10 (October 1993).

Atkins, Margaret, 'Is God kind to animals?', *Priests & People*, 13.4 (April 1999).

—— 'I think therefore I love', *The Way*, 41.3 (July 2001).

—— 'St Jerome and the Lion', *The Ark* 182 (spring 1999).

—— 'St Macarius and the Hyena', *The Ark* 193 (spring 2003).

Balcombe, Jonathan, 'They think, feel pain', *Miami Herald* (10 November 2006).

Barad, Judith, 'Aquinas' Inconsistency on the Nature and the Treatment of animals', *Between the Species*, 4.2 (spring 1988).

Barad-Andrade, Judith , 'Aquinas and Evolution: a compatible duo', *Medievalia*, 13 (April 1993).

Barr, James, 'Man and Nature: the ecological controversy and the Old Testament', *Bulletin of the John Rylands Library*, 55 (1972).

Bartlett, Christopher, 'A Conversation with Andrew Linzey: on Christianity and animals', *The Animals' Agenda*, 9.4 (April 1989).

Begley, Sharon, 'What your pet is thinking', *Wall Street Journal* (27 October 2006).

Berkman, John, 'Prophetically Pro-Life: John Paul II's gospel of life and evangelical concern for animals', *Josephinum Journal of Theology*, 6.1 (1999).

—— 'Medicine, Animals and Theology', *St Mark's Review* (winter 1992).

Bishops' Conference of England and Wales, 'Guidelines for the Use of the CCC', *Briefing*, 24 (26 May 1994).

Børresen, Bergjlot, 'Friend, Foe or Food? Social vs Predatory Emotions in Dealings across the Species Barrier', Paper given at workshop for Human Animal Relations, Oslo University (November 1999).

Bowman, Leonard J., 'The Cosmic Exemplarism of Bonaventure', *Journal of Religion* 55: 2 (April 1975).

Boyle, Nicholas, 'Human rights and our human God', *The Tablet* (18 March 2006).

Braaten L. J., 'The Groaning Creation: the biblical background for Romans 8:22', *Biblical Research: journal of the Chicago Society of Biblical* Research, Vol. L, 2005.

Brett, Stephen F., 'Reception and the Catechism', *The Homiletic and Pastoral* Review (October 1994).

Buckley, Francis J., 'What to Do with the New Catechism', *Church*, 9 (summer 1993).

'C', 'Animal Legends', *The Ark*, 45 (April 1952).

Clark, Jeremy, 'Shambo looked like a finalist for "best in show", not a condemned invalid', *The Spectator* (2 June 2007).

Clark, Stephen R. L., 'Animal Wrongs', *Analysis*, 38.3 (June 1978).

Cohn, Priscilla, 'Animal Rights, Animal Liberation and Animal Welfare', paper delivered to the IV International Meeting for Animals, in Tossa del Mar, Spain (September 30–October 2, 1994).

Conti, Bishop Mario, Speech to the Scottish Order of Christian Unity, 23 August 2001, *Briefing*, 31. 11 (16 November 2001).

Cronin, G., 'The Bestiary and the Medieval Mind: some complexities', *Modern Language Quarterly*, 2, (1941).

Dennehy, Raymond, 'The Ontological Basis of Human Rights', *The Thomist*, 42 (1978).

Dixon, Beth, 'The Feminist Connection between Women and Animals', *Environmental Ethics*, 18.2 (summer 1996).

Douglas, Mary, 'The Forbidden Animals in Leviticus', *Journal for the Study of the Old Testament*, 59 (1993).

Elvins, OFMCap, Mark, 'Animal Rights', *The Ark*, 189 (winter 2001).

Evdokimov, Paul, 'Nature', *Scottish Journal of Theology* 18 (1965)

Eyre-Smith, E., 'De Salute Gregis', *The Ark* 51 (April 1954).
—— 'Letter', *The Ark*, 72 (April 1961).

Eyre-Smith, J., 'The Horse', *The Ark* 69 (April 1960).

Feiss, OSB, Hugh, 'Attitudes towards Animals in Medieval Monastic Literature: lessons for today', *The American Benedictine Review* 53:1 (March 2002).

Fox, Michael W., 'Animal-Insensitivity Syndrome', *The Ark*, 205 (January 2007).

Frey, R. G., 'Animal Rights', *Analysis* 37.4 (June 1977).

Gaspari Pietro, Cardinal, 'Letter in the name of the Pope, to the Toulon branch of the Society for the Protection of Animals', translated by E. Eyre-Smith, *The* Ark, 49 (August 1953).

Giefer, Evelyn Elkin, 'Religion and Animal Rights', *Mainstream* 27.1 (spring 1996).

Gunn, Alistair S., 'Traditional Ethics and the Moral Status of Animals', *Environmental Ethics*, 5.2 (summer 1983).

Hanlon, Michael, 'Do animals deserve human rights too?', *Daily Mail* (1 November 2006)

Hauerwas, Stanley, & Berkman, John, 'The Chief End of All Flesh', *Theology Today*, 49.2 (1992).

Hendrickx, Marie, 'For a More Just Relationship with Animals', *L'Osservatore Romano* (December 2000, also 24 January 2001).

Highfield, Roger, 'So who are you calling a bird brain?' *The Daily Telegraph* (15 November 2006).

Hoffman, Paul, 'St Thomas Aquinas on the halfway State of Sensible Being', *The Philosophical Review*, 99 (1 Jan 1990).

Iltis, H. H., 'Man first? Man last? The paradox of human ecology', *BioScience* 20 (1970).

Jakobovits, I. 'The Medical Treatment of Animals in Jewish Law', *The Journal of Jewish Studies*, 7.3–4 (1956).

Jamieson, D., Regan, T., 'Animal Rights: a reply to Frey', *Analysis*, 38.1 (January 1978)

Johnson, Luke Timothy, *Commonweal*, 120 (7 May 1993).

Johnson, Philip E., 'Metaphysics matters' (book review), *First Things*, 97 (November 1999).

Johnson, Samuel, *The Idler*, 17 (5 August, 1758).

Jones, Deborah M., 'Animal Rights: another perspective', *Faith*, 36.2 (May-June 2004).

Kerr, OP, Fergus, 'And was with the wild beasts', *The Ark*, 185 (summer 2000).

Kilmartin, Edward J., 'Reception in History: an ecclesiological phenomenon and its significance', *Journal of Ecumencial Studies* 21 (1984).

Lamb, David, 'Animal Rights and Liberation Movements', *Environmental Ethics*, 4.3 (Fall 1982).

Lampe, G. W. F., 'The New Testament Doctrine of *Ktisis*', *The Scottish Journal of Theology*, 17 (1964).

LeBlanc, Jill, 'Eco-Thomism', *Environmental Ethics*, 21.3 (Fall 1999).

Legge, James, 'Animal Rights: a perspective on the hunting debate', *Faith*, 36.1 (January-February 2004).

Linzey, Andrew, 'Jesus and Animals in Christian Apocalyptic Literature', *Modern Believing*, 48:1 (Jan 2007).

—— 'Towards Ethical Science', Report of the International Animal Welfare Congress, Helsingborg (10 August 1996).

Lumley, Joanna, 'The Church Compassionate', *Priests & People*, 16.7 (July 2002).

Mangan, Celine, 'The Bible: salvation or creation history?', *Priests & People*, 14.2 (February 2000).

Manning, Cardinal Edward, *The Zoophilist* (1 April 1887); *The Ark* 130 (August 1980).

McDonagh, Sean, 'Communion and the cosmos', *The Tablet* (5 March 2005).

McGrade, A. S., 'Aristotle's Place in the History of Natural Rights', *The Review of Metaphysics*, 49 (1996).

McLoughlin, David, 'The treasure-house of faith', *The Tablet*, (28 May 1994).

McPartlan, Paul, 'Mastery or Mystery: the Orthodox view of nature', *Priests & People*, 14.2 (February 2000).

Mullins, Brody 'Puppy Power: how Humane Society gets the vote out', *Wall Street* Journal (7 November 2006).

Murray, Robert, 'The School for Compassion' (poem), *The Month*, July 1991; also

Theology in Green, 5.2 (June 1995).

Pacifici, Mimmo, *Gente*, (February 1990).

Pease, A. S., 'Caeli Enarrant', *Harvard Theological Review*, 34. 3 (1941).

Paul VI, 'The Reply of our Holy Father, Pope Paul VI', *The Ark*, 93 (April 1968).

Pope, Alexander, *The Guardian*, 61 (21 May 1713).

Provilitus, Anthony J., 'On Assigning Rights of Animals and Nature', *Environmental Ethics* 2.1 (spring 1980).

Rausch, SJ, Thomas P., 'Reception Past and Present', *Theological Studies* 47 (1986).

Rudrum Alan, 'Ethical Vegetarianism in Seventeenth-Century Britain: its roots in sixteenth-century European theological debate', *The Seventeenth Century*, 18.1 (spring 2003).

Schönborn, Christopher, 'Major themes and Underlying Principles of the CCC', *The Living Light* (Fall 1993).

Singer, Peter, 'The Parable of the Fox and the Unliberated Animals', *Ethics*, 88 (January 1978).

Sobran, Joseph, 'The Dark Side of Dolphins', *Christian Order*, 47.10 (October 2006).

Tardiff, Andrew, 'A Catholic Case for Vegetarianism', *Faith and Philosophy*, 15.2 (1998).

Trevor, Meriol, 'Cats, dogs, mice, birds, flies and Padre Filippo', *The Ark* 182 (spring 1999).

Van Merrienboer, OP, Edward J., 'St Martin de Porres', *The Ark*, 198 (Autumn 1999).

Wade, Richard A., 'Towards a Christian Ethic of Animals', *Pacifica* 13.2 (June 2000).

Watson, Richard A., 'Self-consciousness and the rights of nonhuman animals and nature', *Environmental Ethics*, 1.2 (summer 1979).

Westra, Laura, 'Ecology and Animals: is there a joint ethic of respect?', *Environmental Ethics* 11.3 (Fall 1989).

White Jr, Lynn, 'The Historical Roots of our Ecologic Crisis' (*Science*, 155 (Jan-March 1967).

Wilberforce, Samuel, 'Review', *Quarterly Review*, 108 (1860).

Journals consulted

American Benedictine Review 53.1 (March 2002).

Analysis 37.4 (June 1977), 38.1 (January 1978), 38.3 (June 1978).

Animals' Agenda The, 9.4 (April 1989).

Ark, The 45 (April 1952); 49 (August 1953); 51 (April 1954); 69 (April 1960); 72 (April 1961); 74 (Dec 1961); 75 (April1962); 79 (August 1963); 93 (April 1968); 130 (August 1980); 182 (spring 1999); 185 (summer 2000); 189 (winter 2001); 193 (spring 2003); 205(spring 2007).

Between the Species 4.2 (spring 1988).

Biblical Literature, Journal of Vol. 97 (1978).

Biology & Philosophy 10.3 (July 1995).

Bioscience 20 (1970).

Briefing 24.3 (26 May 1994); 31.11 (16 Nov 2001).

Bulletin of the John Rylands University Library 55 (1972).

Christian Order 47.10 (October 2006).

Church 9 (summer 1993).

Commonweal 120 (7 May 1993).

Daily Mail, The (1 November 2006).

Daily Telegraph, The (1 November 2006).

Ecotheology 4 (1998); 7.2 (2003).

Ecumenical Studies, Journal of 21(1984).

Encounter (summer 1997).

Environmental Ethics 1.2 (summer 1979); 2.1 (spring 1980); 4.3 (Fall 1982); 5.2 (summer 1983); 11.3 (Fall 1989); 18.2 (summer 1996); 21.3 (Fall 1999).

Ethics 88 (January 1988).

Expository Times, The 83 (1971).

Faith 36.1 (January–February 2004); 36.2 (March–April 2004).

Faith (magazine of the Diocese of Lancing, Ottowa) (16 October 2006).

Faith and Philosophy 15.2 (1997).

First Things 97 (November 1999).

Gente (February 1990).

Guardian, The 61 (21 May 1713).

Harvard Theological Review 34.3 (1941).

Homiletic and Pastoral Review, The (October 1994).

Idler, The 17 (5 August 1758).

Jewish Studies, Journal of 7.3,4 (1956).

Josephinum Journal of Theology 6.1 (winter/spring 1999).

Living Light (Fall 1993).

Mainstream 27.1 (spring 1996).

Medievalia 13 (April 1993).

Miami Herald (10 November 2006).

Modern Believing: church and society 48.1 (January 2007).

Modern Language Quarterly 2 (1941).

Month, The (July 1991).

Osservatore Romano, L' (December 2000); (January 2001).

Pacifica 13.2 (June 2000).

Philosophical Review, The 99 (1 Jan 1990).

Politics 7.3 (September 1987).

Priests & People 11.3 (Mar 1997); 13.4 (April 1999); 14.2 (Feb 2000); 16.7 (July 2002).

Quarterly Review 108 (1860).

Religion, Journal of 55: 2 (April 1975).

Review of Metaphysics, The 49 (1996).

Science 155 (Jan-Mar 1967).

Scientific Study of Religion Journal for the 35.2 (June 1996); 35.4 (December 1996).

Scottish Journal of Theology, The 17 (1964); 18 (1965).

Seventeenth Cenury, The 18.1 (spring 2003).

Spectator, The 120 (18 July, 1711).

Spectator, The (10 March 2001); (2 June 2007).

St Mark's Review (winter 1992).

Studia Patristica 35 (Leuven, 2001).

Study of the Old Testament, Journal for the 59 (1993); 95 (1993).

Tablet, The (28 May 1994); (7 July 1998); (18 March 2006); (5 March 2005).

Theological Studies 47 (1986).

Theology in Green 5.2 (June 1995).

Theology Today 49.2 (1992**).**

Thomist, The 42 (1978); 66.3 (2002)

Wall Street Journal (27 October 2006); (7 November 2006)

Way, The 41.3 (July 2001); 45.4 (October 2006).

Wildlife Society Bulletin, 15.3 (Fall 1987).

Witness, The 76.10 (October 1993).

Zoophilist, The (1 April 1887).

Books consulted

Catechism of the Catholic Church, London, Geoffrey Chapman, 1994, 1997.

Compendium of the Catechism of the Catholic Church, London, Catholic Truth Society, 2000.

Adams, C. J., *The Sexual Politics of Meat: a feminist-vegetarian critical theory*, New York, Continuum, 1990, 2000.

Agius, A., 1960 *Cruelty to Animals*, London, Catholic Truth Society, 1960.

— *God's Animals*, London, The Catholic Study Circle for Animal Welfare, 1970.

Alter, R., Kermode, F. (eds), *Literary Guide to the Bible*, Cambridge, Mass., Harvard UP, 1990.

Anderson, S. R., *Doctor Doolittle's Delusion: animals and the uniqueness of human language*, New Haven and London, Yale UP, 2004.

Arkow, P., *Child Abuse, Domestic Violence, and Animal Abuse*, West LaFayette, Indiana, Purdue UP, 1999.

Armstrong, R. J. et al (eds), *Francis of Assisi: the Saint*. Early Documents 1, New York, New City Press, 1999.

Ashley, B. M., *Living the Truth in Love: a biblical introduction to moral theology*, New York, Alba House, 1996.

Astley, J., Brown, D., Loades, A. (eds), *Creation. Problems in Theology*, 1: a selection of key readings, London, T&T Clark, 2003.

Baker, J. A.. *The Faith of a Christian*. London, Darton, Longman & Todd, 1996.

Balcombe, J., *Pleasurable Kingdom: animals and the nature of feeling good*, London and New York, Macmillan, 2006.

Barad, J., *Aquinas on the Nature and Treatment of Animals*, San Francisco, International Scholars Publications, 1995.

Barber, R. & Riches, A. (eds), *Dictionary of Fabulous Beasts*, London, Macmillan, 1971.

Barbour, I., *Religion in an Age of Science*, Gifford Lectures 1989–1991, Volume 1, London, SCM, 1990.

— *Nature, Human Nature, and God*, London, SPCK, 2002.

Baring-Gould S., *Curious Myths of the Middle Ages*, London, Longmans, Green & Co., 1901.

Barr, J., *The Garden of Eden and the Hope of Immortality*, London, SCM, 1992.

Bayly M. Beddow, *Clinical Medical Discoveries*. London, National Anti-Vivisection Society, 1961.

Bennett, J. A. W., *The Parlement of Fowles: an interpretation*, Oxford, Clarendon 1957.

Berry R. J., *Environmental Stewardship: critical perspectives – past and present*, London, T&T Clark International, 2006.

Berry, T. with Clark, T., *Befriending the Earth: a theology of reconciliation between humans and earth*, Mystic, CT., Twenty-Third Publications, 1991.

Biehl, J., *Finding Our Way: rethinking ecofeminist politics*, Montreal, Black Rose Books, 1991.

Birch C., Eaken W., McDaniel, J. (eds), *Liberating Life: contemporary approaches in ecological theology*, Maryknoll, New York, Orbis, 1990.

Black R., *Christian Moral Realism: natural law, narrative, virtue and the Gospel*, Oxford UP, 2000.

Blum, D., *The Monkey Wars*, New York and Oxford, OUP, 1994.

Bonner, G., *St Augustine of Hippo: life and controversies*, Norwich, The Canterbury Press, 1963, 1986.

Brenner, A. (ed.), *A Feminist Companion to Genesis*, Sheffield, Sheffield Academic Press, 1993.

Breuilly E., Palmer M., *Christianity and Ecology*, World Religions and Ecology, London, Cassell, 1990.

Brontë, A., *Agnes Grey*, London, Penguin, [1847], 1988.

Brooke, J., Cantor, G., *Reconstructing Nature: the engagement of science and religion*, Edinburgh, T&T Clark, 1988.

Brown, A. B., *The Book of Saints and Friendly Beasts*, London, Longmans, Green & Co., 1901.

Browne, R. et al (eds), *The New Jerome Biblical Commentary*, London, Geoffrey Chapman, 1990.

Bruce D., Horrocks, D., *Modifying Creation: GM crops and foods, a Christian response*, Carlisle, Evangelical Alliance Policy Commission Report, 2001.

Brueggemann, W., *The Land: place as gift, promise and challenge in biblical faith*, Philadelphia, Fortress, 1977.

Budiansky, S., *The Covenant of the Wild: why animals chose domestication*, London, Phoenix, 1994, 1997.

Bulgakov, S. N., *The Wisdom of God: a brief summary of sophiology*, Trans. F. Gavin, London, Williams and Norgate, 1937.

Sergius Bulgakov: a Bulgakov anthology, edited by J. Pain and N. Zernov, London, SPCK, 1976.

Bynum, C. W., *Holy Feast and Holy Fast: the religious*

significance of food to medieval women, Berkeley, CA, UCP, 1987.

Carruthers, P., *The Animals Issue: moral theory in practice*, Cambridge UP, 1992.

Cartledge, M., *Practical Theology: charismatic and empirical perspectives*, Carlisle, Cumbria, Paternoster, 2003.

Chapman, J., *Saint Benedict and the Sixth Century*, London, Sheed & Ward, 1929.

Chapman, M. (ed.), 2004 *Celebrating Creation: affirming Catholicism and the revelation of God's glory*, London, Darton, Longman & Todd, 2004.

Chapouthier, G., Nouet J-C., *Universal Declaration of Animal Rights: comments and intentions*, Trans. Shan Benson, Paris, Ligue Francaise des Droits de l'Animal, 1998.

Chesterton, G. K., *Chaucer*, London, Faber and Faber, 1934.

Chittister, J. D. *Heart of Flesh: a feminist spirituality for women and men*, Grand Rapids, MI and Cambridge, UK, Eerdmans, 1998.

Clark, S. R. L., *How to Think about the Earth: philosophical and theological models for ecology*. London, Mowbray (Continuum), 1993.

— *The Moral Status of Animals*, Oxford, Clarendon, 1997.

Clarke, P. A. B., Linzey, A. (eds), *1990 Political Theory and Animal Rights*, London, Pluto, 1990.

— *Dictionary of Ethics, Theology and Society*, London and New York, Routledge, 1996.

— *Animal Rights: a historical anthology*, New York, Columbia UP, 2004.

Clifford, R. J., *Creation Accounts in the Ancient Near East and in the Bible*, Washington DC, The Catholic Biblical Assoc. of America, 1994.

Code L. (ed.), *Feminist Perspectives: philosophical essays on method and morals*, Toronto University Press, 1988.

Coetzee, J. M., *The Lives of Animals*, London, Profile, 2000.

Collins, P., *God's Earth: religion as if matter really mattered*, Dublin, Gill and Macmillan, 1995.

Conlon, J., *Earth Story, Sacred Story*. Mystic, CN., Twenty-

Third Publications, 1994.

Cox, H., *The Secular City*, New York, Macmillan, 1965.

Crawford, R., *The God/Man/World Triangle: a dialogue between science and religion*, Basingstoke, Hamps., Macmillan, 1997.

Cross, J. M., *The Song of the Sea and Canaanite Myth: essays in the history of the religion of Israel*, Cambridge, Mass., Harvard UP, 1973.

Crüsemann, F., *The Torah: theology and social history of Old Testament Law*, trans. Allan W. Mahnke, Edinburgh, T&T Clark, 1996.

Dahood, R. (ed.), *The Future of the Middle Ages and the Renaissance*, Turnhout, Belgium, Brepol, 1999.

Davies, B., *The Thought of Thomas Aquinas*, Oxford, Clarendon, 1992.

Davies, O., *Celtic Spirituality*, Classics of Western Spirituality, New York, Paulist, 1999.

Davies, R. H. C. et al (eds), 1981 *The Writing of History in the Middle Ages*, Oxford, Clarendon, 1981.

Davis, H., *Moral and Pastoral Theology: Commandments of God*, Heythrop Series, Vol. 2, London, Sheed and Ward, 1935, 1943.

Davis H. F., Crehan, J., et al (eds), *A Catholic Dictionary of Theology*, Volume One, London, Thomas Nelson and Sons, 1962.

Day, P. D., *Eastern Christian Liturgies: Armenian, Coptic, Ethiopian and Syrian Rites*, Shannon, Irish UP, 1972.

Deane-Drummond, C., *Creation through Wisdom: theology and the new biology*, Edinburgh, T&T Clark, 2000.

Delany, B., *On the Ways of God*, London, Burns and Oates, 1926.

Delio, I., *Simply Bonaventure: an introduction to his life, thought and writings*, New York, New City Press, 2001.

De Lubac, H., *Medieval Exegesis*: Volume 2: *The four senses of Scripture*, trans. E. M. Macierowski, Edinburgh, T&T Clark, 1959, 2000.

— *The Mystery of the Supernatural*, trans. Rosemary Sheed,

New York, Herder and Herder, 1965.

—*A Brief Catechesis on Nature and Grace*, trans. R. Arnandez, San Francisco, Ignatius, 1984.

De Vaux, R., *Ancient Israel, its life and institutions*, trans. John McHugh, London, Darton, Longman & Todd, 1961, 1965.

De Waal F., *Our Inner Ape*, New York, Riverhead/ Penguin, 1993.

Derrick, C., *The Delicate Creation: towards a theology of the environment*, London, Tom Stacey, 1972.

Devas, D., *The Franciscan Order*, London, Burns Oates and Washbourne, 1930.

Doolan, I., *Philosophy for the Layman*, Dublin, Dominican Publications, 1944, 1954.

Douglas, M., *In the Wilderness: the doctrine of defilement in the Book of Numbers*, Oxford UP, 2001.

Downer, A. S. (ed.), *1950 English Institute Essays*, New York, Columbia UP, 1950.

Eaton, H., *Introducing Feminist Theologies*, Edinburgh, T & T Clark, 2005.

Echlin, E. P., *Earth Spirituality: Jesus at the centre*, New Alresford, Arthur James, 1999.

— *The Cosmic Circle: Jesus and ecology*, Blackrock, Co. Dublin, Columbia, 2004.

Edwards, D., *Creation, Humanity, Community: building a new theology*, Dublin, Gill and Macmillan, 1992.

Edwards, J. R., *The Gospel according to St Mark*, Grand Rapids, Eerdmans, 2002.

Ely, M., et al (eds) *Doing Qualitative Research: circles within circles*, London and New York, Routledge Farmer, 1991.

Evans, E. P., *The Criminal Prosecution and Capital Punishment of Animals*, London: William Heinemann, 1906.

Faricy, R., *Wind & Sea Obey Him: approaches to a theology of nature*, London, SCM, 1982.

Farnum, G. R., *1947 Vivisection: a dark blot on civilization*, Boston, New England Anti-Vivisection Society, 1947.

Farwell Brown, A., *The Book of Saints and Friendly Beasts*, London, Green and Co., 1901.

Fellenz, M. R., *The Moral Menagerie: philosophy and animal rights*, Urbana and Chicago, University of Illinois Press, 2007.

Fox, M., *Original Blessing: a primer in creation spirituality*, New York, Jeremy P. Tarcher/Putnam, 1983, 2000.

— *Bringing Life to Ethics: global bioethics for a humane society*, Albany, NY, State of NYUP, 2001.

Fr Cuthbert, OSFC, *The Romanticism of St Francis*, London, Longman, Green & Co., 1924.

Fragomeni, R. N., Pawlikowski, J. T. (eds), *The Ecological Challenge: ethical, liturgical and spiritual responses*, Collegeville, MN., Michael Glazier, The Liturgical Press, 1994.

Frey, R. G., *Rights, Killing and Suffering*, Oxford UP, 1983.

Fudge, E., *Perceiving Animals: humans and beasts in early modern English culture*, Urbana and Chicago, University of Illinois Press, 2002.

Gaard, G. (ed), *Ecofeminism: women, animals, nature*, Philadelphia, Temple UP, 1993.

Gaita, R., *The Philosopher's Dog*, London and New York, Routledge, 2002.

Gilligan, C., *In a Different Voice: psychological theory and women's development*, Cambridge, Mass., Harvard UP, 1982.

Ginsberg, F., Tsing A. L. (eds), *Uncertain Terms: negotiating gender in American Culture*, Boston, Beacon Press, 1990.

Glazier, M., Hellwig, M. (eds), *1994 Modern Catholic Encyclopedia*, Dublin, Gill & Macmillan, 1994.

Gold, M., *Animal Century: a celebration of changing Attitudes to animals*, Charlbury, Oxon, Jon Carpenter, 1998.

Gompertz, L., *Moral Inquiries on the Situation of Man and of Brutes* (edited by P. Singer), Fontwell, Sussex, Centaur Press, 1824, 1992.

Graham, E., *Making the Difference: gender, personhood and theology*, London, Mowbray, 1995.

Grange, A. M., *The Church and Kindness to Animals*, London, Burns & Oates, 1906.

Green J. P., Sr (ed. and trans.), *Interlinear Hebrew-Aramaic Old Testament*, Vol. I of *The Interlinear Hebrew-Greek-English Bible*, Peabody, Mass., Henrickson, 1985.

Green, L., *Earth Age: a new vision of God, the human and the earth*, New York & Mahwah, NJ, Paulist, 1994.

Gregg, R.C. (trans), *Athanaius: the Life of Antony*, New York, Paulist, 1980.

Grey, M. C. *The Wisdom of Fools: seeking revelation for today*. London, SPCK, 1993.

— *Sacred Longings: ecofeminist theology and globalization*, London, SCM, 2003.

Grisez, G., *Difficult Moral Questions* (The Way of the Lord Jesus series, Vol. 3), Quincey, IL, Franciscan Press, 1997.

Gruber, J. W., *A Conscience in Conflict: the life of St George Jackson Mivart*, New York, Columbia UP, 1960.

Habel, N. C., Wurst, S. (eds), *The Earth Story in Genesis*, Sheffield, Sheffield Academic Press, 2002.

Haldane, J. (ed.), *Mind, Metaphysics and Value in the Thomistic and Analystic Traditions*, Indiana, Notre Dame UP, 2002.

Harrison, C., *Augustine: Christian Truth and Fractured Humanity* (Christian Theology in Context series), Oxford, OUP, 2002.

Harrison, C., *Rethinking Augustine's early Theology: an argument for continuity*, Oxford, OUP, 2006.

Haughton R., 1973 *Tales from Eternity: the world of faerie and the spiritual search*, London, George Allen and Unwin, 1973.

Hebblethwaite, B., *Evil, Suffering and Religion*, London, SPCK, 2000.

Hessel D. T., Ruether R. R. (eds), *Christianity and Ecology: seeking the well-being of earth and humans*, Cambridge, Harvard UP, 2000.

Hildrop, J., (3rd edn), *Free Thoughts upon the Brute Creation, or, an examination of Fr Bougeant's philosphical amusements, etc*, London, R. Minors, 1745.

Hills, A., *Do Animals Have Rights?* Thriplow, Cambs, Icon, 2005.

Hinde, R. A., *Ethology*, London, Fontana paperbacks, 1982.

Hough, A., *God is not Green: a re-examination of ecotheology*, Leominster, Gracewing, 1997.

Hudleston, R. (ed. and trans), *The Little Flowers of Saint Francis*, Springfield, IL: Templegate, 1988.

Hume, C. W., *The Status of Animals in the Christian Religion*, London, UFAW, 1957.

— *Man and Beast*, Potters Bar, Herts, UFAW, 1962, 1982.

Hursthouse, R., *On Virtue Ethics*, Oxford UP, 1999.

Hyland, J. R., *The Slaughter of Terrified Beasts*, Sarasota, FL., Viatoris Ministries, 1988, 1999.

Isherwood, L., McEwan D. (eds), *An A-Z of Feminist Theology*, Sheffield, Sheffield Academic Press, 1995.

John Paul II *Crossing the Threshold of Hope*, New York, Alfred Knopf, 1994.

Kant, I., *Lectures on Ethics* (translated by Louis Infield), New York, Harper & Row, 1963.

Karrer, O. (ed.), Wydenbruck, N. (trans.), *The Little Flowers Legends, and Lauds of St Francis of Assisi,* London, Sheed and Ward, 1947, 1979.

Kaufman, S. R., Braun, N., 2002 *Good News for All Creation: vegetarianism as Christian stewardship*, Cleveland, Vegetarian Advocates Press, 2002.

Kempis T. À., *The Imitation of Christ*, translated by L. Sherley-Price, Harmondsworth, Penguin, ?1413, 1952.

Kenny, A., *Ancient Philosophy,* Vol. 1, Oxford, Clarendon, 2004.

Kreeft, P., *Back to Virtue*, San Francisco, Ignatius Press, 1992.

LaChance, A., Carroll, J. E. (eds), *Embracing Earth: Catholic approaches to ecology*, Maryknoll, NY, Orbis, 1994.

Lane Fox, R., *Pagans and Christians in the Mediterranean World*, London, Penguin, 1986, 1988.

Lauck, J. E., *The Voice of the Infinite in the Small: revisioning the insect-human connection*, Mill Spring, NC, Swan, Raven, 1998.

Lawrence, C. H., *Medievel Monasticism*, London and New York, Longman, 1984.

Lightfoot, J., *A Commentary on the New Testament from the Hebraica. Matthew – I Corinthians*, Vol. 4, Grand Rapids, Baker, 1979.

Linzey, A., *Animal Rights: a Christian Assessment*, London, SCM, 1976.

— *Animal Theology*, London, SCM, 1984.

— *The Status of Animals in the Christian Tradition*, Woodbrooke College, Birmingham, 1985.

— *Christianity and the Rights of Animals*, London, SPCK, 1987.

— *Animals and Christianity: a book of readings*, New York, Crossroads, 1988.

— *Animal Theology*, Chicago, Univ. of Illinois Press, 1985.

— *Animal Gospel: Christian faith as though animals mattered*, London, Hodder & Stoughton, 1998.

— *Animal Rites: liturgies of animal care*, London, SCM, 1999.

— *Creatures of the Same God: explorations in animal theology*, Winchester UP, 2007.

Linzey, A., Cohn-Sherbok D. (eds), *After Noah: animals and the liberation of theology*, London, Mowbray, 1996.

Linzey, A., Yamamoto D. (eds), *Animals on the Agenda*, London, SCM, 1998.

Loening, K., Zenger, E., *To Begin with, God Created: biblical theologies of creation*, trans. Omar Kaste, Collegeville, Minn., Michael Glazier, The Liturgical Press, 2000.

Lossky, V., *The Mystical Theology of the Eastern Church*. Cambridge and London, James Clarke, 1944, 1957.

Low, M., *Celtic Christianity and Nature*, Edinburgh UP, 1996.

MacQuarrie, J., *Twentieth-century religious thought: the frontiers of philosophy and theology, 1900–1970*, London, SCM, 1963, 1971.

Marsh, J., *Christina Rosetti; a literary biography*, London, Jonathan Cape, 1994.

Marthaler, B. L. (ed.), *Introducing the Catechism of the Catholic Church*, New Jersey, Paulist Press, 1994.

Masson, J., McCarthy, *When Elephants Weep: the emotional*

lives of animals, London, Vintage, 1994.

Masson, J., 1998 *Dogs Never Lie About Love: reflections on the emotional world of dogs*, London, Vintage, 1998.

McCabe, H., *The Teaching of the Catholic Church: a new catechism of Christian doctrine*, London, Darton, Longman & Todd, 1985.

McCaughey, T. P., *Memory and Redemption: Church, politics and prophetic theology in Ireland*, Dublin, Gill and Macmillan, 1993.

McDaniel, J. B., *Of God and Pelicans: a theology of reverence for life*, Louisville, Kentucky, Westminster/John Knox, 1989.

McDonagh, S., *Passion for the Earth: the Christian vocation to promote justice, peace and the integrity of creation*, London, Geoffrey Chapman, 1994.

— *The Death of Life: the horror of extinction*. Blackrock, Co. Dublin, Columba, 2004.

McFague, S., *Models of God: theology for an ecological, nuclear age*, Philadelphia, Fortress, 1987.

— *The Body of God: an ecological theology*, Minneapolis, Fortress, 1993.

McNeil, J. T., Gamer, H. M., *Medieval Handbooks of Penance: a translation of the principle libri poenitentiale and selection from related documents*, New York and Oxford, Columbia UP, 1938, 1990.

McPartlan, P., *The Eucharist Makes the Church: Henri de Lubac and John Zizioulas in dialogue*, Edinburgh, T&T Clark, 1993.

Metz, J., *Theology of the World*, trans. W. Glen-Doepel, London, Burns & Oates, 1969.

Meyer, R. T. (trans.), *St Athanasius: Life of Antony*, London: Ancient Christian Writers, 1950.

Midgley, M., *Animals and Why They Matter*, London, Penguin, 1983.

— *Science as Salvation: a modern myth and its meaning*, London and New York, Routledge, 2002, 2004.

— *The Myths We Live By*, London and New York, Routledge, 2004.

Mivart, St G. J., *On the Generation of Species*, London and

New York, Macmillan and Co., 1871.

Moltmann, J., 1985 *God in Creation: an ecological doctrine of creation*, trans. Margaret Kohl, Munich and London, SCM, 1985.

Moore, J. H., [1906], 1992 *The Universal Kinship*, edited by C. Magel, Fontwell, Sussex, Centaur, [1906], 1992.

Moorman, J. R. H., 1976 *Saint Francis of Assisi*, London, SPCK, 1950, 1976.

— *History of the Franciscan Order*, Oxford, Clarendon, 1968.

— *Richest of Poor men: the spirituality of Francis of Assisi*, London, Darton, Longman & Todd, 1977.

Morley, H. (ed.), *Ideal Commonwealths*, New York, The Colonial Press, 1901.

Murphy, C. M., *At Home on Earth: foundations for a Catholic ethic of the environment*, New York, Crossroad, 1989.

Murrey, R., *The Cosmic Covenant*, London, Sheed & Ward, 1992.

Nichols, A., *The Service of Glory*, Edinburgh, T&T Clark, 1997.

Niven, C. D., *History of the Humane Movement*, New York, *Transatlantic Arts*, 1967.

Northcott, M. S., *The Environment and Christian Ethics*, Cambridge UP, 1996.

Osborne, C., *Dumb Beasts and dead philosophers: humanity and the humane in ancient philosophy*, Oxford, Clarendon, 2007.

Osborne, K. B., *History of Franciscan Theology* (Theology Series), New York, Franciscan Institute Publishing, 1999.

— (ed.), *The History of Franciscan Theology*, New York, The Franciscan Institute, St Bonaventure University, 1994.

Page, G., *The Singing Gorilla: understanding animal intelligence,* London, Headline, 1999.

Page, T., *Vivisection Unveiled; an expose of the medical futility of animal experimentation*, Charlbury, Oxon, Jon Carpenter, 1997.

Paterson, D., *Humane Education: a symposium*, Burgess Hill, Sussex, Humane Education Council, 1981.

Paterson, D., Ryder, R. D. (eds), *Animal Rights: a symposium*, Fontwell, Sussex, Centaur, 1979.

Patterson, C., *Eternal Treblinka: our treatment of animals and the holocaust*, New York, Lantern, 2002.

Phelps, N., *The Dominion of Love: animal rights according to the Bible*, New York, Lantern, 2002.

Pierce A., Smyth G. (eds), *The Critical Spirit: theology at the crossroads of faith and culture*, Blackrock, Co. Dublin, Columba, 2003.

Polkinghorne, J., *Science and Creation: the search for* understanding. London, SPCK, 1988.

Preece, G. (ed.), *Rethinking Peter Singer: a Christian critique*, Downers Grove, IL., InterVarsity Press, 2002.

Proffer, K., *Adam, Darwin and Washoe: Genesis and the Talking Chimpanzee*, London, Underhill Management, 2002.

Rachels, J., *Created from Animals: the moral implications of Darwinism*, Oxford UP, 1991.

Rae, E., *Women, the Earth, the Divine*, Maryknoll, New York, Orbis, 1994.

Rahner, K., Vorgrimler, H., *Concise Theological Dictionary*, trans. Richard Strachan, Freiburg and London, Burns & Oates, 1965.

Ratzinger, J., *'In the Beginning ...': a Catholic understanding of the story of creation and the fall.* trans. Boniface Ramsey, OP, Edinburgh, T&T Clark, 1998.

Raven, C., *Science, Religion and the Future*, London, Mowbray, [1943], 1994.

Regan, T., *The Case for Animal Rights*, Berkeley, CA:, University of California, 1983, rev. edn. 2004.

Regan, T. (ed.), *Animal Sacrifices: religious perspectives on the use of animals in science*, Philadelphia, Temple UP, 1986.

Regan, T., Singer, P., 1976 *Animal Rights and Human Obigations*, New Jersey, Prentice-Hall, 1976.

Rickaby, J., *Moral Philosophy*, Vol II, London, Longman, 1901.

Ridley, M., *The Origins of Virtue*, London, Viking, 1996.

Ringler, W. A. (ed.), *The Poems of Sir Philip Sidney*, Oxford, Clarendon, 1962.

Roberts, A., Donaldson, J. (trans. and eds); Schaff P (ed.) 1885 *Ante-Nicene Fathers, The,* Vols 1 & 4, Edinburgh, T&T Clark, 1885.

— *Nicene and Post-Nicene Fathers of the Christian Church.* Series I, Vols 1, 2 & 7; Series II, Vol. 6, Edinburgh, T&T Clark, 1885.

Roberts, C., *Science, Animals, and Evolution: reflections on some unrealized potentials of biology and medicine,* Westport, Conn., Greenwood Press, 1980.

Rollin B. E., *Animal Rights and Human Morality,* Buffalo, New York, Prometheus Books, 1981.

Rose, A. (ed.), *Judaism and Ecology,* World Religions and Ecology, London, Cassell, 1992.

Ross W. D., *The Right and the Good,* Oxford, Clarendon, 1930.

Rowland, B. (ed.), *Companion to Chaucer Studies,* Oxford UP, 1979.

Ruether, R. R., *Gaia & God: an ecofeminist theology of earth healing,* London, SCM, 1993.

— *Women Healing Earth: Third World women on ecology, feminism, and religion,* London, SCM, 1996.

Rumbaugh, D. M., Washburn, D. A., *Intelligence of Apes and other Rational Beings,* New Haven and London, Yale UP, 2003.

Ryder, R. D., *Animal Revolution: changing attitudes towards speciesism,* London: Berg (Basil Blackwell), 1989, 2000.

— 2001 *Painism: a modern morality.* London: Centaur

Salt, H. S. (ed.), *The New Charter: a discussion of the rights of men and the rights of animals,* London, George Bell & Sons, 1896.

— *Animals' Rights: considered in relation to social progress, London, George Bell and Sons,* [1892], 1922.

Santmire, H. P., *The Travail of Nature: the ambiguous ecological promise of Christian theology,* Philadelphia, Fortress, 1985.

Sargent, T., *Animal rights and wrongs: a biblical perspective,* London, Hodder & Stoughton, 1996.

Saunders, N. J., *Animal Spirits,* London, Macmillan, 1995.

Savage J. J. (trans.), *St Ambrose*, New York, Fathers of the Church, 1961.

Schwartz, R. H., *Judaism and Vegetarianism*, New York, Lantern, 2001.

Seager, J., *Earth Follies: feminism, politics, and the environment*, London, Earthscan, 1993.

Sedley D., *Creationism and its Critics in Antiquity*, Berkeley, CA, University of California, 2007.

Sevenhuijsen, S., *Citizenship and the Ethics of Care: feminist considerations on justice, morality and politics*, London, Routledge, 1998.

Sheldrake, R., Fox, M., *Natural Grace: dialogues on science and spirituality*, London, Bloomsbury, 1996.

Sideris, L., *Environmental Ethics, Ecological Theory and Natural Selection*, New York, Columbia UP, 2003.

Simpson, R., *Exploring Celtic Spirituality*, London, Hodder & Stoughton, 1995.

Singer, P. (ed.), *Applied Ethics*, Oxford UP, 1986.

Singer, P., *Animal Liberation: a new ethics for our treatment of animals*, London, Jonathan Cape, 1976.

— *Practical Ethics*, Cambridge UP, 1986, 1996.

Slee, N., *Women's Faith Development: patterns and processes*, Aldershot, Hants, Ashgate, 2004.

Smith, A., *The Glasgow Edition of the Works and Correspondence of Adam Smith*, New York, Oxford UP, 1976.

Snyder, M. H. (ed.), *Spiritual Questions for the 21st Century: essays in honour of Joan D. Chittister*, Maryknoll, NY, Orbis, 2001.

Sommers, C. H., *The war against boys: how misguided feminism is harming our young men*, New York, Simon and Schuster, 2001.

Sorabji, R., *Animal Minds and Human Morals: the origins of the Western debate*, London, Duckworth, 1993.

Southgate, C. et al., *God, Humanity and the Cosmos: a textbook in science and religion*. Book two: *Theology and the New Physics*, Edinburgh, T&T Clark, 1999.

Sparks, H. F. D., *The Apocryphal Old Testament*, Oxford, Clarendon, 1985.

Stevenson, P., *A Far Cry from Noah: the live export trade in calves, sheep and pigs*, London, Merlin, 1994.

Strauss, A. L., Corbin, J., *Basics of Qualitative Research: grounded theory procedures and techniques*, Newbury Park, CA., Sage, 1990.

Strayer, J. (ed.), *Dictionary of the Middle Ages*, Vol. I, New York, Charles Scribner's Sons, 1982.

Stuart T., *The Bloodless Revolution: radical vegetarianism and the discovery of India*, London, HarperCollins, 2006.

Taylor, A., *Plato: the Man and his Work*, London, Methuen, 1927, 1960 (7th edn).

Taylor, P., *Respect for Nature*, Princeton UP, 1996.

Thomas, K., *Man and the Natural World: changing attitudes in England AD 1500–1800*, London, Penguin, 1983.

Tronto, J. C., *Moral Boundaries: a political argument for an ethic of care*, New York & London, Routledge, 1993.

Turks, P., *Philip Neri: the fire of joy*, Freiburg im Breisgau, Herder. Trans by Daniel Utrecht, Edinburgh, T&T Clark, 1986, (English) 1995.

Turner, E. S., *All Heaven in a Rage*. Fontwell, Sussex: Centaur, 1964, 1992.

Vallance R. (ed.), 1950 *A Hundred English Essays*, London, Thos. Nelson & Sons, 1950.

Van Der Ven, J. A, Schulz, B., *Practical Theology: an empirical approach*, Kampa, The Netherlands, Kok Pharos, 1993.

Von Balthasar, H. U., *Theo-Drama: theological dramatic theory:last Act*, Vol. 5, translated by G. Harrison, Fort Collins, CO., Ignatius Press, 1998.

Waddell, H., *Beasts and Saints*, London, Darton, Longman & Todd, 1934, 1995.

Walker, O., *Of Education, especially of young gentlemen*, London, Richard Wellington, 1699 (6th edn).

Walter, R., *A Voyage round the World by George Anson, Esq*, London, Richard Walter, 1748.

Ward B., *The Spirituality of St Cuthbert*, Fairacres, 1992.

Warren, K. J. (ed.), *Ecofeminism: women, culture, nature*, Bloomington & Indianapolis, Indiana UP, 1997.

Welburn, A., *The Beginnings of Christianity: Essene mystery, Gnostic revelation and the Christian vision*, London, Floris, 1991.

Wenham, G. J., *Genesis 1– 15* (World Biblical Commentary), Vol. 1, Milton Keynes, Word (UK) Edition, 1987, 1991.

Westacott, E., *A Century of Vivisection and Anti-Vivisection*, Ashingdon, Essex, C. W. Daniel Co, 1949.

Westermann C., *Genesis 1–11.* Trans. John J. Scullion SJ, London, SPCK, 1974, English edn 1984.

White, A. R., *Rights*, Oxford, Clarendon, 1984.

Winterbottom, M. (ed. and trans.), *Gildas: the ruin of Britain and other works*, London, Phillimore, 1978.

Ziolkowski, J., 1993 *Talking Animals: medieval Latin beast poetry,* 750–1150, Philadelphia, IL, University of Pennsylvania, 1993.

Index

LaVergne, TN USA
13 January 2010
169854LV00003B/22/P